Beginners Please

VERA MORRILL

Ellie

All good wishes

Vera

22. 1. 08

authorHOUSE®

AuthorHouse™ UK Ltd.
500 Avebury Boulevard
Central Milton Keynes, MK9 2BE
www.authorhouse.co.uk
Phone: 08001974150

First published by AuthorHouse 8/8/2007

ISBN: 978-1-4343-0819-1 (sc)

Printed in the United States of America
Bloomington, Indiana

This book is printed on acid-free paper.

For Lesley and Nicholas

Prologue

Elegant in evening dresses of pale gold satin overlaid with lace, (no concessions here to modern trends), they entered the box, the 'Royal' box as theatre staff liked to call it. Hair swept into silver-blonde chignons, diamonds gleaming, they sat down.

A frisson of excitement swept through the theatre. The initial sporadic sputter of applause, gathering momentum until, like a tide, it suffused the whole building.
Smiling, the two ladies rose, inclined their heads in acknowledgement, raised hands in greeting, and sat.

A collective sigh of pleasure rippled through the audience. The famous Golden Girls, here in the flesh and just as identically beautiful as they had always heard. Here to witness members of their own families tread the boards.

Contentedly, the theatregoers resumed their seats and closed their programmes, as the lights dimmed and the curtains opened.

Chapter 1

MARIGOLD

She's done it again! After all this time I shouldn't be surprised, but it's so unfair. Just because she's the younger, by a mere ten minutes and two or three pounds smaller, she's always been handled with kid gloves. For as long as I can remember I've been looking after Daisy, making sure she drank her milk, ate her vegetables and had plenty of sleep so that she'd grow big and strong like me. Let's face it, if she'd been a piglet, then she would have been classified as the runt of the litter and probably disposed of. Now, when we both have to make a new start tomorrow, she's swanning off to work in Newport, staying on the Island close to home and able to see the family from time to time, whilst I have to go to Richmond in Surrey to work with some old biddy, who's probably senile.

I know I'm going to be frightened tomorrow and very, very homesick. I get so tired of Daisy never misbehaving, always doing her Miss Goody Two Shoes routine, but at least she's someone my own age and I can talk to her about anything and everything. All sorts of nasty things might happen to me and what about monthlies? Hasn't anybody thought about that? Who's going to help me when all that starts and I feel poorly? Daisy will be able to talk to Mum about it. And what about boys? I mean there are bound to be boys…eventually. I'm not quite sure what happens in that sex business, if it's anything like the animals on the farm it's pretty disgusting.

At least if Daisy was there we could have talked it through and it would have helped both of us. Now, from tomorrow, I'll be on my own.

Come to think of it there is one situation I wouldn't change with her. Dad and Mum were hoping for a boy when we twins were born, a son who could help Dad out on the farm when he grew up. When we two girls arrived and names were being discussed Mum wanted to call one of us Joanna, which could be shortened to Jo, so that she might believe her dream of a son had come true. Dad would have none of it. "We've got two beautiful girls, little flowers they are and that's what they're going to stay. You can forget that boy's name nonsense." And that's how we got our names, two flowers, Daisy and Marigold. I thank God every night that I'm not called Daisy. For heavens' sake, we've got a cow called Daisy. How could they? At least with Marigold, if it's shortened I get Mari and I can live with that.

I've just thought of something else she's got, that I certainly wouldn't want. That quirky eyebrow of hers. Fancy having one blonde, like our hair almost to the point of whiteness, and one brown, it's weird. I keep telling her she ought to darken the light one with a brown crayon or something. She never does. It never seems to worry her. But then what does?

This basket is really heavy. I think Mum's gone a bit overboard with the food, but she kept saying, "Well there are two of you and you've been happy there and more importantly, I think Miss Webster is a really good teacher who's taught you a lot." Just what help parsing sentences and long division is going to be to me when I'm making beds, or doing any other chores, I can't imagine. I think we could be in for a bit of trouble today, birthday or no birthday. Packing up this little lot took absolutely ages.

DAISY

We're later than I thought. The man Marigold and I call 'Mr. Overalls' passed us on his bicycle just as we were closing the farm gates and we usually meet him near the bottom of the Swanmore Road. He called out 'Mornin' missies, you're late today' and I called back 'Yes, it's our birthday'. We heard his voice in the distance calling out 'Many happy returns to you both'. I hope Miss Webster will understand. Mum so wanted to give us plenty of goodies for the other children – meat patties and apple pies and a special cake for Miss Webster and packing them took longer than any of us expected.

From tomorrow I suppose we'll be working girls and not children any more. Everything has happened so quickly, almost too quickly for us to get used to the idea of where we were going and what we'd be doing. It's just a few short weeks since we called at Southfield House to walk home with Mum after she'd finished work. There were visitors of course, Mum only helps out now and again when Mrs. Murray-Rogers has guests. A group of them were sitting in the garden when we arrived and there were lots of 'Oohs ' and 'Aahs' and 'What pretty gels.' It was all very embarrassing, especially when one old gentleman said 'White-blond hair and those eyes, such a lovely blue-green.' Mum was preening herself, as she always does whenever we receive compliments and then they started asking about school and suddenly we were each having to recite a piece of poetry. Marigold loved it of course, but then she's always been a terrible show-off.

Only with hindsight did I realise that Mrs. Murray-Rogers was quietly checking up on the way we spoke and behaved under scrutiny, very clever. A few days later she asked Mum if she could be of help in finding suitable employment for us and of course the answer was 'Yes, please.' So, in less than twenty four hours, I shall be on my way to Newport and a new life, the thought of which is absolutely terrifying. Marigold will be on her way to the mainland. For neither of us to be at home for Christmas is beyond belief, I daren't even think about it. It's Friday the thirteenth and I know what they say about that, but it is 1918 and the dreadful war has been over for a whole month, so I think that, as the grown-ups keep saying, everything now is going to get better and better.

I wonder if being fourteen makes me a grown-up?

MARIGOLD

It was harder than I thought saying goodbye to Daisy. First of all we had an argument about clothes. Mea culpa, as Miss Webster would say. I started it, I know. Daisy's so good with her needle that her clothes always seem to look more attractive than mine, in spite of the fact they're supposed to be identical. During the row I told her it wasn't fair that I had to go so far away whilst she was staying on the Island. With that she burst into tears and said she didn't want to go anywhere and why couldn't we both stay at home?

She's so soft-hearted, heaven knows how she's going to manage in the big wide world. Dad always says I'm the tough one, so I should be able to cope. Mum came in to see what the fuss was about and soon we were all having a little weep, until Dad arrived and made us laugh by asking if he should bring in the rain butts and store the water, just in case there was a drought next summer. Soon we were all smiling again.

Then he reminded us that Daisy and I were not bound for Outer Mongolia or Timbuktu (wherever they are) and that there were such things as letters and even, in emergencies, telegrams. Dad's like that, somehow he always manages to calm a situation down and makes us start to think logically.

Perhaps that's the differences between the sexes. Mum certainly isn't scatter-brained but she, Daisy and I do tend to get all het up about things before we've really thought them through. Dad doesn't look the thoughtful type. He looks like what he is, a farmer. Big-boned, broad-shouldered and bearded. He gives the impression of being just a heavy weight, but he's far from that. Always gives careful consideration to any problem before he gives an opinion – and he's usually right.

Tomorrow he's taking me over on the ferry and putting me on the London train in the care of the guard. How humiliating is that? Someone is to meet me at Waterloo and will take me off the guard's hands. Anyone would think I was a parcel. One half of me is excited because I've never been off the Island before and the other half is terrified and although I joke about it, it's quite reassuring to know that someone will be with me until I reach my destination.

I know I've often had wicked thoughts about Daisy, but she's my other half, my good half and oh gosh, I'm going to miss her so much.

DAISY   Saturday 14th December 1918

It was a long walk from Newport station and her carpet bag seemed to get heavier as she turned into each new road. Slade Manor she knew was on the other side of the town, but Daisy decided she would probably die of frost-bite before she ever reached it. Mum had knitted her some warm gloves and she was wearing her best woollen skirt over warm drawers and long thick stockings, but in spite of the layers, her nose felt like an icicle and her cheeks were burning with the cutting North-Easterly wind.

At last. She could see the solid bulk of the manor house set back from the Shide road and her pace quickened at the thought of warm fires and something to eat. As instructed she went to the rear of the house and found what was clearly the entrance used by staff and tradesmen in a wing of the building fronted by a large courtyard. She jumped at the sound of the bell jangling and stepped back as the door was opened by a girl a few years older than herself. The girl smiled and ushered her indoors saying "You must be Daisy. Wait here, I'll tell the Housekeeper you've arrived."

Daisy looked around her. She was in an enormous kitchen with the biggest range she'd ever seen. Stirring something in a huge pot was a very large lady, who smiled and raised one hand in welcome. "Hello Daisy, can't stop for a minute or two. Put your bag down dear and your coat over there on the hooks." By the time this was done, the girl, who introduced herself as Alice, was back and together they walked down a long dark corridor. Alice knocked on a door at the very end and then, as a voice called 'Enter' turned the handle and gently pushed Daisy inside. After the gloom of the corridor she was for a moment almost blinded by the light from a large window, but then an austere lady seated behind a desk came into view and she was told to sit down.

The formidable lady was Mrs. Frensham, Housekeeper, who said she was to be addressed as Ma'am at all times. Daisy's appointment as assistant parlour maid, helping out in the kitchen whenever necessary, was confirmed. She was to have one full day off per month and one afternoon off per week midweek, between the hours of two and five o'clock. Mrs. Carstairs, the mistress of the house, also to be addressed as Ma'am, would see her later in the day and pass on any other necessary information.

The next question was totally unexpected. "Did you bring your thimble and sewing equipment with you?"

"Yes…Ma'am."

"Then, once you have unpacked, I want you to report back to me, I have some sewing I would like you to do."

No mention of a hot cup of tea, no warm words of welcome, Daisy left the room feeling very deflated. But not for long. Once back in the kitchen, Mrs. Barton the cook, came quickly across, "Sit down my luv, you look fair shrammed. There, get that down you." 'That' was a mug of cocoa and a large slice of cake. It looked delicious but Daisy hesitated, "Mrs. Frensham said I was to unpack and then there was sewing to do…"

"You can do all that in a minute, right now you need something hot to drink and some food inside you. It's freezing out there, you've had a long walk from the station and unlike me, you've not got a lot of padding to keep the cold out. When you've finished, Alice will take you upstairs, then you can sort your things out properly later on. We'll be having lunch at twelve thirty sharp, so when you come down, collect your sewing and then Daisy my dear, you'll be able to sit down and draw breath."

That night listening to Alice's deep breathing, Daisy reflected on her day. Everyone had seemed friendly, except Mrs. Frensham, but perhaps that was too much to expect. Meeting Mrs. Carstairs had not been quite the ordeal she had expected. The Morning Room was bright with French doors to the garden, an abundance of flowering plants and more pictures than she could count. Mrs. Carstairs was rather aloof and very elegant in a tailored grey dress with wine-coloured trimming.

"It's Daisy isn't it? Mrs. Frensham has explained your duties?"

"Yes Ma'am."

"You are to share a room with Alice, who has been with us for four years. Your uniforms are waiting for you. Blue for the morning and grey for the afternoon, they may require minor adjustments. Mrs. Barton the cook, arranges matters so that you and Alice can accompany Mrs. Frensham to church on Sunday mornings. On those occasions you will wear a hat. Do you have a hat?"

"Oh yes Ma'am."

"Very good, but remember, a hat always, but no feathers and certainly no flowers. No 'followers', that is male friends, until you are sixteen years of age and Mrs. Frensham is to be informed of any such liaison. You come to us, Daisy, through the goodwill and recommendation of our friend, Mrs. Murray-Rogers, I am sure you will do your utmost to fulfil the trust she has placed in you and prove a credit to your family. Now is there anything you wish to ask me?"

"No Ma'am, thank you Ma'am."

"Very well, you may go."

A relieved Daisy retuned to the more relaxed atmosphere of the kitchen, once there trying to assimilate as much information as possible about the staff and her duties.

It was obvious that the war had made staffing a problem for a house such as this. Jimmy, a strapping lad of fifteen, did all the heavy lifting indoors, laid fires etc., whilst Fred, who she was told was well past enlistment age, looked after the exterior and was on hand to help indoors when necessary. Alice was responsible for the main rooms used by the family.

Mrs. Barton explained, "The mistress decided to close the Drawing Room until the war was over, or until things improved. It seemed daft to keep rooms ready with hardly anyone here and let's face it, with the war on, people were not in the mood for entertaining. Everybody seemed to have someone away fighting and it just didn't seem right to have parties and dinners with all that going on. At Christmas we made a special effort and that was for the sake of the children. So, any entertaining that has to be done, is in the Dining and Morning Rooms. This has cut down on our work and of course on the heating, which has been a big help."

Now Alice chipped in, "It's my job to get the rooms ready before the family come down for breakfast. Jim attends to the fires, looks after the carpets and I dust and then take up the food when everything's ready. When they're all at home it's been quite a rush sometimes to get it all done, that's why I'm really glad to see you Daisy, we can do with another pair of hands."

"And the bedrooms?" Daisy wanted to show she was following all this.

"As soon as the mistress has had breakfast she goes into the Morning Room and unless she has an engagement or walks in the grounds, stays there until lunch. That means the Dining Room can be cleared and the family bedrooms put to rights. Mrs. Harris from the village comes in twice a week and helps with bed changing and laundry and we have another lady on tap who helps us with spring cleaning, Christmas preparations and if anyone is coming to stay. It works quite well, they're always on hand if we really need them." Mrs. Barton smiled. "I know it sounds hectic and we are on the go for much of the time, but here is not like some places I've heard of where you never get a minute to yourself and we do manage to have quite a bit of fun down here in our own domain. And Daisy, don't you be put off by Mrs. Frensham's bark, it's much worse than her bite."

Alice's friendly chatter saw Daisy through the worst of her homesickness later that night, but when Alice finally succumbed to sleep Daisy was left alone with her thoughts. One thing's for sure, I'm not going to starve here, Mrs. B. is an excellent cook and she's lovely. Round and cuddly, full of fun and just…comfortable. Although they're not the least bit alike, I think she's going to help me in not missing Mum quite so much. She gulped. Was it really only yesterday that she and Marigold had left school for good? Here she was in a strange house with a stranger in the next bed, the first time in all their lives that she and her twin hadn't slept in the same room. The tears started and as a clock somewhere struck midnight she remembered that she had to be up at 6.30 a.m. and turning her head into the now damp pillow, attempted sleep.

DAISY'S   Journal—Sunday 15th December 1918

However difficult, I'm going to have to make time for this. Mum suggested that both Marigold and I should keep some record of our lives away from home and Dad said it was an excellent idea. As soon as the animals had been fed he was off to Ryde, returning with two quite handsome five year journals. In a strange way, I think he is going to miss us even more than Mum. He loved it at the end of the day when we were chattering about school and telling him about our studies.

Lunch yesterday was an enlightening experience, learning about the family etc. Mr. Carstairs, now referred to as the Major, is a gentleman farmer, but has only just returned home after being away with the army for the past three years. He's now trying to pick up the threads of running the estate and the farm, all of which have been in the hands of local and often, elderly labour. I haven't seen him yet, but Mrs. B. says he looks very white-faced and 'not himself'. The eldest girl, Cynthia, is usually away at school near Brighton, but will be home tomorrow, Monday, for the Christmas holiday. The

11

Carstairs boys, aged ten and eight, are at the local grammar school. I didn't see them yesterday as I was excused church on my first day, but they too, will soon be home all the time for the Christmas and New Year break.

Alice is eighteen and has been here throughout the war years. Before that she was at home helping her mother with younger sisters and brothers. Once her sisters were twelve and ten it was decided they should take over. Their father had been conscripted and sent abroad and with Alice able to send a little money each week they could just about manage. Their father is due home in a few months' time, but he has been seriously wounded. His loss of a leg and partial blindness has been a bitter blow to the family and it's quite possible that if, on his return they're unable to cope, Alice will once again have to assist at home. I was surprised to learn that Mrs. B. who was widowed some ten years ago, lost her son within a few months of him being sent overseas. How can she stay so cheerful? They all seem positive about the future and confident that now the war is over, everything will soon be back to normal.

I'm not sure about Jimmy. Seems a bit full of himself. Reserving judgement!

DAISY'S Journal—Mon. Dec. 16th

Living on a farm, I'm used to hearing signs of activity early in the morning, but getting up at that time is another matter. There was a tap on the door this morning at half past six. After doing the fires, Jimmy's job is to give us a call and leave outside a jug of hot water for Alice and me. We're lucky that there is a small staff bathroom on this landing, with a water closet, such a luxury, but we also have a stand in our room with a washbasin and jug, so that we don't get held up in queues. We were downstairs in twenty minutes, had a quick cup of tea, then dusted the Dining and Morning rooms, the study and the entrance area.

In the hallway I met Major Carstairs. Either the poor man can't sleep or he's desperate to make an early start. His face is ashen. Mrs. B. says he's about forty, but he looks more like a sixty year old to me. He just nodded and said "Good morning" and went in to have breakfast. Mrs. B. said I was to eat with her, then I could go in with Alice to serve the others. Cooked dishes were taken in at half past eight and replaced on the sideboard over burners, so it was only a matter of removing porridge and cereal dishes and ensuring that the teapot was kept filled. David and Michael seemed very well behaved but David the elder, caught my eye once or twice and when his mother was occupied, gave me a wicked grin.

Mrs. Frensham's visits to the kitchen were infrequent and invariably sent a shock-wave through everyone present. The day after Daisy's arrival, she suddenly appeared during the quiet period between lunch being cleared and tea served.

"Daisy, I wish to speak to you in my office. At once please." With that she was gone.

What had she done wrong, or omitted to do? Daisy, in fear and trepidation, followed her quickly.

"Close the door child and you may be seated." This in a slightly mellower tone.

"Mrs. Carstairs' mother, Mrs. Templar, is joining the family party for Christmas. She is in her late fifties and experiencing a little trouble with arthritis. Mrs. Carstairs asks if you would be prepared to assist her in dressing in the mornings and again the evenings. Mrs. Templar has always been a very smart lady, beautifully dressed and I personally feel you could learn a great deal by assisting with her wardrobe. Would you be prepared to do that?"

"Yes Mrs. Frensham, Ma'am, I would be pleased to do so."

"Good, then that's settled," Mrs. Frensham almost managed a smile. "Mrs. Templar arrives tomorrow. You may return to your duties."

The news caused quite a stir in the kitchen.

"Another mouth to feed, another room to prepare. It's never ending." Mrs. Barton chuntered away good-naturedly. In fact she was never fazed by extra chores, taking everything in her stride and always finding enough food to put on the table regardless of how short the notice given. Now she added, "She's a lovely lady, it'll be a pleasure to see her again."

At four o'clock Daisy joined Alice in the Morning Room, standing as instructed, by the long low cabinet along one wall. She watched Alice's positioning of the three-tiered stand with its tiny sandwiches and small cakes.

"Nothing large", Mrs. B. had explained, "always something that can be popped in the mouth easily." Next a small low table was placed in front of Mrs. Carstairs and, at Alice's signal, Daisy took the tray with its silver and porcelain and placed it in front of the hostess. Now they were free to leave, there was extra water and should Mrs.

Carstairs require more tea, she would ring the servants' bell.

On this occasion, only Major and Mrs. Carstairs and their daughter Cynthia, newly arrived from school, were present, and Daisy saw that the Major, as Mrs. B. had said, was very pale. He seemed withdrawn and whilst mother and daughter chatted, he rarely joined in the conversation. Cynthia was like her mother, tall with dark hair cut in the latest smooth bob fashion. Her dominant feature was her very dark brown eyes and although only sixteen, Daisy could see that she was wearing a light make-up. The total effect was of a very handsome young lady.

Only her third day and already Daisy could see that the family who lived here existed in a different world from the one she and her family knew on the farm. Slade Manor was full of beautiful things, furniture and pictures pleasing to the eye. Colours of carpets and cushions and even the flowers, all blended harmoniously The people who lived at Slade Manor never had to worry about preparing food or when the laundry would be dealt with. Everything was just handed to them and all they had to do was to sit back and enjoy it. What a life! One day she thought, I'll live like this and people will be at my beck and call. I'll stay in the very best hotels and…

"Daisy come along my girl, no time for day-dreaming. We've got a dinner to cook. Those boys are in tonight and they're always hungry."

Slade Manor, Daisy decided, was not an attractive house externally. There was no single distinguishing feature like the portico which Daisy had seen at Southfield House. Flat fronted and of dull grey stone, it was set on the side of a slope which fell away at the rear, with the result that some family rooms were at the front overlooking the front garden, with the dining and morning rooms facing to the rear. The two wings were set at right angles to the house thus forming at the rear, the three sides of a square. This area was divided by a high stone wall, so that the kitchen and service rooms, approached inside by several steps down from the first floor, looked out onto a courtyard area, whilst the family dining room faced onto a garden. Much of the furniture had probably been handed down through several generations and was rather too dark and heavy for elegance. Clearly Mrs. Carstairs had tried to counteract this with paler coloured drapes of velvet and brocade and an abundance of flowers, usually carefully positioned in front of mirrors. This was a house, Daisy decided which would always look at its best when fires were burning brightly and lights glowing or, alternatively, when the sun streamed through its windows.

DAISY'S   Journal—Tues. 17th December

The two ladies in charge here could not be more different. Mrs. Frensham (that must be a courtesy title, I think she's a spinster), is all angles and sharp edges, nose, cheeks bones, elbows, whereas Mrs. Barton the cook is all smooth roundness, Her chins wobble when she laughs, her upper arms tremble quite violently when she's kneading the pastry and if you brush against her it's like bumping into a cushion.

Alice is much taller than me and slim, whilst Jimmy is stockily built with a shock of brown hair which is forever falling over his eyes. I'm surprised Mrs. Frensham hasn't told him to get it cut before now.

Something awful happened this morning. Major C. was up early as usual and Mrs. B. told me to hurry and take the tray into the dining room. The Major was just ahead of me as we crossed the hall, when one of the dishes moved and rattled slightly. In one movement he whirled round and knocked the whole tray onto the floor. For a moment I was stunned, as I think he was then, hearing the noise Mrs. Frensham appeared and ignoring the mess on the floor, went straight to him and quietly suggested he should go into the dining room and sit down. I, meanwhile, had burst into tears. Alice came running from the kitchen and I could see Cynthia hovering at the head of the stairs. Fortunately, the tray consisted of the metal containers which sit over the burners, the empty toast rack and the cruet, so there was no precious china broken and no silver dented. Mrs. F. told me to return to the kitchen and that she and Alice would clear the debris.

I was convinced everyone would think I had just been clumsy and dropped the tray, but strangely enough it didn't happen at all as I imagined. Mrs. F. sent for me, asked if I had recovered and then started to explain what she thought had occurred.

Major C. had she said, been involved in a great deal of trench warfare during the past years. She said, "Do you know what that means, Daisy? It means living in deep, often muddy ditches for weeks on end. It means being prepared to be attacked every minute of every day and if you are an officer it means being responsible for the men in your charge and, sadly, having to write to their loved ones in the event of their being killed or seriously injured. There is no respite, food is limited and boring and you are on edge the whole time. I'm telling you all this, so that you will understand what I think happened today. Major Carstairs unaware that you were close by, heard a movement behind him and immediately thought he was back in the trenches, where a sudden sound could mean he was in serious danger. That's why he struck out at the nearest object. Do you understand? It was nothing to do with you personally and you were in no way to blame. I want you to be quite clear about that."

I was so relieved and it was nice to see how understanding she was about Major C. I thanked her for explaining it all and then she told me to go and tell Mrs. B. I was to have some cocoa and a biscuit right away because I'd had a shock. Obviously there's a gentler side to Mrs. F. which I haven't seen before.

Chapter 2

MARIGOLD

I'm not quite sure what I expected of the lady who was meeting me. One thing's for certain, she didn't fit *any* ideas I might have had. About thirty I think, slim and petite, she was wearing the smartest coat I've ever seen. Rather Russian in style, black velvet with braid frogging and silk tassels both front and back and a hat with a small velvet crown banded with black fur. Small she might be, but with an air of authority to which people responded very quickly. Having introduced herself to me as Estelle Evans, within seconds we were in a taxi and on our way to Richmond. There she explained that she was deputising for her friend, Rosalie Reece, an actress, that she herself was an actress and a singer and then, rather ruefully, that work had been in short supply during the war years, most of the theatres having been 'dark'.

Seeing my puzzled expression she explained,

"Sorry… if we say a theatre is 'dark', we mean it's closed. So many men were away fighting and for the first time many women were occupied doing the jobs the men had had to vacate.

"There really were not the audiences to fill theatres and people had much more on their minds than enjoying themselves. Having said that, several of the music halls did keep going and we did pick up some work there."

I noted the 'we', but by this time I was horrified. There must be some terrible mistake. People who went on the stage were surely frowned upon. Mum and Dad couldn't have known who these people were or I would never have been allowed to come here.

Estelle was still talking, "Of course it mattered little to Rose, Miss Reece, with whom you're staying. Her reputation is such that if there was any suitable work at all to be had she would get it and in any event she has made her pile, so doesn't have to count the pennies like the rest of us. Not that I'm criticising her in any way. She is the most generous kind-hearted person I've ever known, as I'm sure you will very soon agree."

It wasn't until I saw Miss Reece's house that I realised just how great the pile must have been to which Estelle Evans had been referring. Situated at a vantage point for a clear view down the Thames Valley, the river bed flanked by meadows and dense woodland, the house was very impressive. A smartly dressed maid greeted us at the portico entrance and we were ushered into the most magnificent room I had ever seen. Rising to meet us was a slim elderly lady, probably in her fifties, with hair which I can only describe as silver-blonde. Taking both my hands in hers she said,

"Marigold my dear, you are most welcome and yes, they were quite right, you are very pretty indeed." Just who 'they' were I had no idea, but I was divested of my coat, seated and offered tea and sandwiches. I was in a complete state of bewilderment. This surely was not the reception for someone who was joining the household as a servant. It was all very weird.

It was at this point I had a horrible thought. Perhaps I had been brought here as part of the White Slave trade! I had heard that they liked very young females, preferably blonde. But surely not? Miss Reece and Estelle seemed so, well…nice.

There was something else. Looking around me I could see dozens of photographs, all beautifully framed. Many were of Miss Reece in different poses and in different costumes, some obviously from Shakespeare's plays and one, in pride of place on the grand piano, was surely Miss Reece shaking hands with Princess Louise, Queen Victoria's daughter. Goodness, if she had met royalty, she must be very famous indeed.

And so I discovered. Following a maid up the staircase, accompanied by Estelle, who chattered non-stop, I learned Rosalie Reece was one of the foremost actresses in the country, particularly famous for her Shakespearian roles. Estelle was astonished that I had not heard of her. "This island you live on, are its inhabitants unaware of what goes on in the rest of the country?" she said in mock horror.

I was about to explain that on the farm we rarely saw newspapers, when the maid stopped and opened a door. I gasped and put my hands to my face. This room was fit for a princess. Cream furniture and carpet and a bed draped and covered with the palest pink. A dressing table set with toiletries, a button-backed armchair in pink velvet and a small desk and chair with writing materials. There just had to be something wrong. Why on earth would anyone greet an unknown girl in the way I'd been greeted and provide such a display of beauty and riches for her personal use?

Estelle saw I was completely overwhelmed and dismissed the maid.

"I told you of her generosity."

"Even so…"

Estelle stopped me in my tracks.

"I can't say any more at the moment, except to reassure you that you are quite safe here, no-one is going to hurt you or make you do anything you do not wish to do. Now if you have a clean blouse and skirt with you, I suggest you go through the alcove there, where you will find washing facilities. Freshen yourself up and unpack and familiarise yourself with your room. There is a clock on your bedside table. Join us downstairs at six o'clock and we will talk some more."

I looked around me, everything, everywhere was prettier than anything I had ever known or used. From the window I could see a lovely garden…What was going on? Completely bemused by this astonishing turn of events, I lay on the bed and within seconds was fast asleep. As arranged, they were waiting for me in that lovely sitting room, where the carpet and furniture were all light and pale. Even the flowers echoed this, vases of white lilies and Christmas roses, with just here and there to add definition were dark, glossy-leafed plants. It was like looking at a beautiful painting.

"Marigold, I am correct in thinking you are fourteen years of age?"

"Yes, Miss Reece. My twin sister and I had our birthdays yesterday – our last day at school."

"That's later than is usual, surely?"

"Yes Ma'am,. Normally children leave the Dame School at twelve years. Our parents couldn't afford to send us to a Finishing school or the Convent school but they felt we would benefit from some further education. They discussed it with our teacher and she agreed we should stay on for an extra two years, during which she would teach us some French and more advanced lessons on the arts and English Literature which was her own particular forte. At the same time we were expected to assist with the younger children and in return Mum and Dad paid a reduced fee."

"Excellent, even better than I thought." Miss Reece nodded to Estelle to continue.

"I know you're still puzzled as to why you've been brought here."

"Well yes…you see I thought I was to be personal servant to Miss Reece, assisting as necessary, learning to look after her clothes, that sort of thing…"

"Well a little of that may come into it, but there is much more to it than that. Have you ever heard of Sebastian Reece?"

"Yes…" what a weird question I thought, "only a few weeks ago as a matter of fact. Miss Webster, our teacher, was talking to Daisy and me about Impressionist painters and she told us he was one of the leading contemporary English artists, a very gifted man."

Here Miss Reece cut in, "My father was that all right. He was also a compulsive gambler and a womaniser."

I was so shocked. I've never heard a grown-up speak in those terms before and certainly not about a parent. Estelle chuckled, "Don't be alarmed Marigold, Rose often speaks of her father like that. It's true he gambled on everything – horses, dogs, stocks and share, you name it. But unlike other gamblers he invariably won and over the years he accrued a great deal of money. From the start he disapproved of Rose going on the stage. Said it would be like art, little or no money and certainly no future to be had in it. It took him a long while to realise just how successful and famous she had become, but even then he was very quick to point out that it had taken her about twenty years to get to the top of the tree."

Where on earth was all this leading, I wondered?

"Sebastian Reece died several years ago and left Rose a considerable amount of money, enough he said in his will, to ensure if no further work was forthcoming, she would be able to live in the style to which she had become accustomed."

"But I still don't see why...?"

"There's more. There was a codicil to the will. A gambler to the last, Sebastian said he now accepted that Rose had done very well, but he was issuing her with a wager, a challenge if you like."

At last we seemed to be getting to the nub of the matter and I listened carefully.

"The wager was that she could not find a young girl, totally inexperienced, put her on the stage and get her to top the bill in a West End production in five years' time. If Rose succeeded, a very large sum of money would come her way. If she failed, the money was to be given to any charity she cared to nominate."

I thought I might faint. "And you think that I could possibly...? Surely not? Is that why I'm here?"

"Yes my dear." Now it was Miss Reece's turn. "Your presence here is not by chance. Since my father's wishes were made known, I have had friends all over the country looking for suitable material. You see there is enough of my father in me to welcome a challenge, any challenge, and this I feel is something I can really enjoy. I must tell you that you are the fourth girl we have had here and by far the most interesting."

I'd like to place a wager myself, that she said that to every one of the girls when they arrived.

"How do you feel about all this?" Estelle asked.

"Stunned, just about sums it up." They both laughed and I carried on,

"I can't really say. I've no idea what would be expected of me, what I would have to learn, what you would want me to do…?"

Miss Reece now, "I would personally teach you the rudiments of acting, speech, stagecraft, deportment and style. You already strike me as being quite a confident young lady. You know some French which could prove useful. There will be singing and dancing lessons and we will together explore the classics and contemporary drama, poetry too, of course and what is developing in the music halls. Anything and everything in fact which provides entertainment. My father's will said "Topping the bill in a West End production," but he didn't actually specify in what genre, so we have quite a wide canvas to work on. We would have to find out what are your strengths and weaknesses."

I shook my head, "Stop, please stop."

"Oh my dear, I'm so sorry. Have we frightened you to death? If you cannot face this there will be no recriminations, we will quite understand."

"No, no, it's not like that at all," I was almost crying, "It sounds absolutely, fantastically, wonderful. When do we start?"

In retrospect Marigold felt she had spent the evening which followed in a dream. One from which she had felt in danger of waking at regular intervals. The ambience of the elegantly appointed dining room, the reflection of crystal, flowers and fruit on the patina of polished surfaces made her head spin. She savoured the perfumes, the colours and the beauty of everything around her but would have been at a loss to say just what food and drink had actually passed her lips.

Rose and Estelle constantly brought her back to reality with their questions about Daisy, the farm, her parents and the Island and from time to time she saw them glance at each other, as if pleased at what they heard. At nine thirty exactly, Rose suggested Marigold should retire.

"Your first lesson. 'Beauty sleep' is rightly so called," she smiled, "It is absolutely vital to the well-being of the mind and body. Shortage of sleep is always reflected in your skin texture. Remember that, when you are tempted by others to join one celebration after another. Equally important is training the mind to remember words. It is a very necessary part of an actor's learning process, which is why I want you to memorise this by tomorrow."

Marigold glanced at the paper handed to her, a poem by Walter de la Mare, one she had heard before, but memorising it by tomorrow?

Rose continued, "You and I will breakfast at eight forty-five and then spend an hour on breathing exercises, Estelle will join us at church and after lunch I will hear your poem and make suggestions as to how you might improve your delivery. I know this has been an exciting and times bewildering day for you, my dear, but you are most welcome in my home, Marigold, and I feel you are going to enjoy the challenges you and I are now going to meet. Sleep well."

Marigold bid her mentors goodnight and clutching the piece of paper to her as if her life depended on it, mounted the stairs. The ensuing conversation downstairs would have both surprised and delighted her.

"Good presence," this from Rose.

"She speaks confidently, is impressed but not daunted by her surroundings and she's not ashamed of her background."

"Yes, I like that. I got the impression that the parents must be very aware of the benefits of education. The fact that they organised two extra years at school was impressive. Her hands show her nervousness and the neck and shoulders are stiff, but it's been a long and exciting day for her."

"Yes, tension obviously."

"She likes sweet things, might have to watch that," Rose chuckled.

"Her clothes are, well... Estelle grimaced. "Can't wait to see her in something decent."

"I agree. She's such a pretty girl, classic features, good high cheek bones and lovely blue-green eyes. That white-blonde hair is such a gorgeous colour, might need a little assistance in future years to keep it like that. I was very impressed by her directness, but about clothes, the dressmaker's coming on Monday morning and my tailor in the afternoon. Should things not work out then, as with the others, some new clothes will be my gift to her for the trouble she's been put to."

Estelle grinned, "You are, as always beautifully organised. Now, I'm going to make my own wager. I think Rose, this is the one. I believe you've got a winner here."

"Well, amen to that. Now it's time for you to go home and for me to retire. I need my own beauty sleep, there are busy days ahead."

DAISY

I was right about Jim. He isn't a nice person. All that grinning and joking in the kitchen is for show. That's not what he's like at all. Yesterday I as shaking dusters outside the kitchen door and he was in the tool shed talking to Fred. I heard him say, "As for Major Carstairs., well he's a nutcase now, should be in the looney bin by rights". Fred grunted something I couldn't hear. Then Jim said "Nice to see Miss Cynthia back though. Now she's a right tasty piece. I mean have you seen the size of her tits lately. I'd like to get a hold of those and show 'er..." There was a sudden growl from Fred and then,

"You can stop right there, you foul-mouthed young varmint. Get out of my sight, you're disgusting."

I bolted indoors, but it shook me that Jim could talk like that, yet never seemed to put a foot wrong inside the house.

Mrs. Templar arrived today and Mrs. B. was right, she is lovely. She's small, tinyframed, like a little bird. Her hair's pure silver and she has been and still is very attractive, with wonderful skin. I assisted her in changing for dinner and later for bed. I'd learned from Alice that ladies are never totally undressed even in front of their personal maids, unless of course, bathing them becomes a necessity. With this in mind, I kept her silk robe at hand so that she was reasonably covered, even whilst changing undergarments. She seemed quite unembarrassed and this in turn made me feel quite comfortable in what was for me a unique situation.

There were whisperings in the kitchen today that Major C. is going to see a doctor, someone who studies heads rather than bodies. The poor man is still very jumpy and Mrs. C. is herself starting to look pale with worry. Everyone is trying desperately to make Christmas as enjoyable as possible for the family, the first time they will all have been together for at least three years.

On the 20th December Fred brought in the tree, set in a large pot. It was placed in the entrance hall and that night Cynthia and her brothers decorated it with candles in glass holders, red ribbon bows and tiny bags of sweets. Then swags of greenery and holly were hung around mirrors and pictures and suddenly everywhere started to look really festive. Mrs. C. took her husband in to watch the children at work and when they'd finished he smiled and put his hand out tentatively to touch their handiwork, then stood back to observe it, as if fearful it would disappear before his eyes. Poor man, even when he smiles his eyes look so sad.

Christmas was quietly happy, although I couldn't help wondering if Mum and Dad felt lonely without us. Marigold and I used to love the scents of Christmas, the greenery from outside, the goose roasting in the oven and the spicy smell of the Christmas pudding. I could experience all that here of course, but it wasn't quite the same as being at home. In our off-duty hours we played dominoes and card games and I even managed to laugh with the others when I put sugar in my tea only to find it tasted awful. We each have out own little caddies for tea and sugar and Jim had exchanged the sugar in mine for salt. Everyone thinks he's such fun, but I feel very wary in his presence and avoid being alone with him.

It was on Twelfth Night that the pattern of life in Slade Manor was ripped apart. Members of the family were assembling for lunch and the kitchen was its usual scene of organised activity. Suddenly from outside came a wail of anguish. Everyone rushed to the door and out into the courtyard, to find Mrs. Carstairs collapsed in a heap at the entrance to the barn. Fred had his arms outstretched preventing entry. The creaking of the barn's crossbar told its own story that Major Carstairs had been able to face life no longer.

Mrs. Frensham appeared from a side door and sprang into action.

"Mrs. Barton over here and help me take Mrs. Carstairs to the study. Jim you are to assist Fred here and then ride over to Carisbrooke and inform Mr. Richard. Daisy, tell Mrs. Templar there has been an accident and she is required in the study; take her there and bring with you brandy and glasses. Alice, you are to stay in the dining room with the children until I am able to join you. Nothing, I repeat nothing, is to be said, other than that there has been an accident. Once I have informed Miss Cynthia and her brothers, then I will stay with them until Mr. Richard arrives. Alice, you are then to stay close to the study in case you are needed. Mrs. Barton, please prepare some food on trays, whatever you think. The boys will eat something, but I doubt if anyone else... Oh and would someone please see that Fred and Jim each have a glass of brandy and that there is food for them." All this was said whilst Mrs. Frensham and Mrs. Barton were gently lifting Mrs. Carstairs from the ground, straightening her clothes and starting to walk her back to the house. As each order was given, so people hurried to do what was expected of them.

For the younger members of the household who had not previously encountered death and knew little of suicide, it was a traumatic experience. Daisy was deeply shocked that the man she had just thought of as unwell had been sufficiently depressed and disturbed to take his own life. For many it seemed that putting the war behind them was not going to be quite as easy as everyone had thought. It was not until after the funeral that a dreadful quiet settled over the house. Mr. Richard, Major Carstairs' brother, had thought it advisable that Cynthia and the boys return to school as soon as possible. They were all shocked and distressed, but as Mrs. Barton pointed out, "They have been used to a life without their father for the past three years, so hopefully they will soon be back to normal – children are very adaptable to circumstances."

For Mrs. Carstairs it was another matter. She had lost her husband, the father of her children and was finding it very difficult to return to any semblance of normality. Mrs. Templar had agreed to stay on until things improved and constantly advised her daughter to forget the nature of her husband's death, stressing that he was a victim of war, just as much as if he had died from a German bullet. Gradually the trauma diminished. Mrs. Carstairs' brother-in-law proved a tower of strength, taking the two ladies for rides along the seafront at Ryde and to the top of the Downs, so that they could look down on the beauty of the fertile Arreton valley. And, as winter released its hold on the gardens and the spring flowers emerged, the household seemed to give a collective sigh of relief and started to enjoy life once again.

DAISY

Daisy had now settled into her own routine, occasionally meeting her mother in Newport on her half day break. After shopping they would adjourn to Harvey's restaurant for tea and cake and the opportunity to talk about anything and everything. The meetings helped Daisy through a difficult patch, a time when she had become very homesick and longed to be back at home in familiar surroundings, with her mother and father.

Letters to her parents from Marigold were now arriving at irregular intervals and Daisy and her mother devoured their contents. Marigold's new life sounded amazing. Daisy knew jealousy was a sin, but felt she could at least be permitted a tiny bit of envy. At least Marigold could never again complain that Daisy was the favoured one and always seemed to get the best of everything and every situation. Being taught to sing and act and with the possibility of going on the stage was incredible. 'Still', Daisy thought 'must be fair, I think she'll be quite good, she always had a flair for that sort of thing. I'll just not think about all those lovely new clothes of hers and that bedroom! Somewhat different from the one I share with Alice.'

Like Marigold, Daisy was surprised that knowing the theatrical background of Marigold's new home, her parents had not dismissed the idea of her going there to live...and with strangers! Her mother was quick to point out that she had talked to Mrs. Murray-Rogers at some length and had always been full aware that Rosalie Reece was famous and did not come into the category of people of rather unsavoury character, constantly unemployed and having to scratch around for a living. She also had the reputation of being kind and in spite of her fame, unassuming.

"But you didn't say. You didn't tell Marigold or me that she was going to live with someone like that." And then, hesitantly, "It could have been me. Who decided?" Her mother sighed, she had feared this question. "The decision was made by Mrs. Murray-Rogers. She obviously knew all about Miss Reece's plans and having met the two of you, she felt that Marigold was the more extrovert and would suit Miss Reece's requirements better."

"Well the extrovert bit is certainly true, but I wouldn't have minded living in the lap of luxury for a while instead of always being at someone's beck and call."

"Daisy darling, don't have any regrets, at least I get to see you now and again and that means a great deal to me. Fate has a strange way of taking over our lives and who knows what might happen in a few years' time."

Daisy was to remember those words and wonder at how accurately her mother had been in predicting future events. But now it was time for news from the farm, which was pretty much as she would have expected. A whole batch of new lambs, two sickly ones having to be bottle-fed and a new calf called Primrose.

"Not more flower names", Daisy laughed, "Dad's going to find it difficult to continue with that if there's a bull calf!" Was it her imagination or was there hesitation on her Mother's part, before joining in the laughter?

It was good to see her mother outside the environs of the farm and not surrounded by household chores. Here, in a different setting, she looked younger, prettier and Daisy realised she was still at thirty-five a young woman. Each time they had to say goodbye, Daisy wondered how long it would be before they would all be together again as a family, Mum and Dad and Marigold.

Chapter 3

MARIGOLD

Christmas at Greenacres was celebrated in a whirlwind of colour and style. Midnight Mass, the sweet voices of the choristers, luncheon on Boxing Day, the room full of Rose's friends, followed by party games and singing round the grand piano and wonderful gifts. As if all the new clothes she'd received on arrival were not awe-inspiring enough, there was now a gold locket from Rose and a pretty nightdress from Estelle. Marigold felt overwhelmed. In the midst of all this her studies had continued. She had learned to use her diaphragm to ensure maximum breath capacity and had laughed when Rose had demonstrated someone running using only clavicular breathing with her shoulders and chest heaving and a great deal of puffing and panting. Funny, as intended, but Marigold had got the message that such shallowness was insufficient for the stage and she must learn to breathe deeply using the full expanse of lungs and rib cage to achieve the resultant enlarged abdomen capacity.

She now knew that Estelle's home was a very short distance from Greenacres. Her parents having been killed in a coach accident when she was a baby, she lived with a lady called Biddy, who seemed to be a combination of former nanny and housekeeper. Estelle was the musical expert, a trained singer, and her requirements from Marigold were endless scale practice and lessons in reading music. For her part, Estelle was delighted to find that Marigold had a natural sense of rhythm, so that once the co-ordination of breathing and accuracy of notes was achieved she was able to, as Estelle said 'relax into the music' and later would be able to concentrate on expression.

Marigold had also learned a little more about the other occupants of Greenacres. Rose's maid, Milly, and her cook, Mrs. Knight, had been with her since the house was built. Currently both lived in, but Milly was courting a young man in Twickenham and planning to marry soon. The garden was starting to prove too much for Bill, the gardener, and Rose was hoping that he would stay on until the young people married, when she planned to offer them living-in accommodation. Milly's young man was prepared to take over the maintenance and any heavy work at Greenacres, plus the gardening. Milly had indicated that they would both be delighted to receive such an offer.

Every day, as she had been warned, Marigold found there were new obstacles to overcome, new challenges to meet. Some proved more tedious than others, but feeling almost daily the marked improvement in her vocal ability, both in speech and music, Marigold knew them to be both rewarding and exciting.

Two months after her arrival at Greenacres Marigold was taken to the Music Hall. The theatre, with its Victorian ambience, was a delight and from the moment the curtains parted until their closure, Marigold felt she was transported into another world where people sang, danced and joked, giving endless enjoyment to everyone present. The thought of being up there with the performers was almost suffocating, but at the same time she knew it to be exhilarating.

At the end of the show she and Rose went backstage to meet some of the performers and Marigold saw for the first time the inside of a stage dressing room. Cluttered beyond belief with clothes hanging from everywhere possible, grease-paint sticks on tiny surfaces serving as dressing tables, wall mirrors, some with messages scribbled in corners, the occasional bunch of flowers in a jam-jar, the performers' quarters smelling of sweat and face powder were not at all what Marigold had expected. Rose smiled at her shocked expression.

"This my dear, is the reality of our profession. What you see on the stage is a façade, an illusion. What we aim is to transport people into another world, away from the squalid and unpleasant things of life, but sometimes in the pursuit of that we ourselves have to make do with whatever is available. Theatres are invariably very cramped backstage, so much space is required for the storage and movement of scenery and props –properties, that is, items needed on stage. These always take priority and only the most famous..."

"Like you," Marigold interjected.

"Well yes, like me, but never forget that was after years of experience, prior to that I worked endlessly in these conditions. Only a few can expect and receive comfort and luxury backstage."

"There is another room you should see," Rose opened the door onto another small room with a few well-worn armchairs, "this is the Green room."

"But why Green? I mean it isn't…" Marigold looked and felt puzzled.

"These rooms rarely are. Not every theatre can provide one of these, but it is where we are able to relax when not on stage, or busy changing. There are one or two rules attached to being in here. Whistling is not permitted, it is considered bad luck."

"Why?"

"I had an awful feeling you were going to ask me that and I'm afraid I don't know. It's just one of those traditions that have been handed down over the years and we all adhere to them. There is something else that might interest you. When I bought my house, I decided it must have a name connected with the theatre, so I settled for Greenacres, green because it is now my very own place in which to be comfortable and relax. And", with a smile, "before you ask me whether you are allowed to whistle there, let me just say that it is very unladylike for young ladies to whistle at any time. Now do you want to see what it feels like to stand on a stage?"

Marigold's expression was sufficient. "I'll take that as a 'Yes'. I'm sure the audience will have left by now. First, we must get permission from the Stage Manager. Sometimes it can be dangerous if scenery or furniture is being moved."

Mick, the Stage Manger, was clearly delighted to see Rose and undeterred, as she was, by his overalls, embraced her warmly. Stagehands rushed up to say hello. It was obvious to Marigold that however famous Rose was in her profession, she had always regarded herself and been regarded by others, as very much part of a hard-working team. "You will soon see how reliant upon each other we all are to ensure that a show goes well. Bad lighting or noise behind the scenes can ruin a show, so at actual performances, the Stage Manager is the most important person in the theatre, as you will soon find out for yourself. For everyone involved it is crucial that the audiences enjoy the show. A poor, badly received show will close and everyone will be out of work, which could mean weeks or even months without money, so you see…?"

Seeing the empty auditorium from the other side of the footlights was awe-inspiring and for a few minutes Marigold stood there just drinking it all in. The boxes with their gold cherubs and red velvet seats, the orchestra pit at her feet and the tiered seats reaching almost to the roof, all had been packed with people just a short while ago.

"No wonder it's called the Gods up there", Rose said. "Right at the top it's cheaper and the seats are not so plushy, but some of our best audiences sit up there spellbound and as you heard tonight they really join in the singing with gusto. It's lovely that with so many hearts broken after the horrors of war, people are still able to come here and even if it's only for a short while, they can forget their troubles and heartache.

"Now it's time I took you home. Don't worry, we'll come again, and next time we'll visit one of the theatres during the day when it's quiet, so that we can have a really good look around and I can explain more fully what goes on."

❀ ❀ ❀

DAISY'S Journal

Mrs. Templar went home today and I was sad to see her go. She has been so kind to me and taught me so much, in a very unobtrusive way. One day she saw me knock on the door of the study, where I knew Mrs. C. was reading. Later she took me on one side and said "It's never correct for those in service to knock on the door of a downstairs room, you must just enter. Upstairs is of course another matter – always knock, even if you know the room should be empty". And about clothes, when I commented one day, how people in high society always seemed to have the most wonderful matching ensembles, she said,

"That doesn't happen by chance of course, Daisy. A good lady's maid will ensure that when material is purchased for any outfit, summer or winter, daytime or evening, an extra length of material is always bought, so that a hat might be decorated, a scarf made, a jacket edged and so on with the same fabric. And remember if you are asked by a mistress whether an outfit suits her or not, if you don't like what she is trying on, tell her so. She will eventually know that you are giving an honest answer and learn to trust your judgement. Far better than approving an outfit and for her to be told by others that she does not look her best. It may take courage at first, but will be well worth it in the long term."

How simple things seem when one hears them explained.

Mrs.Templar has been invited to join some friends who are holidaying in Tuscany, and as Mrs. C. seems much improved, she has urged her mother to go. I had thought

Miss Cynthia would be here for the summer break, but now learn that she too, is to holiday with friends in Scotland. With the boys spending their summer with cousins in the West Country, I said to Mrs. B. that it was a good thing that Mr. Richard was a regular visitor, or Mrs. C. would be very lonely indeed. Mrs. B. clicked her teeth and muttered something which sounded suspiciously like "Much too early, people will talk, if they're not already doing so."

Oh dear, it seems that nothing in life is ever straight forward. Mr. Richard has been here often and I've been pleased to see Mrs. C. has taken more care with her appearance when she knew he was visiting. Not that she's ever untidy, I can't even imagine that, but on the occasions when he's expected, she puts on smarter dresses and wears pieces of jewellery, which have not seen the light of day for some time. Her brother-in-law has a slight limp, which is why he was not sent away to fight, but he is handsome and makes her smile. When this happens her face is transformed and she becomes very striking indeed.

I had a nasty experience a few days ago. I had an irritating tickly cough which kept me awake for some time. Eventually I decided to go down into the kitchen to get a glass of milk, which I thought would be soothing. The entrance opens onto a small flight of four stairs, so that one looks down on the whole kitchen area. To my horror the floor appeared to be moving At first I thought I must be dizzy, or delirious, then as I looked more closely I realised that what I was seeing was a whole carpet, not of material but of black beetles! The milk forgotten, I was out of the door in a flash and back up to my bedroom, my cough cured by the shock. Mrs. B. laughed when I told her, said they were harmless enough and Fred did put powder down at regular intervals. They never *touched the food and that was her main concern, but for my part, I resolved never again would I make a late night visit to the kitchen.*

My monthlies started yesterday. Hallelulia! I think I might have done something before Marigold at last!

MARIGOLD

Amongst Rose's friends was one to whom Marigold had taken a particular liking. About fifty, Monty Seymour was a dapper little man with dark twinkling eyes and a magical virtuoso on the piano. After one wonderful evening when he had accompanied Estelle and a group of friends round the piano and then proceeded to play both jazz and classical numbers, Marigold expressed her amazement at his ability to Estelle.

"Monty is such a brilliant pianist and has a wonderful voice, he ought to be on the stage."

Estelle almost choked over her glass of wine, "You really are off the beaten track on that little island of yours, I can't believe you've never heard of Monty Seymour – although come to think of it he's been off the boards for about five years and you would have only been nine at that time, so I suppose…"

"So he was a performer?"

"The best! Stage name was just 'Monty'. His shows were always a complete sell-out. Years ago he and Rose had a bit of a 'thing' going. Nothing came of it of course. They were both far too busy trying to get their careers established. He married in his thirties a very well-to-do young lady, the Hon. Lydia Warren, no less. Bit of a scandal there though, about six years ago they were in the Greek Islands, holidaying on a yacht with a well-heeled group of young socialites when Lydia was drowned. She wasn't missed for an hour or so. Most of the others had gone ashore and Monty went down and read the papers in their cabin then had a snooze, thinking Lydia was still where he'd left her, sunbathing on deck. When the alarm was raised, no-one had seen anything. Her body was never found and I'm afraid there was a lot of mud-slinging as far as Monty was concerned, rumours that the marriage was in difficulties, that sort of thing. You see he came out of it so well- a fine house and all her money. There was a police investigation of course, but without the body there were a lot of grey areas, questions unanswered."

"So he gave up the theatre?"

"Yes, but there's the rub and that's why there was so much gossip. He'd apparently been making noises about wanting to quit for some time, but knew if he wasn't working it would be obvious that Lydia was keeping him. After her death he stopped his stage work almost immediately and he's never looked back. He bought a small theatre, gave it a face-lift and put on his own shows. It's proved very profitable."

"I can't believe there's anything devious about him – he seems an absolute angel."

"Well he's certainly that", and as Marigold registered surprise at Estelle's emphatic response,

"I didn't mean it in the sense you did. An angel in the theatre is what you would call a 'backer' or 'sponsor'. In other words, not only does Monty stage his own shows, but he also looks around in the provinces and further afield.

If he finds anything he thinks is a sure-fire success then he will put up the money to ensure it can be staged."

Marigold looked across at Monty enjoying his drink and talking animatedly to Rose. So he wasn't just the carefree friend who enjoyed music, this was a seriously shrewd business man and, what was that other word she'd heard used for the first time yesterday? A French word... entrepreneur. She would remember to use that, she liked the sound of it.

Tomorrow morning, Marigold knew it would be back to basics. A few days ago, discussing speech, Rose had said that there were undertones of the Isle of Wight dialect in her speech which would have to be eradicated. This had come as a surprise, Marigold had always thought that her mother and Miss Webster had gone to great lengths to ensure that she and Daisy spoke what her mother called King's English.

"I've not dealt with it before, but to me there are occasional sounds of a form of Cockney," this from Rose.

"Goodness, I remember ages ago Mum was told by our local Minister that our Isle of Wight dialect was a debased form of Cockney, she was quite upset at the time, but it sounds as if his reference book was right."

"It's only now and then, certainly not constant, but we'll concentrate on rounding the vowel sounds next and then..."

"Yes, Miss Reece and then...?"

"When I am feeling really grumpy and want to tax you to the limit, I shall give you a piece of poetry and ask you to say verses in as broad an Isle of Wight dialect as you can manage and standard English alternately."

"All I can say is 'Help'."

The question of how to address Miss Reece had always seemed something of a problem to Marigold, Estelle had always been Estelle because that was how she had introduced herself initially and in any event she was much younger. But whilst Marigold always addressed her benefactor as Miss Reece, in her thoughts she invariably thought of her as Rose. Knowing her own mother's ideas about young people being too familiar with their elders and whilst the people who were in and out of Greenacres constantly, seemed to call everyone 'Darling' or by peculiar pet names, she knew any change in the situation must come from Rose herself. So, for the time being 'Miss Reece' it remained.

As for Rose ever being grumpy, Marigold couldn't imagine it. With everyone Rose met she seemed friendly and outgoing. Marigold thought the word 'charming' must have been invented with her in mind, for although an actress, this was not acting, it was a genuine interest in others and thought for their well-being. Marigold hoped that there might at some time be an occasion when she could see Rose on stage playing a villainess. It seemed impossible to imagine her submerging her natural warmth to convey wickedness.

Now Rose was as usual, shooing her, albeit gently, to bed, with yet another paragraph to learn and the warning of an early start again next day. Climbing the stairs Marigold thought Mum and Dad need have no worries about me being thoroughly spoiled. It's all absolutely lovely, but there are rules and I am being worked quite hard!"

DAISY'S Journal

I'm still wary of Jim. One afternoon I glanced out of the study window and saw a flash of movement in the kitchen garden. Knowing Fred was off duty, I thought I'd better investigate. I went quietly round the side of the house and saw Jim kneeling on a box and peering through the hedge into the rose garden beyond. A few more steps and I could see what he was looking at. Cynthia newly returned from Scotland, was lying on the garden seat, shoulders and legs bare, enjoying the sun. Then I saw something else. Jim was rubbing the front of his trousers as if to get rid of a stain, but as he continued rubbing, so he was getting redder and redder in the face. Suddenly I knew what he was doing and the realisation made me gasp aloud and quickly turn away from the window. I'd only heard whispers about it at school and Mari and I had said it was probably one of those stories children make up. Now I knew it to be true and the thought made me flush with embarrassment and shame. I returned to the kitchen, undecided what to do. Those nasty remarks he's made earlier to Fred and now this. Should I tell someone? More importantly, how could I? Jim would probably think up some excuse and people would think I was exaggerating and laugh it off. I tried to put it out of my mind.

Two days later Alice had to go home. Her father has now returned and their lives are going to be quite complicated for some time. Obviously Alice is needed to assist her mother. Mrs. Frensham came and sat with us in the kitchen, almost unheard of! The boys were to start at boarding school and with Miss Cynthia also returning to school this week, Mrs.

Frensham had worked out a possible time-table for us all. She herself would serve afternoon tea and assist at dinner time, leaving me to serve breakfast. There would be only Mrs.C.'s bedroom to attend to and the lady from the village would assist with this and our staff rooms and continue to deal with laundry. Jim was to carry on with his usual chores of delivering hot water in the mornings, attending to the fires and cleaning carpets as necessary. He was also to assist Mrs. B. with preparation of vegetables and washing up after all meals. I could see he didn't like that! Mrs. F. said we would try this for a week and if there were problems, it might need rethinking.

And that it certainly did. It turned out to be the worst day of my life. By the time I went to bed my head was spinning with the new arrangements and I was thankful to be able to curl up and go to sleep.

I woke with a start, it was still dark and I could hear Alice breathing. A sudden shock of realisation, as I remembered Alice had gone home. Who, or what was it? The next moment I felt the heat of breath on my face and hands thrusting inside my nightdress, one clutching my breast and another forcing my legs apart. I gasped aloud, rolled out of the bed on the side away from whoever it was and made a dash for the door. There I almost fell over a large jug. Of course...Jim, and he had his excuse at the ready. I grabbed the jug and with one heave threw it, water and all, in his direction, then ran like a mad thing down the corridor, screaming.

Lights appeared, two doors opened simultaneously and Mrs. B. and Mrs. F. appeared sleep-dishevelled and alarmed. Mrs. B. stopped me in my flight and, her arms wrapped tightly round me, we turned in time to see a soaking Jim emerge from my room, dripping water as he rushed downstairs.

Within moments I was wrapped in a blanket and bundled sobbing into Mrs. B's still warm bed.

"Just tell me one thing Daisy, before Mrs. F. and I go down and deal with him, has he hurt you in any way?"

"No, he was touching me," again the tears choked me, "and I woke up and ran away."

"Listen to me Daisy, I am going to lock this door," she showed me the key, "no-one can come in. No-one. In a few minutes Mrs. F. and I will be back with a hot drink for you. You are to stay here tonight and I will take Alice's bed. By the time you get up, Jim will have left for good."

And that's what happened. They were quickly back with the news that Jim had been banished to the barn with a pillow and blanket and would be leaving at first light. They'd brought hot milk with honey and something else in it, something I hadn't had before, but it made me feel drowsy and finally I was able to sleep.

Mrs. Frensham's first duty the next morning was to inform Fred that Jim was no longer at the Manor. He showed no surprise. Non-committal as always, he asked no questions, but said at once, "I know someone who'd do very nicely for what you want".

This was just what Mrs. Frensham had been hoping for.

"He's eighteen, enlisted when he was still seventeen, done his training and was just about to be shipped out when it were all over, thank God. He's a good lad from a decent home. He won't give you no trouble like that other one – a queer fish he was. Too big for his own boots.

Good riddance to 'im. Young Michael's a neighbour of mine, used to help me in my garden when he was a little 'un. His folks'll be glad of the extra cash."

"Ask him to come and see me straight away, Fred, and we'll fix something up. As long as he knows he'll have to live in."

"Don't see as 'ow that'll be a problem. They be short of space now. I could see 'im at lunch break if you likes."

"Do that and ask him to come and see me at three o'clock today. Thank you Fred."

Next was a visit to the mistress of the house, who was shocked to hear of the night's events. Yes, she had heard what sounded like a scream coming from the staff rooms and assumed Daisy was having a nightmare; when all went quiet she thought it had been resolved.

So the matter was speedily dealt with and Michael was welcomed into the fold. And what an asset he proved to be. Diligent, polite, a hard and willing worker, with the bonus of having a lively sense of fun. Not, as Daisy remarked to Mrs. Barton, in Jim's brash showing-off manner. Michael's sense of humour was more subtle, in fact it sometimes took those with him a few moments to realise that he was, ever so gently, poking fun. His months in the service had seen him mature from boy to man, teaching him discipline and preparing him for hard work. He had also been trained to shoot and, as Fred remarked to Mrs. Barton, "There could well be toimes when we'm glad of another gun on the farm, when they foxes get on the rampage."

The running of the Manor farm was increasingly becoming a problem. Whilst Richard Carstairs was currently acting as overseer, it was not an ideal situation.

He was a trained architect, whose knowledge of farm management was limited. Just how long they could manage without a regular trained manager was questionable.

MARIGOLD'S Journal

I can't ignore Dad's journal gift any longer. It's been staring at me reproachfully for months now, but with all the things I have to memorize there seems little time for writing. I've decided I could just try recording special events so here goes!

I am now a fully fledged young woman. Two days ago my monthlies started, or periods, as Rose tells me is the correct name. No fuss and palaver here about that. Belt and towels already waiting for me with full instructions as to how to deal with them. Typically Rose instructed me, "When this happens during the run of a performance, ensure you get extra rest, otherwise you will go on stage looking washed out and that would never do." My main concern is whether Daisy has started yet. Can't wait to hear.

Yesterday evening Monty and several friends were visiting Rose and as always I was included in the gathering, whilst always mindful of the fact that my expected retirement time was nine thirty. Before Monty left he came over, put a hand on my shoulder and said to Rose, "I believe this girl of yours has a birthday soon. With your permission Rose, I would like to give her a birthday treat. I thought you and she might like to join me for tea at the Grosvenor on that day and afterwards be my guests at the theatre. There's a play at the Haymarket with which you are all too familiar, Rose darling, 'She stoops to Conquer'. For Marigold it would be a new experience and, I hope, a pleasurable one. What do you think?"

"I think that as always, dear Monty, you are both kind and thoughtful and we will be delighted to accept your kind invitation.". I too, stuttered my thanks upon which he kissed me on the forehead and said, "It will be my pleasure to escort two such attractive ladies. I shall look forward to it." I sometimes think anticipating a treat, is almost as good as the actual event. For several days I was so excited that Rose had, for the very first time, to chastise me for not paying attention.

Monty and Rose were of course instantly recognised at the Grosvenor and people scurried around as if they were royalty. A pianist was tinkling away on a grand piano and the tune changed to 'Happy Birthday' when the waiter appeared with a cake adorned with fifteen lighted candles. There was something else. When we examined the cake it was decorated with the draped curtains of a stage proscenium arch and round the side was a succession of tiny theatrical masks. (Obviously some prompting on Monty's part). After I had wished and blown out the candles, I was allowed just a few sips of champagne with a slice of cake and having handed out pieces to guests seated round about us and to the pianist, the waiter removed what was left with instructions that it was to be wrapped so that we might take it back to Greenacres with us.

As for the play, according to Monty, it was a Restoration Comedy and a delightful romp. 'A romp' perhaps, but even I, soon became aware of the careful timing of each funny line and gesture and the total absorption in their parts, no matter how small, of each player.

When I thanked Monty he said, "Marigold, today you are fifteen, and I expect and look forward to seeing you on the stage before you are seventeen."

I'm sure it was obvious from my expression that the thought of trying to live up to everyone's expectations absolutely terrifies me.

DAISY'S Journal—December 1919

Amazing news, Mother is pregnant and she and Dad are obviously delighted. Perhaps they'll at last get the son they've always wanted. The baby's due in July, so they've both kept it a secret for the past weeks, just in case as Mum said, 'Anything went wrong'.

Today I received my first letter from Marigold. We have both been very remiss in not writing to each other, but I know that she and Mum correspond regularly and M. receives my news, as I receive hers. All the same it was quite wonderful to see her handwriting, which is almost identical to mine and with the letter what was clearly a birthday card and something else, both of which are to be left unopened until my/our birthday.

I know from Mum that Marigold's birthday is already planned and I fear that mine will be very humdrum by comparison. When I attempted to go home on one of my whole days off, I found that the journey to and from the farm took so much time, there was very little left to spend with Mum and Dad. We decided that it was better for me to continue to meet Mum on those occasions and who knows perhaps if Dad can leave the farm, he may come too.

When I reply to M., I must ask her if she's yet started her monthlies, if so, she hasn't told Mum which is surprising. I can tell she's loving her new life and who wouldn't? She doesn't have to work every day as I do. In fairness, I think she'll be really good on the stage. She always loved dressing up and pretending to be a king or queen. I had to kneel down in front of her and she would tap me on the shoulder with one of the spare fencing poles and say 'Rise Sir Knight'. Once though she was a wicked queen who locked me in a cupboard, the trouble was she then forgot all about me and went off to play at something else. Dad rescued me ages later and M. was sent to her room in disgrace.

Marigold receives five shillings a week pocket money and this with all her expenses paid wherever she goes, but as she says, there are occasionally things she wants to buy like birthday presents (a broad hint). My own money seems a pittance in comparison. However, I'm fortunate to be in a good home where the work is regular but not arduous and, now that Jim has gone, the company is congenial.

I have been saving and bought a pretty card and a scarf which I hope she will love. It is pale blue georgette with tiny silk flowers embroidered at each end. They look very much like marigolds. I know it will suit her because I tried it on, casually draped round my neck as I had seen in one of Mrs. C.'s magazines. The colours were just right.

Fifteen in just two days, how this year has flown.

Daisy having related to Mrs. Barton the exciting plans for her twin's birthday, that good lady decided that Daisy herself should be treated to something special. A word in Mrs. Frensham's ear and their plan took shape.

"Daisy, Mrs. Frensham would like a word with you." As always, it was a nervous Daisy, who tapped on the Housekeeper's door.

"Come in. Ah Daisy, sit down for a moment. I understand you have a birthday on the thirteenth."

"Yes, Ma'am."

"In that case I am sure you would prefer to exchange your full day off to that day, so that you might make the most of it."

"Yes Ma'am, thank you Ma'am, I could see my parents and…"

"May I suggest that they meet you in Newport for lunch. I know you enjoy meeting your mother at Harvey's for tea, perhaps both your parents could come up on that occasion and you could all have lunch together. The shops will be ready for Christmas and there is usually a Christmas Fayre or Bazaar at the Parish Church. Afterwards I would like you to bring parents back here for tea at, say, four fifteen."

"Here Ma'am?" Daisy was nonplussed.

"Why yes Daisy, I think it is time your parents saw where you work and the people with whom you work. Do you think they would be happy to do that?"

"I think they'd be delighted Ma'am. My mother always likes to hear about my friends ." And then hastily, "Not that I gossip Ma'am, it's just…"

"No Daisy, I am quite sure you are not a gossip. Mrs. Barton and I were most impressed with the grown-up way in which you deal with that unpleasant incident recently.

You did not talk to other people about it, just went about your work in your usual and I might say, efficient way."

Daisy blushed at this unexpected praise.

"I will invite Alice to join us and I am sure Mrs. Barton will as always prepare food fit for a king, or in this case, a birthday girl."

Stunned, Daisy returned to the kitchen. 'Us' Mrs. Frensham had said, so she too would be sitting down with them. Amazing! And how lovely it would be if Alice could come, they had so much news to catch up on.

And so it transpired. Lunch at Harvey's with her parents, a visit to the shops where her birthday gift was a dress smarter than any she had previously owned and from there to the Manor where Mrs. Barton had excelled herself. Scones warm from the oven, Mrs. B.'s own raspberry jam, ham rolls, trifle and the centrepiece, a cake decorated with daisies. There were gifts of flowers and chocolates, rosewater from Mrs. Frensham and stationery from Michael. The package from Marigold contained a brooch, a small enamelled daisy. The colours were clear and bright and Daisy loved it. If Mrs. Griffin, Daisy's mum felt any tinge of regret that she was not entertaining both her daughters on their birthday, she gave no such sign, appreciative of the thought that had gone into giving Daisy a wonderful day.

Just before their departure Mr. and Mrs. Griffin were taken upstairs to meet Mrs. Carstairs. It was the briefest of meetings instigated on the spur of the moment by Mrs. Frensham. Having spent some time in the company of Daisy's parents Mrs. Frensham could see that Daisy's quiet composure and her commitment to any task in hand were the products of her upbringing, the values instilled in her from birth. Her education had been the very best the Griffins could afford, with the result that Daisy was articulate and well-mannered.

As she explained to Mrs. Barton afterwards, "I do sometimes feel that the people we serve live in such a rarefied atmosphere, they expect everyone else to talk like yokels and behave boorishly and people like Jim don't help in correcting that. I thought Mrs. Carstairs ought to see that the Griffins and people like them are not only the salt of the earth but also know how to speak and behave correctly. And another thing," Mrs. Frensham was warming to her theme, "since the war we now know that women can hold down all manner of jobs and are able to take their place with men as equals in society. Mark my words, Mrs. Barton, the next few years will bring a lot of changes. Nothing is ever going to be the same again." Unaware of Mrs. Frensham's philosophising, Daisy was in a state of euphoria. Her mother looked well and, apart from the early weeks of weariness, was finding this quite an easy pregnancy. Alice, looking very much the young lady, had made them laugh with her tales of how she coped with two younger sisters and the tricks they played on her. Daisy could see that Michael was quite taken with Alice and thought it would be wonderful if a grand romance had begun on her own birthday. Far from being humdrum, it had been a very special day and she would have much to tell Marigold in her next letter.

Chapter 4

MARIGOLD

Marigold's next visit to the theatre was very much business only. Rose's instructions, as with her lessons, were clear and concise.

"First of all I want you to sit in on an audition, then the first read through of the play, the first rehearsal and so on. In this way to prepare you for what lies ahead and hopefully reduce some of the tension which always arises from stepping into the unknown. There will of course always be some tension and that is desirable, indeed necessary, it helps the adrenalin to pump more freely and the performer to give of his best.

"As I do not wish my presence to inhibit anyone, I have arranged for you to be accompanied by a friend, Celia Jordan. Celia was in a Chekhov play with me some years ago, she is now experienced and sensible. You will be going to the St. John's Church Hall in Kensington, where they are auditioning for a play by a new young author. Take with you a pencil and paper and make notes of anything which interests you, which we can discuss later. Note particularly voices at this stage, whether they are audible and pleasing to the ear. A voice which does not use the rising and falling cadences is monotonous and risks sending its listeners to sleep. Ask yourself if the speaker conveys the energy of the piece and, if he or she is performing an excerpt with two characters, whether the essence of each one is clearly defined."

It was difficult to imagine Celia herself on the stage. She seemed to be a different breed of actor from the ones Marigold was acquainted with at Greenacres. She was quiet, almost sombrely dressed and her pale oval face, devoid of make-up, seemed plain. Marigold felt that she would be best summed up as 'colourless'. Later Rose was quick to point out that the very ordinariness of Celia's face and figure often turned to her advantage, as she said, "It is easier for an artist to paint on a blank canvas than a decorated one. Celia is almost like a chameleon, she can acquire the face and personality of many different characters, simply because her own appearance is relatively bland."

The presence of Celia and Marigold had been agreed and they sat out of the way, several rows behind the Producer, his secretary and two other people. Celia explained that one of these was obviously the playwright, asked out of courtesy, and the other a second Producer/Director who would take part in the selection process. About the applicants for role of male lead there seemed little doubt of the outcome, one being a very experienced performer who had Marigold shivering at the way his voice silkily flattered through a speech hinting at wickedness. A young woman's part was next and Marigold's choice was a girl with red hair, a strong voice and a wide range of facial expressions.

Celia disagreed, "She's altogether too overpowering in appearance and manner for this role. Sometimes an emotion or mood is conveyed by the merest flicker of expression, a nuance in the tone of voice. I preferred the little brunette; you feel drawn to her presence on stage, even when she is still, you sense her reaction."

Sure enough the brunette got the part and Marigold wondered if she herself would ever be able to draw together all these disparate strings and turn herself into an actress.

Their next visit to hear the selected cast read the play through for the first time was even more interesting. The characters started to emerge as individuals and Marigold could see the selection of players had been wise ones. The play, a comedy, called for careful timing and here the experienced performers shone.

"Now they've read through the play for the first time, do they go away and learn the whole of their parts?" Marigold asked.

"Not necessarily. People tackle this in different ways. Some will do just that. Others will learn according to the rehearsal structure, that is, part of a scene, or a whole act."

During the ensuing weeks Marigold watched the play take shape and with Celia's guidance made notes about the workloads of the Stage Manager and his Assistant, the painting of the set and the bringing together of the furniture and the properties involved. She sat and listened whilst they met and discussed the lighting and sound required and any special effects.

"A contemporary play such as this is fairly straightforward," Celia told her, "a period play, which involves getting everything, furniture, props, and costumes exactly right is much more difficult."

One table backstage puzzled Marigold: it seemed to hold a motley assortment of things, a torch, an envelope, a sandwich on a plate, a tray set with cups and saucers, a teddy-bear. Celia smiled, "Don't touch anything there on pain of death. It's the Props. Table, everything needed on stage or for people to carry on with them. It's in the province of the ASM, Assistant Stage Manager and he or she will have seen that the items are set out in the order in which they're needed for each scene. At the end of the evening she'll retrieve them from the set, the stage that is, or collect them from whoever handled them last, checking them off on her list. It's all too easy for an actor to slip an object into his pocket, go off and change and then the item would be missing when it's vital that it be either on stage or on this table."

MARIGOLD'S   Journal

I do believe I'm at last beginning to realise just how much actors have to be coaxed and chivvied in rehearsal and how critical it is for sound effects to be tailored to fit the action to achieve what the Producer clearly wants, a smoothly-knit whole. Last night Rose, Celia and I saw the first night and I felt quite proud of all of them. Proud on their behalf, that the comedy seemed so slick and delighted that the audience were apparently enjoying every minute of it. At the end we went backstage and Rose asked me, of all people, to introduce her to the cast and backstage teams.(I thought Celia looked rather po-faced, I think she assumed she would do the honours).

Seeing the cast's faces at meeting Rose, makes me realise just how important a lady she is to people in this profession and how very fortunate I am to have her tutoring me.

Back at Greenacres the endless routine of learning continued, how to faint on stage, to laugh and to cry, registering excitement and fear. Learning short passages each night had given way to extracts from plays, often now, as she had seen at the audition, portraying two characters. Night after night Marigold fell into bed exhausted yet exhilarated by every new milestone that had been tackled, if not yet completely overcome. Late Spring saw Celia and Marigold back in the theatre, this time the small theatre close to Greenacres in Richmond, and for four weeks Marigold 'shadowed' the Assistant Stage Manager, until she learned the hard way the vital importance of every property being in the right place at the right time, and that windows and doors must be checked for every scene. Ensuring whether the curtains on set should be open or closed, room lights on or off, the fire operative or not and whether there been a seasonal or time change between scenes or acts, which would mean that flowers or plants might require replacing.

Towards the end of this period, Rose dropped another bombshell.

"I am holding a soiree soon, Marigold," and smiling at Marigold's expression, "that's just a posh way of saying in French, a party with music. I think the time has come to make your musical debut. You will be amongst friends so there is no need to feel too alarmed about it. Estelle will help you choose a suitable piece as a solo item and then I would like you and she to perform some sort of double act. I don't mind if it's singing or acting or both. It will be wonderful experience for you and I think you'll enjoy it."

"It has to be 'Alice Blue Gown' with your colouring and that new blue dress. It's well within your vocal range and would be most suitable age-wise". Estelle had made up her mind. "The other item, I'd like to give some thought to, leave it with me."

Eventually Estelle decided on her own version of the song Vesta Tilley had made famous, 'I'm following in Father's footsteps'. Estelle was dressed in a man's suit and wore a battered hat and Marigold wore short trousers, ragged shirt and a boy's cap. Estelle had written a second verse, 'I'm following in Junior's footsteps' and with each of them singing in turn and then as a duet, it worked well.

The numbers were a great success. Marigold had one moment of sheer panic when she missed the note cue for her next line, but Monty smiled reassuringly and gave her the note again and she was back in harness. Another lesson! Concentration was everything. The slightest wayward thought, visual distraction and in that split second you could miss a vital cue, equally important in both music and speech. She knew from Rose that the ultimate sin verbally was slowness in picking up cues, which branded one as an amateur.

As Rose had explained repeatedly, "In normal speech, people speak and cut into other people's sentences quite frequently, so unless a significant pause is necessary to the plot, you must cut in with the next line as quickly and smoothly as possible." With music you were listening for the note cues and Marigold was disappointed that she had missed one.

Estelle brushed aside her apologies and complimented her on her singing and overall performances. Rose was, as always, analytical, "Your moves were good, but do ensure that your hands reflect your emotions, whether relaxed, tense or fearful. In the Vesta Tilley number they could have been stuffed more into your pockets. It all adds to the characterisation. Don't forget either that if you're in a period play, it's likely that the woman you're portraying did no manual work at all, so your hands will have to be whitened with make-up. If you forget to do this and only remember whilst waiting in the wings for your cue to go on stage, just raise your hands above your head for a few moments and the blood will drain away from them leaving your hands lily-white."

MARIGOLD'S   Journal—January 1920

I can't believe it! Mother pregnant, at her age. The parents both seem delighted, but I do wonder if they know just what they're letting themselves in for.

I've decided it would be impossible to get too big-headed in this environment. I feel in any performance, there is always going to be something upon which one could improve. Come to think of it, that's probably why these artistes say they never read what the critics have to say, it's sometimes so destructive they'd probably never tread the boards again.

Today Rose showed me some of her most treasured costumes. She has one room which has wardrobes all round the perimeter. There are magnificent regal dresses stitched

*with jewels and pearls, artificial, of course. The Tudor
garments were stunning, but my favourites were of the
Victorian and Edwardian vintage. Everything is a lesson
here and she showed me that even the simplest summer day-
dress must be sculpted and lined for stage wear, otherwise it
would not hang properly. I loved her Puck outfit and told
her that was a part I would so love to play. Rose's eyes lit up
when she talked about her excitement as a young woman
playing such a lively character. "Who knows," she said, "that
might be your first major role."*

    The thought delights and terrifies me.

DAISY'S   Journal

*Something terrible has happened here. I woke up during
the night and wondered for a moment what I was hearing.
It sounded like wet washing on the line slapping in a stiff
breeze. Suddenly I realised the sound was not slapping but
crackling and rushed to the window, where my view is from
the right wing of the house, looking across the courtyard to
the barns and storehouses. The barn was blazing and I now
heard other sounds, the horses neighing and stamping their
feet in terror, people shouting. Pulling on my coat and shoes,
I ran down the back stairs, seeing Michael's figure several
yards ahead of me.*

    *It was obvious from the start that the barn could not be
saved, but Michael managed to get the two horses to safety
through the rear door and Mrs. B., Mrs. F. and I pumped
water from the courtyard well to splash over the store rooms.
We were joined by Mrs. C., Cynthia and the boys and formed
a chain, using all the buckets and large containers we could*

muster from the kitchen. Our biggest worry was that Fred if he was busy, often stayed overnight in one of the small store-rooms there and no-one knew whether he had gone home or not. As yet there was no sign of him and with one of the stores well alight we were all anxious. It took us about twenty minutes to get the store rooms sufficiently soaked to gain entry. Sure enough there was Fred, unconscious from smoke inhalation. Mrs. C. had already telephoned for the fire brigade which arrived just as we were dragging Fred into the fresh air. The men there knew exactly what to do until the doctor arrived, then the ambulance came and Fred was whisked away to hospital.

Once the firemen were sure that the smouldering barn no longer posed a threat to the Manor itself, we all went into the kitchen and Mrs. B., Mrs. F. and I made cups of strong tea for everyone. Mrs. C. was clearly distraught and whilst the boys finished their cocoa, Mrs. F. suggested that Cynthia should take her mother upstairs and give her some brandy. This is the second time I've seen Mrs. F. in a crisis situation and there's no doubt about it she is able to take control immediately and seems to know exactly what is needed with great attention to detail and the well-being of everyone involved.

Barns, I know from living on a farm, are always fire hazards and it was not until Fred was with us again three days later that seeds of suspicion were sown as to how and why this had happened. Fred was in no doubt whatsoever that this was Jim's doing. Apparently Jim had said often in the village pub and elsewhere that he would be getting his own back for his instant dismissal, which he claimed to be totally unfair. The police were informed. They came to the Manor and asked questions, but when they looked at what *remained of the barn, it was obvious that all the suspicions in the world would not prove Jim's guilt.*

Since this happened Mr. Richard has been staying here. Mrs. B. makes it quite obvious that she does not approve and mutters darkly about 'tongues wagging' and even, 'no smoke without fire'.

Above stairs Richard Carstairs sat with his arm round his sister-in-law's shoulders.

"Julia my dearest, I don't want to force decisions on you whilst you're so obviously still shocked, but I really do think what I am suggesting would make a great deal of sense and be for your good and that of the children."

"But the gossip, it's so soon after Richard's death."

"It's a year and a half my darling. And why should we care what people think, if it is the best for us and for the family? Farncombe Manor only came to me because I was the eldest son. It's much, much too large for a bachelor as you well know, but with a growing family space is important and if you wished your mother to come and live with us, there would be no problem. I have tenant farmers working my land, with enough to spare should Cynthia and the boys want to take up horse riding. It makes sense on every level, certainly financially, running one property instead of two and most important of all because I want to have you with me in our home, so that I can love you and take care of you the way I've always wanted."

"I can't believe..." Julia hesitated.

"What can't you believe? I must have convinced you by now. I've always wanted you and bitterly regretted not speaking up before Robert staked his claim. Once he'd done so and you'd accepted, there was no going back, but losing you has been an on-going festering pain for all these years. Now we have the opportunity to make a fresh start together. I think you've always been fond of me and whilst that isn't the same as love, I'm willing to take the chance that it will grow into that and I'm willing, however difficult, to put my own feelings on hold until it does. We have to try to put behind us the sadness of Robert's death. He won't be forgotten by any of us, he's the father of your children and to me a dearly loved brother, but life goes on and we must live it and enjoy it."

"So, you're suggesting…"

"That we put Slade Manor on the market immediately. Have a quiet wedding next month just before the children return to their schools. In this way they would avoid all the upheaval. Some of the staff we can retain, this we'll discuss in detail. When the children have left, you could decide which items here you wish to have moved to Farncombe. You will have to examine the contents there too, to see if there is anything you feel you can't live with. I want you to feel you are creating our home. At the same time we can always store family heirlooms for such occasion as Cynthia or the boys might wish to make use of them."

Julia smiled, "You really are trying to think of everything."

"Well, there is something else. Moving you away further afield, would mean less likelihood of that idiot

Jim trying any more stunts like he did the other day. Next time it could prove even more serious."

Julia shuddered, "When I think of what might have happened to poor old Fred. He wouldn't be able to come to Farncombe of course."

"Don't worry about Fred or any of the others. Any we can't accommodate with work, I'll see are well compensated. Now, are you ready to explain this to the children?"

"I don't think 'ready' is quite the right word, but with your support my dear, I'll do my very best."

"Good, I'll ring the bell."

As was fitting, once the children had been told, Mrs. Frensham was the first to be informed. She showed no surprise and formally congratulated them.

"There will be work at Farncombe for some, but I am afraid not all of the staff here. My own housekeeper has been with me only a few years and I regret I cannot offer you the equivalent position you hold here. I do however, have one suggestion you may wish to consider. Mrs. Carstairs' mother, Mrs. Templar, who you already know, is to be invited to live with us and I wonder if you would consider joining our staff as a permanent assistant to her. She will become increasingly dependent upon others and it would be nice to think that this could be someone with whom she feels at ease."

On being summoned before Mrs. Carstairs and her brother-in-law Mrs Frensham had anticipated the move and expected the worst. Where was she a spinster, at fifty years of age, to find other accommodation? With no training other than household skills and certainly no income the future looked very bleak. Where was she to live, how could she support herself? Now Mr. Richard was offering her a lifeline, a comfortable home amongst people with whom she was familiar. A silent prayer of thanks and, "I am most grateful to you Sir and to you Madam. I will be delighted to accept. Mrs. Templar is a charming lady and I will be only too happy to assist her and you, in any way I can."

Further announcements were made later that day in the Morning Room. Fred was given notice, together with a small annuity which was enough to make him smile from ear to ear Mrs. Barton, if she wished, was to take over from the Farncombe Manor cook who was due to retire and Alice and Michael were also to join the staff there. Mrs. Barton like Mrs. Frensham was delighted that her future was assured and Alice and Michael were pleased to learn they would now still work with people with whom they were comfortable and importantly for them, be able to maintain their own developing relationship.

All seemed resolved until the next day, when Daisy was summoned to the telephone. She had only twice spoken on the phone before, to summon a member of the family to speak but this call was for her and she was trembling as she held the receiver. It took her a few moments to recognise her father's voice." "Daisy love. It's good and bad news I'm afraid. Mum's had twins – boys this time, but one of them is very small and he might not…Mum's had a really bad time. Lost a lot of blood and is very weak. The doctor's worried about her. The district nurse is coming in, but there has to be someone here all the time to watch her and these bairns. I don't think I can…" His voice broke. "Please love, I know it's

short notice but can you come home? I really need you…"
His voice broke again.

"Oh Dad, don't be so upset. Of course I'll come. I'm sure we'll be able to work something out here, but there won't be a train tonight. I'll get there as soon as I can in the morning."

"God bless you darling. Thank you, thank you."

There was never any doubt about her going and Mrs. Frensham and Mrs. Barton did all they could to help. Michael volunteered the information that things had improved at Alice's home and she would probably be able to fill in and do Daisy's work. He would go and see her right away and help carry her suitcase. Mrs. Barton took several pies and a ham from the cold store and packed them with ice.

"So you don't have to worry about food for the next few days. You'll have enough to think about without that." Mrs. Frensham brought a lawn nightdress and a bed jacket saying, "You'll be needing plenty of these. Now go up and pack and Michael can take you to the station in the morning."

That proved unnecessary, as on retiring, Mr.Richard announced his intention of taking Daisy to the farm by car. Daisy's last thought before she slept was 'They've all been so very kind. I'm leaving them all behind and I'll probably never set foot in Slade Manor again. I should be rejoicing at having two little brothers, but oh Mum I do so want to see you and reassure myself that things are going to be alright. Wait for me…"

Chapter 5

At half past eight the next morning Daisy left Slade Manor. A formal handshake from Mrs. Carstairs, was followed by a surprising peck on the cheek from Mrs. Frensham and the warmest of embraces from Mrs. Barton. There were tearful hugs from Alice and Michael and tears too from Daisy, knowing that she was leaving behind not only friends, but a period in which she had matured from the raw schoolgirl who had arrived, to a more knowledgeable young woman. Tears too of fear, that she was moving into another unknown situation.

In the car already were her possessions and the hamper from the kitchen which seemed to have grown in size overnight and Mr. Richard, ignoring her tears, motioned that she was to take the seat alongside him. For the first time ever Daisy found herself being driven in a private car. In spite of her worries, she started to look around, taking note of where they were, areas she had not seen when travelling by train and when he saw she was composed again, Richard Carstairs started to speak.

"Daisy, after I've dropped you at your home, I'm going to see Mrs. Murray-Rogers, who knows a lot of people in this area. We will arrange that someone comes to assist you as soon as possible. Is there a spare bedroom at the farm?"

"Oh yes, Sir…"

"Then I suggest whoever we send stays overnight and remains with you for several days. In this way you will both be able to get sufficient sleep, always a problem I gather with new babies in the house and together you'll be able to establish a routine. Once things improve her duties could be scaled down and she could come in daily, I'll leave you to decide about that."

"But Sir…"

"I don't want you to worry about money Daisy. I will ensure this lady's wages are paid. You have been a good and reliable worker for Mrs. Carstairs and I, we that is, want to repay you for that. Alice will come with us when we move to Farncombe, but should you be in a position to return to service with us and wish to do so then I want you to get in touch with me and say so."

Passing her an envelope he continued,

"In here is money should there be any emergency, extra medicines needed, that sort of thing. There is also my business card with my office number and Farncombe Manor's number. In your local Post Office there will be a telephone and a telegraph system, so you can always get a message to me if there is a problem. Now promise me you'll do that."

"Yes Sir, I will. Sir, I can't thank you enough. Everyone's been so kind." Daisy stumbled over the words.

"Everyone is concerned at what has happened. It is such a lot for someone as young as you are to have to cope with."

Unloading the car, he thought again what a slender slip of a girl she was to be taking on the running of a household with an ailing mother and two babies, one of them frail. But he had done what he could...With a farewell salute he drove away.

There was no response to Daisy's tap on the door, she could hear a baby wailing upstairs and turning the knob went in. Confronting her was a sight far worse than anything she had feared. Her father was slumped in his usual armchair, seemingly oblivious to the chaos around him. A bucket by the sink was piled high with dirty nappies, giving off a distinctly unpleasant odour. The table and sink were littered with dirty crockery and half-eaten food and Daisy gasped in horror as one of the farm cats jumped up on the table and started eating from one of the plates. In a flash she grabbed the cat and thrust it outside the door, then turned to her father.

"Dad, it's me , Daisy. I'm home."

His eyes flickered over her. "I can't do it lass, can't do it, don't know where to start start." It wasn't possible. This was her father, the rock of the family. The man who ran a farm, organised milking and lambing schedules without turning a hair.

Daisy hugged him. "We're going to do it together Dad. First of all I want you to clear the table and make sure there's plenty of hot water. I'm going up to see Mum and the babies."

He nodded slowly, but she wasn't sure he'd absorbed what she had said.

Upstairs was like stepping into another world. Clearly the District Nurse had had a hand in this. Her mother, ashen-faced lay sleeping and in the two cribs were the babies. One was clearly about average weight, he lay eyes wide open, unblinking as she smoothed his cheek and held his hand. The other was tiny, probably about half the other's weight she guessed. He was grizzling and fidgeting, either hungry or needing a nappy change. So… that must be the first thing to tackle.

Her mother stirred, groaned and opened her eyes. Daisy kissed her on the forehead.

"Mum, are you in pain?"

"Oh my darling, it's so good to see you. Yes, the pain's bad, the doctor had to do a lot of stitching. He's given me tablets, over there on the table. I could have one now please, with a glass of water."

Daisy collected them and helped her up on the pillows. "Mum, what about the babies, are you able to breast-feed?"

A wry smile from her mother. "Well, let's say I'm trying, but the doctor says it won't be very successful until I've built up some strength again. The nurse is bringing powdered milk and bottles today. She'll show you what to do, it's just so that we've always got food, if we feel they're hungry."

"This little one seems hungry now."

"That's Timmy. I think he's trying to catch up, he's always hungry. The other's Joe, you see I've got my Joe after all."

"I can't believe history's repeated itself like this. Did you know it was going to be twins?"

"I was suspicious – but it's not quite the same as you and Marigold. You were never as frail as Timmy and not nearly so small." She sank back on the pillows.

"Mum, you're tired. Look, if I give you Timmy, will you see if it will help if you try to feed him? It will keep him quiet whilst I'm getting sorted."

The baby settled at his mother's breast, Daisy went downstairs to find her father back in his chair, but having done what she had asked. The impact of the kitchen's appearance was already improved, the stove was burning and there were two kettles being heated.

"My things are still outside Dad. Could you bring them in for me? I need to make sure the food I've brought is stored in the cool as soon as possible."

Again he obeyed her instructions without saying a word and when she asked if he would take her things upstairs and then see if their patient and the babies were alright, he moved immediately but without comment. The food safely stored, she took the nappy bucket outside and left the contents standing in clean water. Now to tackle the sink! Not until every cup and plate had been washed and dried, the kitchen table wiped down, did she feel reasonably satisfied and at that precise moment the District Nurse arrived.

"My goodness, you've worked miracles in a short time," said that good lady, looking around approvingly.

"Well that's the easy bit, I need to know what to do for Mum and the babies."

Her father was on the landing and as he left to go downstairs Daisy said,

"Dad, Mum has got to have a lot of fluid if she's to feed the babies. Will you make a pot of tea for all of us please? I'm sure the Nurse would be glad of a cup."

The Nurse explained that she would continue to come in twice daily for at least another seven days to ensure the wound and the stitching were clean and healing. She then demonstrated how cow's milk must be sterilised, if using it became necessary. A nappy cream and baby powder would also be needed. The infants, she said, would benefit from the fresh air and, having noticed the farm cats outside, suggested protecting the pram with a net of some sort to avoid accidents should the cats become too curious.

Daisy found that the big pram kept in the loft all these years was already in the spare room, so before all this happened her father had been preparing, getting out the cribs etc. Now he seemed like a broken man, able to take instructions, but other than that…

In his absence, she asked the Nurse about it. "He'll snap out of it eventually. He's still in a state of shock, as severe as if he had been involved in an accident. During labour we thought we were losing your mother, he knew that and just couldn't handle it. Went completely to pieces. Eventually the doctor gave him an injection and he went to sleep. I had to stay all night because of course we couldn't leave your mother and the babies. The next day the word had got around and two ladies from the village came in and did what was necessary. People came in and fed the animals, they all rallied round. Nobody was eating, so there wasn't much food to prepare, but it was important that the babies were watched and kept clean and that your mother had her medication and plenty of fluids. I'm hopeful she will sleep herself well again, but we're seeing she has extra iron and as soon as she feels like eating it will be good for her and help build up her strength".

Daisy showed the Nurse some bottles she'd found in the hamper. "Would it be alright for her to have this?"

"Porter! Excellent. Full of iron. Normally we wouldn't advise any alcohol whilst breast-feeding, but in this case it's just as important for her to get the nutrition. Now you're here Daisy, your father will be alright. Mark my words, in twenty-four hours he'll be a changed man. You're on the right track. Just keep giving him things to do and gradually he'll start doing things again without being told. It's Mum you'll then have to watch closely."

"What do you mean? I thought she was out of the wood, I mean... Is there something else I don't know about?"

"All mums with new infants are under strain, they've been weakened by the stress of labour and your mother more than most. She has had two babies and will be doubly anxious as to whether she can ever cope again. Yes, I know, you are a twin, but the last time this happened was fifteen years ago and she was younger and fitter. We have to ensure that she doesn't become seriously depressed and develop very much the same symptoms as your father has at the moment. She'd not be able to function properly and that would be disastrous for everyone."

"So how can we avoid it?" Daisy felt this was another difficult new territory into which she was being projected.

"First of all make sure she doesn't get up too soon. She must stay in bed for at least another week. When she does start getting up, make sure she rests each afternoon and that she has some assistance during the night if the babies are troublesome. She needs all the rest she can get."

As the nurse left, Daisy felt herself reeling under the impact of so much to think about, so many pitfalls to avoid, but the next two hours saw her so busily occupied there was no time for self-pity. The babies had to be changed. Trying to do this on the bed in the spare room was not ideal and Daisy decided that the large ottoman on the landing was a better option. The top was padded and she covered this with blankets, a waterproof sheet left by the nurse and topped the whole with a large towel, moving a small table alongside it with all that might prove necessary, plus a bucket for soiled nappies. She stood back pleased with her handiwork, feeling it would save her a great deal of rushing from one place to another and ensuring that the babies could be changed whilst her mother was resting. The infants did seem to be breast-feeding, but whether the milk was going to prove satisfying enough for two babies was another matter.

Downstairs she found her father again in his chair with his eyes closed. She herself felt exhausted, but knew there were too many chores still to be tackled to even contemplate a rest. The next few minutes proved to be like an answer to a prayer. Answering a tap on the door, a large-boned young woman almost fell into the room.

"Hello, you must be Daisy. I'm Sue, Mrs. M., Mrs. Murray-Rogers that is, asked me to come. You look done in my love. Bet you wish you could have a nap, like Dad here. Have you had any food? What were you going to eat later?"

Daisy stunned by this spate of words said, "I thought ham, I brought some with me".

"Now look my love, tell me if I'm being too bossy as my friends say I am. Is there any bread?"

"Yes, in the hamper I brought… two new loaves."

"Great. Point me in the right direction and I'll go and make a few sandwiches whilst you make us all a pot of tea. We can talk over food, then I'll meet your patients and afterwards deal with those nappies outside and any more that are lying around. The sun's shining, there's a nice bit o' breeze and it will both dry them and keep them nice and soft if we can get them out on the line".

Daisy took to her immediately. She was like a whirlwind but full of fun and able to laugh at situations and at herself, which was like a breath of fresh air after the worries of the last few hours.

In no time at all they had eaten, Mrs. Griffin's bed had been changed, the nappies were blowing on the line, Mr. Griffin spurred into assisting Sue and Daisy bring the twin pram downstairs, and Sue's belongings installed in the spare room. She was clever too! Having learned from Daisy Mr. Griffin's problem, she started subtly to assist in getting him moving again. Daisy was astonished when after the broadest of hints from Sue about getting low on fuel, her father suddenly rose from the chair and said, "I'll attend to that."

The relief at having another female in the house was tremendous and the District Nurse smiled her approval at what she saw during her evening visit. It was decided that Sue would be on call the first night for, as she said, she had not been on the go like Daisy, since early morning. Nor, she added, had she been under the same strain mentally. Repeatedly Daisy blessed Mrs. Barton's kindness and foresight. The contents of the hamper were a life-saver during the early days. Jacket potatoes and one of her meat pies solved the problem of dinner that first night and for the first time Mr. Griffin spoke. "This looks good," he said, picking up his knife and fork. Sue winked at Daisy as if to say, "We're getting there."

Only when she got to bed did Daisy think about Marigold. "Oh help, I hope Dad let her know what was happening, or she'll be absolutely furious, as I would be if it were me." She must ask him in the morning if he'd been in touch with Marigold, find out what was happening outside on the farm, get to know whether the babies' births had been registered and send a word of thanks to Mrs. Murray-Rogers for sending Sue. Knowing the night hours were in her capable hands was sheer bliss!

Marigold had received the news, though not directly from her father. Mrs. Murray-Rogers had very sensibly decided after speaking to Richard Carstairs that Daisy's sister should be informed and had rung Rosalie Reece at Greenacres. Upset at the news and that she should have learned in such a roundabout way, Marigold knew in her heart of hearts that she would not have wanted to drop everything in which she was immersed to go to the Island. It would have been so awkward. Rose had said it could be managed, but had puckered her face in such a way as to indicate it would prove difficult to organise, and Marigold felt a sense of relief knowing that with Daisy installed at the farm she herself could explain her absence by saying the news had come too late to make the necessary arrangements etc.

Since leaving the farm she had returned only once and that had been at Rose's suggestion, indeed insistence. In the Spring she had arranged for Marigold to travel down one Saturday morning, returning on Sunday evening. This time she had not been sent as a parcel, but sat importantly alone, having heeded Rose's warning that she must select a carriage containing women only.

It had been quite an experience and seeing her father waiting for her at the ferry terminal at Ryde had made her feel quite emotional. Nothing at the farm had changed, other than her mother's pregnancy, but her parents had seemed content and self-sufficient. She had pondered on that. There had never seemed to be any question of how much she and Daisy were missed and how sad they were that Marigold herself was so far away from home. Perhaps they can't go down that road, she thought. After all they suggested and organised everything. To express regret now would be in a way an admission of defeat. And then, more charitably, but they want us to do well and feel fulfilled and they're happy in each other's company. Obviously they're delighted about the baby and their own lives are busy and full, as mine is and Daisy's appears to be, so why should I be a grouch and expect them to be moaning and groaning about our absence.

Here at Greenacres, the challenges were never ending. She was currently learning about make-up and costumes. Rosalie had taken her first of all to the stage make-up firm of Leichner's and there she watched as a Mr. Bloom transformed her from a fifteen year old to a lady of eighty years, complete with neck jowls, bags under the eyes and wrinkles. She was amazed at what could be achieved with padding inside the mouth, removal of eyebrows and the substitution of different ones and the reshaping of the mouth. She saw that faces could be made to look wider or longer with careful shading and highlighting, how make-up could portray the very sick or a healthy rural complexion. The list was endless.

Mr. Bloom explained, "We always use our own greasepaint sticks, they are made from the purest materials and will not damage the skin. Actors are exposed to very strong lighting which creates heat in which the skin would dry out, so we are very careful about ingredients. Look at Miss Reece. Her skin is beautiful, yet she has been using greasepaint for years."

Mr. Bloom smiled reassuringly. "Just one or two basic rules: never pile layer upon layer, unless as I showed you, you are having to create a different face. Always cleanse your skin after a performance, remove every trace of grease paint with cream, then wipe off and wash thoroughly."

Later at Greenacres Rose had produced a box of greasepaints and suggested she experiment. "Think always of the character you're portraying, I've seen people dressed as nuns, sporting highly rouged cheeks, thick mascara and enough blue eye shadow to sink a ship."

With Autumn almost on them Rose had decided practical experience was now needed. A local amateur group was planning to stage a pantomime, 'Dick Whittington', and Rose had arranged for Marigold to audition, which would involve both singing and reading. "This will be very low key, you understand, but you just need to get the feel of being on stage, working as part of a team and the discipline of being there both for rehearsals and performances. This group may not be so professional as the one you watched rehearsing before, but they do have an excellent director and what they lack in talent you will find they make up for in enthusiasm. Good rehearsals will provide you with the confidence to go out in front of an audience rather larger than the one you had at the soiree."

Estelle did not agree. As Marigold left the room, she heard her for the first time expressing her dissent.

"It's too soon and it's lowering her standards".

"Estelle, she has to learn from the start about the in-fighting in dressing rooms, how not to become involved and stay on good terms with everyone. Marigold needs the discipline of being in the right position off- stage ready for an entrance and, as to lowering her standards, John Finch is a first-rate director. She's got to have some dancing lessons too. I know she'll only be in the chorus, but there'll be some routines to learn and the more she knows, the more at ease she'll be."

Estelle was not convinced. "I hope you're right. I would have preferred to see her stick to the classics. Don't you think you're expecting too much too soon?"

"No, she's a clever girl and anxious to learn. Don't worry, she's getting plenty of grounding in the classics, there's hardly a day goes by when she's not reading some Shakespeare." And with a deliberate attempt at easing the tension, "What I would really like is to see her play Puck, I'm working on that."

Estelle had to smile. "I don't doubt it for one moment."

She had planned a hectic schedule, but Rose Reece was well aware that Marigold had a filial duty to visit her mother at the earliest possible moment and started to look at dates to see when this might be arranged. When a letter from the Isle of Wight arrived the next day it determined the matter. Daisy wrote that whilst her mother was making some progress it was very slow. Timmy had put on a little weight, but there was still concern for the two of them. Christening the babies had been delayed until the end of September and if Marigold could join them on that occasion it would be wonderful and give her mother a real boost.

There was no hesitation on Rose's part. "Of course you must go. You have not yet met your new brothers nor seen your mother since she was so seriously ill. Neither have you had a break from the programme we've been following. I think you should stay at least four days with your family. This way you'll feel refreshed and all the more able to tackle what lies ahead in the coming months. Rehearsals for the pantomime will not start until mid-October and we'll fit in as many dance lessons as possible before your break. No, that should all work very well."

And so it was arranged. There were gifts to be bought for the babies, clothes to be packed and the dancing lessons! Rose explained: "There may well be some tap dancing required in the panto, so we'll cover that, some classical dancing and also modern ballroom steps. It's just as important that you learn to do the Charleston as it is that you walk and talk correctly and look delicious. There's bound to be an after-show party and you don't want be sitting out of the dancing like a wallflower. Basic steps only will probably be needed in this production, but should you want to go into a musical…"

One thing's for certain, Marigold thought, Rose is never lacking in enthusiasm. She goes from one subject to another like a whirlwind and she always seems to be thinking about three months ahead. It should be fun being in a pantomime, but before that I'll be seeing my lovely Island again and my other half. I wonder if she's changed.

Daisy had written about her father's strange behaviour during her mother's illness, so it was with relief that when Marigold greeted him at the ferry terminal everything seemed perfectly normal. She was embraced in his great bear hug and welcomed the familiar smell of pipe tobacco, soap and hints of the farm.

"Goodness lass, you look a right young lady now. Let me have those bags, once we're on the train you can tell me all your news."

Crossing the Solent again had been a delight. Yachtsmen were making the most of the good weather before boats were laid up for the winter, and their sails billowing in the breeze formed a rainbow of colour, which was a feast to Marigold's eyes. The Island looked so beautiful and she sank back on the carriage's padded seat with a contented sigh. It was lovely to be going home, there was so much to talk about.

There were tears at first of course and Ted Griffin once again threatened to bring in the water butt. Marigold cuddled each baby, exclaiming over their tiny hands, noting their knowing eyes and concealing her alarm at her mother's frailty. She shuddered at the thought of what might have happened during the period when she had decided she must remain in Richmond. She had feared recriminations about that, but none were forthcoming and she was able to relax and examine each member of the family and note the changes since they had last met. It was Daisy about whom she had to suppress genuine amazement and as they dried their tears, Marigold tried to lighten the atmosphere.

"You've grown up, little sister. We're now the same height, although I think you're slimmer. Not eating your greens again, I expect, I can see I'm going to be back in my old job of keeping an eye on you for the next few days. You look well though. The Isle of Wight air is obviously more healthy than that in London."

Daisy was quick to retaliate, "You've certainly put on weight, but then you always did have a fancy for sweet things. Your curves might be in the right places now, but you'd better watch you don't become too curvaceous. Only opera singers are allowed large bosoms!"

They all laughed and the tone was set for a relaxed atmosphere, as relaxed that is, as it could be with two babies requiring a great deal of attention. There was more laughter when she described her musical performance with Estelle and how she had to practice phrases to improve her lip and tongue agility and improve her diction. She had them all trying to say, 'Here's a pot of paint and a pair of pale pink plates, plus a perky parakeet that perkily pecks at any pretty petal,' until they collapsed in giggles and Daisy was delighted to see her father joining in and once again appearing to be his old self.

It was however the changes Marigold saw in Daisy which continued to bemuse her. The next morning it was Daisy who seemed to take the household by the scruff of the neck and get everything moving. She it was who prepared breakfast for everyone and then shooed Meg Griffin upstairs to feed the babies in peace, whilst the twins cleared the kitchen. Sue arrived in her usual boisterous fashion bearing sandwiches and cakes and was duly introduced. Her exclamation, "My, you're like as two peas in a pod!" caused some hilarity; then Marigold asked "Ah, but can you spot the difference, there is one." Eyeing them from top to toe, it was a few moments before

Sue noticed Daisy's darker eyebrow and heard Marigold say, "Daisy, isn't it time you did something about that? You could dye the light one so they are at least both the same."

Daisy's reply was, for her, rather acid. "It may have escaped your notice, but I've had rather more to think about just recently, than worrying about a stupid eyebrow."

The discussion came to a sudden halt as Ted Griffin came in from the milking shed and it was when Daisy asked Marigold to be ready to leave at quarter to ten, that she realised an outing was planned.

Sue was to stay with Mrs. Griffin and the babies and would as she said "get they nappies on the line as soon as possible". She and Meg would have lunch together and "Yes," she told Daisy, "I know what we agreed we'll have for the meal tonight. I'll see to that. Oh yes," this to Mr. Griffin, "and I'll feed the hens." At last Marigold was told what they had planned for her as a surprise. She and Daisy and their father were going to Nunwell House to see the Isle of Wight Hunt meet there. Marigold had always loved horses and had cried bitterly when the two they had at the farm were requisitioned at the beginning of the war. It was now a good number of years since they had seen the Hunt assemble. Their own pony and trap was already waiting.

This, Marigold realised, was Daisy's idea and her organisation. The quiet unassuming girl she had left behind on the Island almost two years ago was now someone with quite a wealth of experience. Whilst she herself had been having lessons in speech and deportment and been taken on luxurious outings, her twin had seen life as it really was. Obviously in the servants' quarters at Slade Manor she had learned much about organising and preparing meals, house cleaning and dealing with laundry and now in the last few weeks she had cared for a very sick patient and mastered the art of looking after two infants at the same time. Not bad for a fifteen year old.

Later, learning of Richard Carstairs' generous provision of assistance in the form of Sue, she found that Daisy had now written to him thanking him for all he had done and explaining that Sue's services were now being reduced to mornings only and that her father was financially able to meet this cost. It was hard to believe that Daisy had done all that was necessary in fulfilling these courtesies and had obviously done it very efficiently. A charming reply from Richard Carstairs had again stated that he should always be called upon if assistance was needed and that Daisy would be welcome to join the Farncombe staff if she so wished. Marigold was impressed. By contrast her own life had been so easy. Yes, she had been working at her studies, but with food put in front of her when required, her own lovely room kept clean and tidy and every new step of the challenge facing her, carefully structured by the meticulous Rose, in contrast to her sister she had been spoon fed.

Another thing she had noticed, Daisy's speech was slightly different. Whilst living on the Island Marigold knew she herself had been relatively unaware of the local idioms and the dialect there. Now she was acutely aware of speech patterns and she knew that Daisy's, like her own, had changed. Clearly living in a large house where the mistress and her family and the housekeeper spoke correctly had had its own effect. "They say young people are born mimics and they're right, there's definitely a difference."

With their father at the reins, she and Daisy boarded the trap, waved goodbye to their mother and Sue and left for Nunwell. She had forgotten what a beautiful scene the meeting of the Hunt was. The lovely old house still fronted by late roses and the horses, glossy and beautiful, were snorting and shivering with excitement. The hounds in their enclosure were desperate to get started, anxious for the traditional hunting cup niceties to be finished with as quickly as possible.

When the horn sounded, even their own little shaggy pony seemed to want to join in the chase. The hounds were released and the stream of horses pressed through the gate and were off. For a time they followed in the trap, catching glimpses of hounds working the woods and clusters of riders, but at last there was little else to see from the trap and it was agreed that they drive up to Brading Downs for their picnic lunch and then, at Marigold's request, go into Sandown so that she could enjoy watching the sea for a while.

It proved a lovely day. To drive again through the Island lanes, the hedgerows netted with honeysuckle was a delight and Marigold realised that although Richmond and the Thames had its own beauty, she had missed her Island with its quaint thatched cottages and banks of hydrangeas. Reminding herself of her good fortune in having been presented with a wonderful opportunity, she told herself sharply that one cannot have the best of all worlds.

On the return journey to London she pondered on her visit. Within the span of those few days, her mother's colour seemed to have improved and her father seemed more purposeful. She felt her parents had enjoyed watching their girls together again and seeing that she herself was well and happy in what she was doing. Daisy, with Sue's help, had everything under control. Certainly the christenings had been well planned and if both she and Daisy, standing as godmothers, had shed a few tears as they made their vows, then that was only what one would expect on such a special occasion. At home she had taught Daisy the Charleston and some ballroom dancing steps and entertained them all with her version of Hardy's 'The Ruined Maid', spoken in a broad West Country dialect. She had learned how to make a shepherd's pie and how to wash nappies and knew how to prepare a baby's bottle for those emergency middle of the night feeds. Now she had a busy few weeks before her and must concentrate on adjusting to what lay ahead.

Chapter 6

As Rose had anticipated, Marigold was to be in the chorus of the pantomime, appearing in various characters as a villager, a lady at court and a fairy in a dream sequence. In the latter she was to sing two verses solo. Once rehearsals started, the weeks rushed by with the pressure of evening rehearsals and Marigold's own daily lessons. Costumes were hired in bulk and then had to be sorted and tried on, with adjustments made where necessary. As they moved towards the opening night, her sixteenth birthday passed without the celebrations of the previous year, but after rehearsing, the cast did assemble on stage that evening, a cake provided by Rose appeared and together they sang 'Happy Birthday'.

Marigold found, as Rose had said, that every audience was different. She loved it when the children responded to the comic characters and felt the warmth coming back across the footlights when the audience joined in the singing. Her solo had passed without incident and when the show closed on January third, she blessed Rose's foresight with regard to the ballroom dancing. For the first time she was able to join in as everyone took to the floor and did the Charleston.

The pantomime over, there was no respite. Marigold found that Estelle had also been working on her behalf and had managed to get her an audition for a slot in the next Hackney Empire Music Hall. They were elated when this proved successful. She would be bottom of the bill, of course, with two solos, one in each half of the programme. In the first half she was to sing 'Alice Blue Gown' again, this time in front of, they hoped, a full theatre. In the second half she was to sing the number Marie Lloyd had made famous, 'The boy I love is up in the gallery' and for that she had to work on a slight Cockney accent, just broadening some of the vowel sounds.

There was now considerable discussion under what name Marigold should be billed. For the amateur production her own name Marigold Griffin had been used on the programme, but looking ahead Rose and Estelle felt a decision should now be made about a stage name. Several suggestions were forthcoming and the final choice was left to Marigold, who opted for Mari Gold. They all agreed that this was easy for the public to remember and if at a later stage, it seemed preferable to revert to Marigold with no surname, it would not confuse the issue.

Her dresses were selected with care. A girlish full-skirted blue for the Alice number, her hair loose and for the Marie Lloyd item, a more grown-up typically modern dress, Empire line in aqua, worn with rows of Rose's long stage pearls and with her hair looped into a French knot. As the dress rehearsal approached Marigold was terrified. She couldn't do it! She'd faint with fright. Hearing a snigger from the wings as she missed her note cue, she thought she'd die of humiliation, but the Musical Director smiled encouragement, gave her the cue again and as her sweet clear voice rang out in the empty auditorium the whispering stopped as the other performers listened intently. They knew of course it was to be her professional debut and the ripple of applause and pats on the back when she finished were sufficient to tell her they approved.

Estelle accompanied her backstage for the performance, helped her dress and checked her make-up, before going to join Rose at the rear of the orchestra stalls. The audience loved her. Her fresh youthful appearance was appealing and after the applause there was a rustling of programmes to check on who the newcomer was. Completely different in style, they listened intently to see how a young girl would tackle the number introduced by an experienced performer. They noted the accent and the right note of lovesickness and again showed their approval.

"All in all quite satisfying, for such a public debut," Estelle said.

"I call that a serious understatement," Rose replied. And to Marigold, "You have done us both proud. Very well done. Now you will see, we will go from strength to strength."

Next day a line in the Theatre Critics' column endorsed their jubilation. It read, "A fresh young talent is treading the boards. Look out for Mari Gold. A name to remember!"

As always, Rose's mind was leaping ahead to the next assignment. But now she felt there was a very real problem. Her plan was that Marigold should audition for a place with a touring company which would start rehearsing in April, with the tour leaving in May. The Company was performing 'A Midsummer Night's Dream' and she intended Marigold to audition for both Puck and the Fairy. She would be pleased to see her secure either of these roles. But who could accompany her? At sixteen she was very young to be exposed to the rigours of touring in a play. The cast would be billeted in two guest houses, usually males and females separated and Rose did have a friend Lilia, who was almost certain to be cast as Hermia. Nevertheless, she worried that Marigold would be very much out on a limb and lonely.

Explaining this to her, Rose said, "I did wonder..." she hesitated.

"Yes, you wondered..?"

"I wondered if Daisy would accompany you."

"Daisy?" Marigold was staggered.

"Your mother now seems to be fully recovered. The babies are what, nine or ten months old and this lady, Sue, is still assisting. I wondered if Daisy could now be spared. All her expenses would of course be covered by me. The important thing is that you would have someone of your own age, close to you, with whom you could share both troubles and joys and there are very often both in this kind of venture. I would of course ensure that you were both under the same roof as my friend Lilia, to whom you could turn if there was a real problem. What do you think?"

"I'd love it. I can't imagine anything I'd like better." Marigold was ecstatic.

"But...I'm not sure if Daisy would be prepared to leave the Island and wouldn't there be long periods when I'd be busy and she'd have nothing to do? She might be terribly bored."

"I'd be very surprised if in a touring company of this nature they didn't quickly find her a job of some sort and I certainly don't think she'd be bored. Now, would you like me to make the approach to your parents?"

"Oh, please. It would be so wonderful if they agreed."

And agree they did. A personal note from Daisy added to their comments, in it she thanked Rose and expressed her delight at the opportunity to see beyond the confines of the Island. To Marigold she wrote how excited she was at the prospect of being a small part of her exciting experiences and that she couldn't wait for that date in April when a whole new world would be opened up for her.

MARIGOLD'S Journal

I can hardly believe it, Daisy's coming to join me here at Greenacres. Wonderful! Someone to pour out my troubles to, like the fact that I have to get to grips with all this Shakespearian text and Celia coming with me to 'The Taming of the Shrew'. She's staying here overnight so that we can have 'an informed discussion about it' tomorrow. Ugh! When we're together she dismisses my ideas as rubbish but in Miss R.'s presence says they're sensible and shrewd. She's treacherous. The other really good news though is that Miss R. is going to turn one of the rooms here into a small sitting room which Daisy and I can regard as our own. Roll on April!

After Celia's departure, Marigold asked Rose about Celia's background.

"Brought up by her father, Stephen Murray. It's quite a sad story. Stephen and her mother Gillian, both on the stage, were very good friends, all of us starting out on our careers. Following Celia's birth Gillian became very withdrawn, then started to act more and more strangely. After a time it was felt unsafe to leave her with the baby and she was taken into care, where her condition deteriorated rapidly and she was placed in a mental institution. Stephen brought Celia up and I think did a good job. She was keen to follow him onto the stage, so he helped her to do so. I'm her godmother and have always tried to keep an eye on her."

"Is she still with her father?"

"No, I'm afraid he died in that awful flu epidemic two years ago, just as we were all celebrating the end of the war. As her parents were such dear friends, I've always tried to keep an eye on Celia. I'm rather worried that rumour has it that she's more than friendly with a man called Charles Lord. He fancies himself as a Director, but I'm not very impressed. He's inclined to cut corners and it shows. There's something about him that…But I mustn't fill your head with my whims. Take people as you find them, must be your motto."

And that's the whole point thought Marigold. I *find* Celia peculiar and somewhat devious. It's a good thing I don't have to see too much of her. Marigold's delight at learning that she had won the coveted role of Puck was slightly diminished by the knowledge that Celia had also been auditioned and was to play Titania. She chided herself that it was unimportant, after all there had been no argument between them and there were no overt signs of Celia's disapproval – at least not in the presence of others. And with Daisy at her side!

Daisy's arrival created both joy and surprise. Rose had not expected even an identical twin to be quite so identical. Studying the two slim blonde sixteen year olds together she realised what a stunning combination they made. Daisy had a quiet charm and whilst not so extrovert as Marigold, Rose felt there was a vein of steel in her, a sense of purpose and resolve which would not be easily daunted. Now Rose felt she could relax. Whilst singly, each would be very vulnerable as any young, striking girl would be, together they could prove a force to be reckoned with.

Daisy was, as Marigold had been before her, overwhelmed by the opulence of Greenacres, but quietly expressed her appreciation of its beauty and her gratitude for Rose's generous hospitality. Visits into Richmond and Kingston and finally, London itself, left her speechless as she tried to take in the size of the emporia, the roads, the volume of traffic. It was all a far cry from the Isle of Wight.

At the end of April they left for their first venue, Norwich. Playing three nights at each theatre they were to visit eight major cities and would be away for nine weeks. Two days were allowed prior to a performance, the first for the erection of the set and putting lighting and sound in place. In the evening of that first day there was a quick run through to allow the cast to familiarise themselves with entrances and exits which might have been re-sited. The second day was scheduled as a full dress rehearsal, with any 'difficult' patches repeated several times if necessary.

To Daisy it was like stepping into a different world. She could now see the reason for Marigold's enthusiasm. There was a glamour about dressing up and going out into a blaze of light in front of an attentive audience. Yes she realised, it must be frightening at times, but seeing the performers at the end of the evening tired, but glowing with satisfaction, said reams about just how rewarding it must feel.

Marigold had not mentioned her feelings about Celia to Daisy and it was not until their second venue, Leeds, in the scene involving Titania, Oberon and the Fairy that Marigold became aware that she was being deliberately masked on stage. She had been told to stay in the dominant position, upstage centre, and was surprised to find Celia moving centre downstage so that effectively Puck was not visible to much of the audience. Still speaking, Marigold moved discreetly to the left, only to find that another move from Celia masked her again. Twice more she moved and with the same result. Forcing herself to concentrate for the rest of the show she did not erupt until she was back in their bedroom, alone with Daisy.

"I still can't believe she did that. She knew of course that Jonathan wasn't out front tonight, or she wouldn't have dared."

"And Jonathan would have noticed?"

"Noticed! He would have been livid. As Director, Jonathan has plotted every move we make on that stage, for maximum effect. He told me exactly where I was to deliver my lines. The others won't say anything, wouldn't want to tell tales. I don't know what to do. I wonder if I ought to tell Lilia, Rose's friend, she wasn't on stage at the time, so wouldn't be aware. It was so blatant. It just couldn't have been a mistake, not from a seasoned performer."

"I'd sleep on it if I were you. Perhaps she wasn't feeling well, time of the month that sort of thing, there could be a variety of reasons. Leave it for the moment. I'll keep an eye on Celia, perhaps if she knows you suspect something, she won't get up to any more tricks."

At the Chester venue with just ten minutes to curtain up, Puck's jaunty little hat was missing from the dressing room. Only Daisy's diligent scouring of the set and wings resulted in it being found wedged behind one of the spare scenery flats. The situation was saved but Marigold was once again on edge and Daisy found herself checking and rechecking every item of clothing and items required on stage.

It was not until Warwick that another incident occurred. The second scene was set in a woodland clearing and at the rear of the set a metal frame had been constructed and covered with greenery. Up this Puck had to climb, whilst delivering his lines. As Marigold put her foot on the first rung and her hand on the one above she felt sharp stabbing pains. Reaching to the next rungs she found it was exactly the same and was hard pressed not to cry out with the pain. Now she could see the thorny branches interlaced with the artificial greenery. The thorns had pierced the soft felt soled shoes she wore and her hands were already bleeding. Somehow she finished her lines and descended, with each step driving the thorns further home.

Off stage a first aid box was quickly produced and her hands cleaned. Removal of the thorns had to wait until conclusion of the play. Instructions were passed to the fairies that they must on no account climb the frame and the play continued. At the final curtain Director Jonathan was incandescent with rage. "I have never in twenty-five years experienced anything like this. Surely no-one could have thought it a joke? If anyone knows who is responsible for this cruel act I want to know immediately. I don't know how Marigold did it but she has my warmest congratulations for bravely keeping going in spite of the pain and ensuring that the play continued to run smoothly. Well done."

There was no response of course and later, whilst Daisy with eyebrow tweezers, painstakingly removed thorns from her feet and hands, Marigold exploded again, tearful both in fury and pain.

"Whatever next, Daisy? Is she trying to kill me? I can't tell Lilia now, it's so awful I don't think she'd believe me and I still can't understand why?"

"Let's think this through Mari. In the first incident, it could have appeared to others that your moves were at fault, then the missing hat suggested you were careless and now this. If you had 'dried' and the play had come to a standstill you would have looked an idiot. If you had stopped and not climbed further, there may have been only the slightest pinprick. In that case you would have looked very foolish, especially if the thorn branches had magically disappeared without whoever put them there being seen.. It would have seemed to everyone that you'd brought the play to a halt just because you'd pricked your finger on the frame. Whoever's doing this is just trying to discredit you so that people start to feel you're a liability."

"Daisy, thank goodness for your sensible head. You always were one for logic. I think you're absolutely right, but as to 'whoever's doing this', well, I don't have to go any further than Miss Celia."

There was no further unpleasantness. Celia, if Celia it was, must have realised that there would in future be strict surveillance of the set and dressing rooms and was taking no chances. 'The Dream' as even Daisy soon learned to call it, was a sell-out, with Rose and Estelle attending the final showing at Richmond. Marigold's performance was lively and polished and they congratulated each other and her on her success. If Marigold seemed suddenly cool when they were joined by Celia at the after-show party, they assumed that she was tired after a gruelling few weeks.

By contrast Daisy was bubbling with good humour. She had visited eight major cities, made numerous mugs of tea, helped iron costumes and wash smalls and insisted that she knew every line of "A Midsummer Night's Dream" by heart. Most amusing of all her speech was now peppered with theatrical terms. Laughingly, Estelle said to Rose "I've got a feeling you might soon have another protégée on your hands. Why do I think she's now smelled the grease-paint and there will be no going back?"

"You could be right. When Daisy arrived and I first saw those two girls together, do you know what my reaction was? It was what a wonderful double act they would make. But that's enough shop-talk for one evening. What have you been up to this week, I haven't seen you for a few days?"

"I had dinner with Monty on Wednesday. At the Savoy. Rose, isn't he just the most lovely man? He's not just generous and charming, he's so entertaining to talk to, well-informed and so kind. I just love being with him, he's such good company. Don't you agree?"

Rose hesitated…"Of course he's everything you say Estelle, but he's also at least twenty years older than you are. It would be nice to find someone nearer your own age."

"I doubt they'd be capable of Monty's courtesies, or his intelligence. One thing he did say was that he's met a young man called Coward, Noel Coward, who's apparently been on the stage since he was just twelve years old. He's now twenty two and has been writing plays for quite a while. There was one which he'd co-written with a friend, which they managed to stage in 1917. It never made the headlines, but I suspect the war didn't help there. Now he's got one or two others in the pipeline, his own work, and would very much like to meet you. Apparently his one ideal is to write something and have you in the starring role. So I don't want any more of that 'I'm over the hill' nonsense."

Rose laughed "Flattery will get you just about everywhere! I'll give Monty a ring and tell him to bring the young man over for a drink sometime, then we can both give him the once over. This might just be the one you've been looking for."

It was Estelle's turn to laugh. "I very much doubt it, a) he's the other end of the age scale from Monty, fifteen years too young and the other thing I didn't mention is b) he prefers men."

"Ouch! What is it about our profession…? Ah well forget about marriage plans, we'll still invite him. I'd like to hear just what he has in mind. There could be something in this for you too. I know you've had several music hall slots, is there anything else in the pipeline?"

It was Estelle's turn to hesitate. "I've been a bit reluctant to mention it, but next week, I'm reading for the lead in 'The Second Mrs. Tanqueray'."

"If the reluctance was because I once played the role, forget it. At your age and with your ability it's more than likely that this will now often happen. Don't think I'm going to shed bitter tears about it, I'll be truly delighted if you get it and happy to give any advice… but only if you want it!"

Daisy had assumed that her invitation to join Marigold on tour, had extended to that period of time only, and two days after their return approached Rose to ask when she would prefer her to leave.

"My dear Daisy, I certainly don't want you to leave." And seeing her amazement, Rose smilingly added, "I think you have done a really good job at helping Marigold through a quite traumatic experience. Touring with a play and particularly for the first time, is both exhausting and stressful and having you with her undoubtedly helped to counteract that. You obviously enjoyed yourself and at the same time learned a great deal. If you are willing, I'd like to suggest that we build on that, always assuming your parents are agreeable. You know now what we are working towards and what I suggest is that you remain here, sit in on all our lesson periods, participating if you wish, and certainly travelling with Marigold as necessary."

Daisy's face said it all. For a while she was unable to speak. Being involved with theatrical work, albeit on the fringe, had been thrilling and now it was to continue, with perhaps even more involvement.

"Tell me Daisy, do you sing?"

"Why yes, Miss Reece, Marigold and I often sang duets together at school, but I'm not very good at reading music…"

"Then we must have a word with Estelle, let her listen to you and give you some help as necessary. I'm giving one of my evening get-togethers soon, where my guests entertain each other. It might be nice if you girls were able to perform for us together."

Now it was Daisy's turn to be alarmed. Singing in school was vastly different from having to do so in front of Rose's stage friends. Still, if Marigold had managed to do it… For the next two days any spare moments found the two girls, their heads together, busily writing, or staring into space. At the end of it they had agreed, providing they had Estelle's approval and assistance, on their number. They both loved Music Hall with its variety of music and so had decided on Burlington Bertie but with a difference. Their two characters would be the original, plus their own creation, Kensington Gertie. Each would sing one verse and together they'd sing the chorus.

Bert, played by Marigold, was to be in a dilapidated morning suit, whilst Daisy as Gert would wear a bedraggled evening dress and sing,

I'm Kensington Gertie, My best friend is Bertie, We go for a stroll down the Mall,

We call on the King, if by chance he is in, And exchange a few words with our pal.

104

His guards all salute me and laugh at my dress
They all think it's passé, but I know it's classy
I'm Gert, Gert, my best friend is Bert
We're frightfully top drawer you know
All the ladies admire me, The gents they desire me, We're
Bertie and Gertie from Bow.

Estelle certainly did approve and said to Rose, "What they've done shows real ingenuity. They've both got a flair for comedy and young Daisy has a great voice, as good, if not better, than Mari. I know the others won't dress up but I think the girls will enjoy doing so and it will help Daisy for a first performance to have costume and a character to hide behind. Leave it to me to help them get organised, there are things in my stage wardrobe which will be just right."

As requested, Monty brought the young Noel Coward to Rose's party. Obviously talented, and when he followed Monty at the piano and accompanied himself to a comedy piece he had written, there were murmurs of appreciation and applause. Then it was the turn of the twins, with Monty's introduction of 'It's now time to hear from Rose's Golden Girls'. The 'luvvies' loved them. When it was learned that it had been the twins' choice and their wording for the extra verses there was even more praise. It was on this evening that their joint stage name was born, from henceforth when performing in public they would always be known as The Golden Girls.

Seeing Monty and Estelle whispering confidentially in a corner of the room, Rose's raised eyebrows registered faint disapproval, but she was later mollified to learn Monty was merely saying that he thought he had something in line for Marigold's next assignment. It was on this evening too, that the young Noel managed to buttonhole Rose. "This play I'm drafting, one part is so definitely 'you' darling. Having admired you from afar and dreamed of you being in one of my humble offerings, I'd be sad if you couldn't find your way clear to do it." Experienced enough to know that it was wise never to commit oneself without finding out a great deal more, Rose kept her own counsel.

His further comment, "I'd better look to my laurels or your Golden Girls will beat me to the top and steal any thunder I might make," was reassuring. If this intelligent, multi-talented young man saw potential in the twins then she and Estelle were obviously on the right road with regard to their tuition.

Monty's 'something in the pipeline' proved to be the second lead in a comedy "Darling Lou" by a new author, Willard Jones, to be staged at the King's Theatre, Southsea in the summer. Auditions were to be held in two weeks with rehearsals starting in June. Monty himself was backing the play and said with a smile that regardless of the auditions, the part would be Marigold's if Rose so wished.

Daisy was always amazed at the speed with which decisions were made and arrangements put in hand. It was a small cast and Daisy would be in charge of the wardrobe and assisting the A.S.M. when and if necessary. At Rose's suggestion once the cast was confirmed the girls were to go to Southsea two days before rehearsals started and then visit their family on the Isle of Wight.

The only sour note as far as Rose was concerned was learning from Monty that Celia's friend Charles Lord was to direct the play. Let it be, she thought, he must surely be improving his technique by now, it's two or three years since I last saw his work. She personally thought the piece rather light-weight, but as second lead Marigold would get critical appraisal and Rose knew how necessary it was to keep her name in the forefront of the news, which would be seen and noted by producers, directors and the general public.

Chapter 7

The twins' visit to the Island was reassuring. Their mother looked much better and the babies were amazing. Now one year old, they were inquisitive and entertaining and, of course, hard work. But Sue was still very much a regular feature in the household and Meg Griffin clearly relied upon her a great deal. Returning on the ferry they agreed that the farm seemed once again to be a happy and contented home.

Seeing the King's Theatre for the first time, the girls loved its Victorian ambience and Marigold quickly settled into her role, with Daisy often on 'the book', prompting for rehearsals. In the early days, Marigold had been warned about the persistence of 'stage door Johnnies', but it was not until this production got under way that she learned just how persistent they could be. One young man in particular was there every night, bringing her flowers and begging her to go out for a late supper with him. For the first week of the run she kept him at a distance but on the penultimate night before closing, he was waiting once again and pointed out the new Ford car parked at the side of the road.

"If you won't eat with me, please, please, come for a drive tomorrow afternoon," he begged.

"I don't know…I'd have to be back no later than six thirty. I'm supposed to be in the theatre at least an hour before curtain up which is seven thirty."

"No problem. Goodness, we'll be back ages before that. Just go for a spin and perhaps a cup of tea somewhere. I'll pick you up at three o'clock. Can't wait."

Daisy was uneasy from the start. Always practical, she liked Marigold to be within striking distance of the theatre the whole time, but Marigold brushed her doubts aside.

"I promise you I'll be back here by five thirty. Rose and Estelle are coming tonight, so I'll want to get myself ready in good time."

When the clock registered six thirty and no sign of Marigold, Daisy began to worry. Mari might be extrovert and occasionally scatter-brained about some things, but about anything to do with her stage aspirations she was deadly serious. Perhaps they'd had an accident, or the stupid boy had let his car run out of petrol. But it was a casual drift of conversation between two of the cast, which turned her fretting into panic.

"Have you seen that dishy Simon, who's been pestering Mari?"

"Celia Jordan's cousin you mean, the one with that gorgeous new Ford."

Daisy didn't wait to hear any more. Celia might not have put in an appearance, but her cousin had. Just what was he up to? If Mari was not here in time for curtain up, or worse if she didn't appear at all, any future in the theatre for her could be forgotten. Unless of course, perish the thought, that absence was due to an accident. No, she brushed that aside, this was surely another much more serious attempt to discredit Marigold and ruin her career. Funds did not run to understudies in the provinces and without a member of the cast, the audience would have to be turned away. Suddenly, her mind made up, Daisy started to undress, slipping on Mari's dressing gown. Quickly she applied the make-up she'd seen Mari use and by seven twenty-five was ready and dressed in the role of Madeleine. When the 'Beginners please' call came, she gritted her teeth and moved into the wings.

Seated in the orchestra stalls, Estelle squeezed Rose's hand on Madeleine's appearance. The first act was in two scenes. Rose knew 'Darling Lou' was no masterpiece, but it was light, amusing dialogue and they were particularly concerned with Marigold's performance. As the lights came up at the scene end Estelle said,

"The girl's lost a bit of weight since that dress was fitted, it's not nearly so snug".

"No, and there's something else. I really thought I'd eradicated every trace of Isle of Wight dialect, but I did notice a couple of slips."

"Nerves, I expect. Understandable. She knows we're here too, her most critical audience, it's bound to be unsettling."

"Still…"

The second scene had been running for several minutes when Estelle picked up her opera glasses and then gave an audible gasp. Rose looked at her reprovingly and then was surprised to find her hand being squeezed and the glasses thrust into it.

"Look at her face," Estelle whispered.

A few seconds and Rose knew. That eyebrow dark in comparison to the other, identified her. The girl giving a flawless performance, the girl they were watching, was not Marigold, it was Daisy!

They found her at the end of the act, in the dressing room, shaking with reaction and it was then that an ashen-faced Marigold burst in on them. Seeing Daisy in her Madeleine stage dress, she was about to burst into tears, when Rose took over.

"Estelle, black coffee straight away. Daisy, costume for Act 11 please. Marigold sit down and I will do your make-up. No time for tears or explanations, we'll go into that later. Deep, deep breaths Marigold. Here's the coffee, plenty of sugar. Now girls it's going to be fine. Your first line, Marigold?"

"I regret to say this Dennis, but Lou has been lying to you'"

"Good, now you're on course, stay focussed. You are now Madeleine and you're going to give the performance of your life."

And so she did. The knowledge that once again she'd been tricked, now fuelled her anger and with that the adrenalin kicked in and she was, as the part demanded in the next act, incisive and arrogant.

Their Post Mortem was lengthy. Mari had, she said, been driven for some distance and into a rural area. When the car came to a shuddering halt with Simon's pat exclamation that something was wrong, she had waited whilst he supposedly made adjustments. As the time passed, she became first of all suspicious and then certain what was happening and left the car, walking to a main road. Eventually she had got a lift back to Southsea. The girls recounted their experiences whilst on tour and how Celia appeared to be the culprit and when Daisy

111

related the conversation she had overheard, it seemed conclusive.

The final performance passed without incident. At the after-play party Willard Jones, the author of 'Darling Lou' told the twins he had been so inspired seeing them together and knowing they were under Rose Reece's wing that he had already started on a play with the two of them in mind, its working title being 'Double Trouble'. Together they laughed and decided not to attach too much importance to this, Marigold having been warned many times that stage people were often flamboyant and talked rather grandly about what they had and were about to achieve. There was the usual kissing and hugging at the after-play party, promises to keep in touch which everyone knew would never materialise and it was over, another play 'put to bed', with each of them now anxious to move on to whatever might be offered next.

Back at Greenacres Rose phoned and asked Celia to visit her.

"I think you have some explaining to do", Rose said on Celia's arrival.

To her amazement the response was, "I think you have a great deal of explaining to do also."

"What on earth do you mean?"

"I know all about what happened between you and Dad. I know I'm your daughter."

Rose stared at her open-mouthed, "Have you taken leave of your senses? What on earth are you talking about?"

"Dad always told me that I was just a few months old when my mother was taken into care. I don't believe that. When I was growing up and visiting her she often said, 'You're starting to look just like your mother. One day you'll be famous like her'."

"But she wasn't herself… You knew that."

"I've looked at your stage records during that period and I know that you did nothing on the stage for about six months, just about the time I was born. I know, I think I've always known, that I was your daughter and Dad's."

"Celia, I cannot imagine how you came to such a ridiculous conclusion, but you are most definitely mistaken. Gillian gave birth to you just as your father said. I never had, at any time, an affair with Charles. He, your mother and I, were dear friends and that is all. If you're not convinced then I'm sure there's probably some medical test which would prove that what I'm saying is true. I am, of course, your Godmother. Your mother sadly, was having at that time wild fantasies and illusions, you must have been aware of that from the staff caring for her. Perhaps she confused the term mother with Godmother.

"Of course in her possessions there would have been photographs of me and there would have been mementoes of your early weeks, the fact that they might have been packed away together holds no significance, I was after all Gillian's best friend. But there's something else I want to know, why should this strange idea of yours make it necessary for you to harm Marigold in any way, she's only a young girl, who's done you no wrong?"

"She's taken my place, that's why. I'm the one who should be here with you, living with you in this lovely house, not this upstart girl from the back of the beyond."

"Celia, I've already explained that your wild accusations are completely without foundation. I suggest you see a psychiatrist, I seriously believe you need medical treatment. Now I want you to leave my house. If", Rose added, "I were to spread the word of your behaviour to other directors and producers, you would never again be employed on the stage."

"And *if*", Celia sneered, "I were to report that someone with no experience whatsoever, had acted as a stand-in for a professional without permission, your precious Golden Girls would soon be back where they belong, on the farm."

"Leave my house now, I don't want to see you in it ever again."

Closing the door behind her Rose wept bitter tears. Tears for two dear friends lost to her and for the disillusionment of seeing a young woman she had cared about, beginning to show the early signs of her mother's derangement. Rose was obviously distressed when Marigold and Daisy, hearing the front door close, hurried down to find her. She did not recount the conversation with Celia, other than to say that Celia had not denied their accusations. Marigold persuaded her to have some brandy before retiring and called her maid to ensure Rose had calmed down and was in bed before they too retired. At last, after a traumatic day for its occupants, the house reeled to a standstill.

Rose was in bed but not asleep. After all these years the truth was in danger of beginning to surface. Celia had been wrong about many things, but dangerously near the truth, too near it for comfort and now Rose herself was on the horns of a dilemma. Why hadn't she spoken before? What would the reaction be? Would she alienate those whom she loved more than anything in the world?

Soon, very soon, she would have to make a decision. Why, oh why had she started out on this road of deception in the first place? With a fervent prayer, that somehow she would find the strength to do what was necessary, she tried to sleep.

It was to be forty-eight hours, with the final performance and the return journey home behind them, before the enormity of what Daisy had done penetrated deep into the consciousness of those most closely involved. Daisy herself shuddered every time she thought of what might have happened. The Stage Manager might have seen and ordered the curtain to be lowered. Others on stage might have realised and reacted accordingly; she herself might have 'dried' mid sentence or died of fright! And yet, and yet, in her heart of hearts she knew that ultimately she had been exhilarated and that after a few minutes on stage she had felt in command and enjoyed herself. A wonderful, wonderful feeling.

Marigold's first thoughts that her 'little' sister had saved her from shame and humiliation were followed by a shock-wave of amazement. How swiftly and efficiently Daisy must have acted to do what was necessary. Not one member of the cast or the back-stage crew had noticed anything untoward, so throughout two scenes Daisy had played the part of Madeleine, exactly as Marigold had been doing for the past weeks at rehearsal and in performance. That vein of steel she had first seen in Daisy during her visit to the Island for the christenings now revealed itself as something to be contended with and admired. No longer the quiet, gentle unassuming little twin, this Daisy was a force to be reckoned with.

Repeatedly Estelle mulled over the events of that evening. What she had witnessed went beyond all the bounds of probability. Here was a girl who had never before performed in public, never performed on a stage and certainly never been confronted with a theatre packed with people. Yet, she had steeled herself to go onto the set, speaking lines to which she had previously only listened, carrying out moves she had only watched and most importantly conveying to the people both on stage and those watching, the character of the role she was playing. And she had done it. Without a prompt, without a tremor in her voice, without becoming confused and showing it, she had been for two scenes, Madeleine. This was the sort of raw, natural talent which could never be instilled. Yes, it was possible to coach with various techniques, but flair for acting was instinctive and came from within and this girl certainly had that. So, were there now two potential stars in Rose's household? And if so, what next?

Rose's appearance the morning after Celia's visit alarmed the twins. So much so, that Marigold left Daisy talking to Rose and slipped out to telephone Estelle asking her to call as soon as possible. She arrived an hour later and immediately called Rose's doctor, who unequivocally insisted that Rose should return to bed and stay there for a minimum of two days. Quietly the doctor intimated to Estelle that there were indications of a slight heart murmur and he wanted the assurance that for at least a month there should be no meeting deadlines or sense of urgency. Brushing aside Rose's objections regarding what she had planned for this period, Estelle insisted that she was quite able to cope with further coaching for the girls and that she had already spoken to Rose's agent asking that she should be contacted should anything remotely suitable for Marigold become available. Within twenty four hours Rose was starting to look much improved and Estelle started to make noises about a holiday.

A few discreet enquiries, some dropped hints and an invitation was forthcoming for them to make use of a house on the banks of Lake Garda, an area of which Rose was particularly fond. In September there would be few visitors and the weather should still be beautiful. To the twins' delight and amazement they were to be included in this expedition. There would be a servant at the Italian house and Biddy, Estelle's maid of all work, was also to accompany them. They travelled by Pullman to Dover, then by cross-Channel ferry and from there by rail to Verona. A magical car ride to the north of the lake, surrounded by mountains and overlooking the vast span of water and they had arrived. The house was a joy, situated in a prime position, its balconies affording every opportunity for enjoying the beauty of its environs, whilst simultaneously relaxing. The Swiss influence was apparent everywhere and a day's outing across the border took them deeper into the spectacular mountainous region, where even the menus reflected the difference from those offered on the banks of the now Italian Garda. The girls and Estelle enjoyed a sail on the lake, with Rose waving from the balcony and following their progress through binoculars.

A visit to Verona found them all admiring the statue of Juliet outside the home of the Capulets and gazing in awe at the size of the amphitheatre there. Marigold's comment was, "And we thought some of our theatres were big!"

Often the girls discussed their good fortune.

"It's not three years yet since we left school and look what has happened to us." This from Daisy.

"You know when I first arrived at Greenacres, I thought they might be part of the White Slave trade. I just couldn't relate the treatment I was receiving to the fact that I'd understood I was to be some sort of servant."

"Like me you mean?" Daisy laughed. "I didn't have a glamorous start to my adult life, but I've no regrets, it taught me a great deal and I did meet some lovely, kind people. I also think I learned quite a bit. It's almost impossible not to listen and learn, when you're in rooms where adults oblivious to your presence are discussing things of importance. At Slade there were comments about the strategy or lack of it during the war and how some of the senior Ministers in charge didn't seem to worry how many died as long as the troops managed to move forward a few yards, or held their ground. It was as if all those lives were expendable. I heard a lot about politics too and how, now the war is over, the Suffragettes are picking up the threads of their own battle to win the vote. And then there were the tips useful to all women, correction ladies."

"Tips?" Marigold asked, "What sort of tips?"

"Well I happen to know that a lady wears pearls before six in the evening and diamonds afterwards. It's absolutely not the done thing to do it the other way round. That is surely the most valuable piece of information any young lady could have. I mean, how could we possibly manage without it?"

"Well as neither of us possess either pearls or diamonds, I don't think that's going to present much of a problem at the moment," and with that they both collapsed in giggles.

"Mari there is another thing," Daisy sounded very serious.

"Yes, what?"

"It's the journals. Can we dump them? I mean at Greenacres we never have time and they do give me an uneasy feeling."

"What ever do you mean?"

"Well supposing I wrote something really rude about you. One day you might find it and then…"

"Then I would beat you to a pulp. Seriously, couldn't agree more. By the time I've learned a chunk of verse or prose each evening, I'm far too tired to write down reams"

"Right, so we're agreed?"

"Definitely, all I can say is…Hallelujah!"

Returning to Greenacres they all felt refreshed, with Rose appearing to be her old self and anxious to get started on the next challenge. "Peter Pan" was due to be staged as the Christmas production at the Lyric Theatre and Rose's agent suggested that Marigold might read for the part of Wendy. If Daisy wanted to go along to the audition, a number of 'boys' would also be required in the Neverland scene.

"We can always disguise Daisy so that she doesn't look like Marigold's twin," Estelle said to Rose. "Fortunately they're not tall girls so I think Marigold might be lucky, although much would still depend on the heights of those cast to play Mr. and Mrs. Darling."

"It would be great if Daisy could also get into the cast. Now she's got the stage bug, a part where she just acclimatises herself to movements around the set, a big audience etc. would be perfect for her. Although," Rose added, "after what she achieved without any of that preamble, makes her either a brilliant mimic or..."

"Or, a natural,", Estelle cut in, "which I'm convinced she is."

Daisy's appearance at the audition was not to be. Within a week of returning from Italy, Rose received an S.O.S. from someone she knew in Kingston saying that a morality play which he was about to stage in his local church, had just come to a grinding halt because the central character of Youth had contracted chicken pox.

Knowing that Rose was coaching a young girl, Peter asked if she could possibly take over the part. Rose knew the play, which told the story of Youth being torn in different directions, between vices and virtues, with good emerging triumphant at the end. It comprised just two short scenes, a total length of some forty minutes.

"Obviously my friend, Peter, had Marigold in mind, but I think Daisy could do it," Rose mused.

"She's a quick study, she'd learn it in no time and because it's fairly stylised there would not be a huge amount of moves for her to master in such a short time," Estelle was also thinking aloud.

"The thing is, Estelle, would you be prepared to oversee Marigold at the audition and from then on? After what happened before, I'm nervous about letting her go anywhere unsupervised."

"No problem. I'm about to start rehearsing for 'The Mikado', but having played Yum Yum for what, five times already, I do know the score from A to Z and if I have a rehearsal clash, then I'll ensure someone else is always around."

"Thank you, my dear, that would enable me to accompany Daisy to the local commitment, which wouldn't be quite so arduous."

"Exactly, and after what the doctor said, we wouldn't want to be blotting our copy book now would we Rose?"

"Stop fussing! So we'll get the script for Daisy tomorrow and she must start learning right away. The other script for Marigold to see is in the post and should be here tomorrow also. So, it will be action stations."

"Yes, and Rose, I've been thinking what might be an idea. Why don't we let the girls read 'The Seagull' next and 'The Sisters'? Have you got a volume of Chekhov's plays? I really would like to hear them tackle something meaty and get them to start thinking about the characterisation and the interaction on stage."

"You're not trying to steal my role by any chance?" Rose laughed.

"Not likely. No, another thing I'd like to try with them are some of the Gilbert and Sullivan numbers. They have a real sense of comedy and I'd like to tap into that."

"Steady... now who's the one who's trying to run before we can walk? Having been in most of Chekhov's plays, I might have some of my old scripts upstairs, I'll have a look, but not before we get some of these other matters sorted." Rose's tone now became serious, "Don't let Celia near Marigold, will you? If Celia reads for a part in this play, I don't want Mari to be involved."

"That could be tricky. You can't let Mari miss chances just because Miss Celia is likely to behave oddly."

"I'm sorry, but it's too dangerous. You might have forgotten me telling you the whole sorry story, but I can never forget. Celia's mother went completely off the rails and is in a mental institution. Celia's already shown that she has some very peculiar tendencies and I just wouldn't want anything to happen. I am after all, as far as these girls are concerned, in loco parentis."

"Of course, I do understand, I'll see that the girl's quite safe and if Celia should present herself at the audition I'll let you know. Now that's quite enough shop talk; I think we should have a glass of sherry and listen to some nice soothing music."

If Daisy was disappointed at not accompanying Marigold and Estelle to the London production, she was much too polite to show it. Rose's generosity to them both had been beyond belief and if this was to help out one of her friends then so be it. Daisy was also well aware that with regard to the stage Rose was first and foremost a professional. If Rose felt this was to be good experience then she was probably right.

And by doing this instead of doing humdrum jobs backstage, Daisy knew she would be assured of a part in her own right. She'd heard about morality plays but this would prove another completely different genre to anything else she had seen or read. No, her London debut would just have to wait!

The play was to be staged in a church on a temporarily erected stage. Entrances and exists had sometimes to be made through the main body of the church so that the characterisation had to start immediately one set foot in the auditorium. There were only seven other characters and they had been rehearsing for several weeks so were already word perfect and knew their moves. Daisy retained the script for the first rehearsal with them, merely as a confidence booster, but from then on to the amazement of Peter and the cast she was able to discard it and concentrate on body language and facial expression. Rose watching from one of the pews was delighted. The girl was charming. Whether conversing with elderly or young members her courtesy never faltered. Always she was listening and, as Rose already knew, usually learning from what they had to impart.

There were to be just two performances on the Friday and Saturday, allowing the church then to be cleared for Sunday services. Daisy was nervous and on edge during the run up to starting time and Rose said to her several times, "Daisy, slow down, deep deep breaths."

The evenings were now dark and lights had been placed in sconces to ensure players coming through the auditorium could see their way to the stage. Half way through the second scene there was a loud banging on the church's outer door and a crash as it was flung open. The players stood transfixed on the stage as firemen saying they had been called to a blaze, burst in asking where the fire was. Realising that what had been seen from outside was not flames but the flickering sconce lights, they were about to withdraw when one of the men called that there was something in the vestry. There it was found that a waste-paper bin was alight and this had already spread to curtains. It was quickly dealt with and once assured that there would be no further problems, the firemen withdrew, leaving a bemused cast to pick up the threads of their play. Later the cast and backstage team were able to laugh about it, saying they would dine out on the episode for years to come and that whilst they had heard about 'setting the stage alight with a performance', they hadn't realised it was to be taken literally.

Rose was not laughing. Someone had called the fire brigade deliberately in order to disrupt the play, someone had started a fire in the vestry and everything pointed to the fact that Celia's hand was in this. Had she assumed that Marigold was taking the lead role, as Peter had initially intended or had she now changed her tactics and was targeting Daisy as well? Daisy was not made aware of the darker side of Rose's thoughts relating to what happened that night. She laughed with the others about the bursting in of the fire brigade. She now knew quite a lot about morality plays and their staging, particularly in York. Rose had insisted she learned all about their origins and their part in the foundations of theatre.

"You see Daisy, stagecraft and knowledge of the theatre is a vast non-finite subject. With each new role, there's an extension of your vocabulary and the necessity to express, often in depth, different emotions. It's all an educational process, both mental and physical. That's why we're all so tired at the end of a show because our brains and our emotions have all had to be used and at the end of a particularly demanding play you will find yourself physically drained. Have no doubt that with every single role you play in the theatre you will have learned more about the human condition.

"Forgive me my dear, this wasn't intended as a lesson. My congratulations again. You have performed very well indeed and conducted yourself well throughout. I know that Peter and members of the cast found you a joy to work with and are deeply grateful that you were prepared to step into the central role at such short notice. I am delighted they gave you flowers; they are very well deserved."

Marigold, as expected, secured the Wendy part, and with Estelle becoming increasingly busy with the November production, Daisy now accompanied Mari to rehearsals. Soon she was assisting the Wardrobe Mistress, Jenny, and also in charge of culling the 'Boys' together whenever they were needed. Of necessity their seventeenth birthday had to be celebrated early and Rose announced that Monty was taking them all to see Estelle in 'The Mikado'.

Their enthusiasm afterwards knew no bounds.

"I just loved it, the libretto is so witty and the music..."

"And the costumes and what about the make-up?"

"It was just fantastic and Estelle well, she was just brilliant."

The girls' delight spilled over with Monty interrupting them to say "I gather you approved? I'm glad you enjoyed it. Estelle sings like an angel and always looks so delicate on stage. But Rose, you and I know and I think you girls also know by now, that she is quite a determined little lady. That's one of her greatest attributes she, as they say, 'paddles her own canoe' and is not easily deterred from that."

Later that evening Daisy asked Marigold,

125

"What was it that Monty said, which seemed to upset Rose?"

"I didn't see her upset, what are you talking about?"

"Well, she wasn't weeping and wailing, I don't mean anything like that, but surely you noticed after he'd been heaping praise on Estelle, Rose suddenly went very quiet."

"No, I didn't notice, but perhaps…?"

"Yes, perhaps?"

"Well Estelle herself did once tell me that years and years ago Rose and Monty had quite a fling, which cooled because they were both so busy and going in opposite directions. Perhaps even after all these years there's still just the teeniest bit of jealousy."

Daisy was instantly dismissive, "At their age, never!"

The magic of a children's show at Christmas was to stay with them forever. The excited bustle, as the theatre filled for a matinée. Children looking around them in awe at the splendour of the furnishings and then the expectant hush as the lights went down. Always the children exclaimed when Peter Pan first appeared and gasped in horror when Captain Hook strutted arrogantly into view. It was, as Daisy said, just what theatre should be all about, transporting them for a short time into a completely different magical world.

It was in this state of euphoria that the girls both decided they were in love, unfortunately with the same young man. Derek Lane was just twenty-three years of age, a lively East Ender. Tall, with dark curly hair, brown eyes, and a grin which almost split his face in two, they both found him fascinating. From the start, except when Marigold was wearing her Wendy outfit, he was unable to differentiate between them. This of course added to their delight and excitement. The matter of the quirky eyebrow was never ever discussed and he continued in blissful ignorance, sometimes telling Daisy she was beautiful and playing her part so well and sometimes congratulating Marigold on being prepared to take a back seat whilst Daisy earned all the plaudits. It was all innocent and enjoyable fun.

Apprenticed to an electrician at the age of fourteen, Derek had spent hours at weekends helping his uncle at the Lyric Theatre to erect scenery. Once he had been allowed to witness a number of performances he was enthralled and badgered stage managers and directors unceasingly until he was at last given a job backstage as general assistant, filling in wherever required. His speech peppered with Cockney rhyming slang delighted the girls and at home they clowned around copying his accent both in speech and song. They knew that soon the run of the play would be over and once again they would be saying goodbye to another cast and having to move on to pastures new.

"But", Daisy said dramatically, "as they say, the course of true love never runs smooth. Ah me, c'est la vie."

"May we have a reprise on that please madam, I'll just get the violins out."

Marigold copied her mournful expression and together they laughed.

Chapter 8

Rarely was Estelle at a loss to work out what was wrong, but this was one such occasion. At first she had thought herself to be imagining things, but not any longer. Every now and again there was a definite chill in the atmosphere emanating from Rose and, she now realised, it was always when Monty's name was mentioned. And, she reflected, it had been quite a while since he had been invited back to Greenacres, yet his own generous invitations had still been forthcoming. And now this, that the four of them should join him for late supper at Claridge's on Christmas Eve, following the 'Peter Pan' performance, staying overnight and for the Christmas Day festivities and entertainment.

Amazingly, Rose had hesitated, saying, "Mari will have been performing all evening, she should be resting."

Monty protested, "But this will be a rest for all of you. No organisation of food, no entertaining, for a change you will have it all done for you."

Rose tried to lighten the atmosphere, "I'm not sure the girls are ready to be exposed to this sort of opulence, they might get ideas above their station."

"Never!" Monty was emphatic. "They're far too well grounded and intelligent for that. They would love it and if it makes them set their sights high and realise just what can be achieved through diligence and using one's talents, then surely that's not a bad thing." As always, Monty's persuasiveness started to take effect and Rose smiled.

Estelle added quickly, "And you have to admit Rose they've been really good girls, worked their socks off and done everything you and I have asked of them."

"Well, there's no denying that. Alright, you win. But Mari will have a show on Boxing Day, so it's essential we see that her sleep patterns are adequate to cope with that." Estelle sighed with relief, but looking back on the incident wondered again, why Rose should have made such heavy weather of it all.

Arriving on Christmas Eve with the hotel in festive mode, the girls decided that Claridge's must be the most beautiful hotel in the world. The uniformed staff smiling and courteous, the magnificent lounges, the dining rooms, the bedrooms and oh…their bathroom! They stood and gazed at it in wonder on that first night. Fitments of peach with here and there touches of the palest coffee, silver and peach shower curtains, a bath big enough for four and, as Daisy quickly pointed out a vase of peach coloured flowers and, unbelievably, a telephone! It was exquisite.

The array of food and its variety was bewildering, its presentation so pretty that Marigold remarked on more than one occasion, "It's much too attractive to disturb with a knife and fork."

Presents had been despatched to the Island and, at Monty's suggestion an extra Christmas telegram was sent with the girls' love to their parents and the little boys.

On Christmas Day there were presents, silver bracelets from Monty, velvet dressing gowns and slippers from Rose and jewellery boxes bearing their initials from Estelle.

Monty raised his glass and asked Rose and Estelle to drink a toast to the Golden Girls, who he felt were destined for great things.

"Now," he said to the twins, "I want you to join me in a toast to two other gorgeous females, your mentors and the two special ladies in my life, Rose and Estelle." As she and Rose smilingly responded, Estelle watched her friend closely. She had not been mistaken. After all these years she knew Rose too well. Her lips smiled, but in her eyes was a wariness, a flicker of alarm. Either she or Monty had seriously upset Rose in some way. Whatever the problem was, it had not gone away.

January saw both girls on a rigorous programme of classical studies in the morning, dancing lessons and music in the afternoons. For the first time they auditioned for Shakespearian roles. The theatre at Stratford was alternating 'Hamlet' and 'The Tempest', so the parts of Ophelia and Miranda were being read for by a score of hopefuls. To Rose's delight Mari secured the latter role and although the director said he had been much impressed with Daisy's performance, he felt that as yet, she had not had sufficient experience to play a major part in a professional performance. He was however, prepared for her to understudy the Miranda part, thus allowing her to attend rehearsals, seeing how the moves were plotted and the character developed.

She would also have to learn the part of course and become very much an integral part of the acting team.

Rose was delighted with the offer. Daisy, being Daisy, accepted the logic of everything that was said and pointed out to Marigold tongue in cheek that this was just another example of how the younger twin always had to follow where the other led and never had the same opportunities. They were in fact appreciative of the fact that once again they would be together whilst away from home and could be mutually supportive.

Early February saw them ensconced in a guest house with other females involved in the two productions. The girl who had secured the role of Ophelia, Tessa Rainer, became a firm friend. She was twenty one and they were impressed to learn she had studied for a year at The Royal Academy of Speech and Drama. She was equally impressed to learn that they were being coached privately by none other than Rosalie Reece and receiving music lessons from Estelle Evans.

"My goodness, you must be destined for stardom. That makes my background look decidedly paltry. My mother has been telling me how brilliant Rose Reece is and how I should try to emulate her, since I was just a little tiddler."

Nothing was said about the wager. It had long been agreed that it was politic not to discuss that with anyone other than Rose, Estelle and Monty. Tessa came from Surrey, her mother was an artist and her father a bank manager, so as the girls discussed later, the family was obviously quite well-to-do, which was why they had been in a position to pay for her training. Again they realised just how fortunate they had been.

"Fell on our feet, we did. First you and then me," Daisy said. "If it hadn't been for Rose, I'd still be feeding the hens and helping Mum with the washing up."

"You're really missing that aren't you?"

"Yes, like a hole in the head! Oh, I miss seeing Mum and Dad more often and it would be great to see our little brothers, but as they say, you can't have your cake and eat it too."

"Correction, little sister, what they say is 'One can't have one's cake and eat it'. One must learn to get things right."

One early spring-like day with no rehearsal scheduled, Tessa's parents drove up from Surrey and took the girls out to lunch. The Rainers had found a small hotel out in the country where the food was first-rate and the girls welcomed the opportunity to get away from the somewhat claustrophobic atmosphere of the theatre and into the fresh air. After an excellent lunch the girls walked across the fields, picked early primroses and even to their delight, found mushrooms. The Rainers, happy that their daughter had such pleasing company for the following weeks, drove further afield until they came across a small tearoom, where they indulged in scones warm from the oven, homemade jam and clotted cream. They all laughed when Daisy admonished her sister, "Remember Marigold, one scone only, one must watch one's weight if one is to tread the boards!"

Rehearsals were going well and they had the added advantage of being able to witness on numerous occasions, the play other than the one they were in, thus becoming totally familiar with both productions. On two occasions the director asked Daisy to take over the role of Miranda for the afternoon, so that she would be prepared, if it ever became necessary, for her to stand in. It was all very satisfying and enjoyable and they both agreed that what Rose had always said that good rehearsals were what inspired one's confidence was very true. Working as a unified team, should anyone (heaven forbid) 'dry', they should as professionals be able to cover and maintain the smooth running of the production.

Both plays were received well and played to packed houses. The critics were kind. One wrote, '*I advised you a few months ago to look out for this new talent. Now Mari Gold plays a classical role with confidence and conviction. Rumour has it that working behind the scenes is a lady with a wealth of talent and expertise. Who knows, perhaps she already has plans for Mari? Certainly for a young girl to have this broad band of experience is most unusual and one cannot help but wonder, what next?*'

Everyone said it was an awful accident and such dreadful bad luck. But Daisy and Marigold both knew at once, this was not an accident and luck, bad or otherwise, had played no part in it. With just five performances to go everything was going extremely well until...

Marigold's scream brought Daisy whirling round from the costume rail to see Mari clutching a hand which was pouring blood. Grabbing her by the wrist, Daisy thrust her arm into the air and grabbed at a long white stocking, attempting to wind it below what seemed to be the source of the problem. Mari's scream had brought others running and suddenly the dressing room was full.

One hurried away immediately to call an ambulance, someone else held Mari's arm aloft, whilst another helped Daisy to form a make-shift tourniquet. There was so much blood it was impossible to see what the problem was until one of the cast picked up the stick of grease-paint which Marigold had been using to whiten her hands.

"Good grief," she exclaimed, "look at this."

'This' was a sliver of glass embedded deeply into the greasepaint with just one razor-like point now visible.

"Thank God, she didn't get that anywhere near her face," someone said, and there were horrified murmurings at the thought of what might have happened.

Marigold meanwhile, ashen-faced and shivering with shock, was seated, wrapped in a blanket, with one arm still elevated. Brandy was suggested and decided against.

"This will need stitching," someone said "definitely no alcohol."

At last the ambulance men arrived and Mari was helped to the door. As Daisy moved forward to accompany her, the Director put a restraining hand on her arm.

"Sorry my love, you're needed here. Margaret will go with Mari. It's a deep cut and I think it might have just nicked a vein, but once it's stitched and she's over the shock she'll be fine. We'll take you to see her at the end of the show and I guarantee she'll be as right as rain. I'm afraid for us the show must go on and that means you must now do what you've been trained to do. "Jean," calling to another understudy, "Stay and help Daisy please. Someone clean up this blood and get this girl just one mouthful of brandy – no more. Now Jean, you know the drill, Daisy needs helping into her costume and you assist her in making-up as quickly as possible please."

The Director picked up the offending grease-paint stick. "I'll take charge of this."

Turning back to Daisy he hugged her warmly and said, "Daisy my dear, you are going to be absolutely fine."

Leichner's examined the grease-paint and their findings were unequivocal. All their grease-paint was put through a fine filter before it went into the stick moulds, there was absolutely no way in which in its fluid state, it could have contained any abnormality. If the stick had been placed on the glass and then pressure put on it, then it could have penetrated the stick, but the paper sleeve around the stick would have been broken, so in that case it would have been obvious. Perhaps, they suggested, someone had broken something and the girls themselves had created the problem without noticing it. The matter was dropped. Daisy and Marigold knew full well that the stick had been used the previous evening and had been perfectly all right then. They agreed that this was undoubtedly another of Celia's tricks, but just how she had managed it was unfathomable. Somehow, she had substituted the stick Mari had used the previous evening for the new 'doctored' stick, but the Stage Door steward Bert, was insistent that he had known everyone who came into the theatre that evening. So she must have had an accomplice.

"Which makes it all the more worrying. I've really kept my eyes peeled all the time we've been here, never seen sight nor sound of her, nor that awful cousin of hers, so who on earth could it be?" Marigold realised that Daisy was weighed down with guilt because in spite of her surveillance something awful had happened – again.

Daisy now carefully made a comprehensive list of all those involved at the theatre with either of the two productions. The majority she knew well, as performers or the main back-stage teams, but there were one or two about whom she felt vague and it was on these she decided to concentrate. It was whilst poring over her list that she found the answer. One of the 'Hamlet' prompts listed, Daisy knew only as a young woman with auburn hair and rather heavy make-up. She seemed to do her job and then disappeared with no socialising whatever, which was why Daisy and Marigold had never had any conversation with her. Now the solution leaped out at her, the girl's name was Alice Rose. Alice, an anagram for Celia…so they were right in their suppositions. A casual enquiry of Bert at the Stage Door elicited the response she had been expecting.

"Bert I wanted a word with Alice, the 'Hamlet' prompt, have you seen her lately?"

"Not today Miss, she popped in yesterday late afternoon, but only for a few minutes. Shall I give her a message for you?"

"No, thank you. I'll catch up with her later."

So, they were now certain. An auburn wig, a girl expert at make-up, never allowing the voice to give her away. If there had been doubts before, there were none now.

Rose was devastated. The thoughts of what might have happened if Marigold had dragged the stick of grease-paint across her face were horrific. She not only saw the point of the anagram, but that about which the others knew nothing, the assumed surname Rose. She dreaded what must be done next. She would have to see

Celia and threaten her with police action. But the girls' findings were largely supposition what could they actually prove? How could Rose insist that the girl had medical advice if she refused to do so and, what was even worse, what would she do next if she was hell-bent on destroying the career prospects of both Marigold and Daisy?

With regard to the latter she had been singularly unsuccessful. Marigold, on medical recommendation, missed three performances. She had lost a lot of blood and the side of her hand would always bear the scar where ten stitches had been necessary. But as the Director had said, once the effects of the shock had settled and she'd had plenty of rest she was ready and raring to go back and resume her role. For the critics the incident had provided a field day, an event which made a good story-line and bore out the old adage 'any publicity is good publicity'. One twin having to go to hospital with a badly cut hand and the other standing in for her, how unlikely an event was that? All complimented Daisy, many fulsome in their praise.

'Another Gold girl with maximum talent. They must breed them well on the Isle of Wight! Daisy Gold, understudying her sister in the role of Tempest's Miranda proved herself more than capable. Both these girls seem able to meet any challenge which comes along. Attractive and talented, like their name, pure gold. No wonder Monty Seymour, the entrepreneur, refers to them jokingly as The Golden Girls'.

For Rose, only a few more precious months to achieve her goal. In spite of their caution, the theatrical world was now starting to whisper about the wager. It was common knowledge that she had trained the twins. But this business with Celia could destroy all her work. Should anything go wrong now, any scandal be apportioned to her, the whole edifice of her success, her wonderful career and reputation would come crumbling down. And what about these girls who had trusted her and were already looking forward to great things happening to them also? And what about Monty, dear loving Monty, who had not changed over all these years, always there for her, a supportive loyal friend? Worst of all, what about Estelle? How would she react? Could she ever forgive Rose? It didn't bear thinking about.

After no contact for two years, Daisy was surprised and delighted to receive a letter from Mrs. Barton, the cook, now resident at Farncombe Manor with the Carstairs family. As Daisy said to Marigold, "It totally reflects her happy nature. I was so lucky to meet her on my very first day in the big wide working world. And when I think of what she has had to endure, being widowed so young and then losing her only son, it makes me ashamed of complaining about small inconveniences."

Daisy my dear,

You'll be surprised to receive this from me, I've no doubt. But we do often talk and think about you and Mr. Richard tells us whenever there is something in the paper about you and your sister. My, my how well you are doing. I can hardly believe that my little Daisy is performing at all these places in and around London. What sights you must have seen travelling all over the country. I am so pleased for you.

We are very fortunate here. Mr. and Mrs. Carstairs are so happy together and lovely people to work for. They were quietly married as planned and now have a baby son of their own- he's a darling. Miss Cynthia is due to marry the brother of one of her school friends and is going to live in Sussex. The older boys are away still at boarding school and doing well.

You'll be sad to hear that dear Mrs. Templar died soon after moving to Farncombe, Mrs. Frensham could have stayed on but not as housekeeper, there's already one here, Mrs. Miles. She, Mrs. F. that is, got a position at Nunwell and, wait for it, has now married the butler there. I would have missed her company if it were not for our lovely youngsters here. Michael and Alice manage to keep me laughing and they too are marrying in the summer. Mr. Richard has promised them a cottage on the estate, you can imagine how thrilled they are about that.

Occasionally Mr. Richard gives us news about your family at Swanmore. I gather your little brothers are also thriving and that your mother is fully recovered from her nasty experience when they were born.

You would see such a change in Mrs. Carstairs. Mr. Richard looks after her so tenderly and she is now warm and friendly to everyone. She insists I have a few hours' break each day and told me to make use of the small rose garden which is so pretty and totally sheltered. With the other children away, the baby is her delight. Daisy, my love, she's so relaxed and happy, you'd hardly know her.

Well my dear, I think that is all our news. Everyone here sends you congratulations and their love. Who knows perhaps in the years ahead there might come a time when

*some of us could actually come up to London and see you on
the stage- that would be truly, truly wonderful.*

*Daisy, you were such a good girl here, I am sure you
deserve every success.*
My regards to your sister
Love,
Dolly Barton

Mrs. B.'s penultimate paragraph sowed the seed and
Daisy determined that one day she would try to ensure
that those on the Island who had been so kind to her
when she most needed help, would do just what Mrs. B.
had said, come to London and enjoy seeing their Island
girls on the stage.

The promised script from Willard Jones arrived the
day after Mrs. Barton's letter. It was better, far better than
Rose had expected. There had been a shallowness about
'Darling Lou' of which she could not approve, but this had
some depth and a good story line. Two sisters Hannah
and Hester, with just one year difference in their ages had
been at loggerheads since birth. The play showed them
disagreeing and quarrelling about everything, clothes, boy
friends, but largely, after the sudden, unexpected deaths of
their parents, about money. In the absence of a will the
elder sister Hannah had inherited everything. Hester had
contested this and taken the matter to court, but amidst
a great deal of acrimony had lost her case. Raging against
the injustice of it all Hester set out to get her revenge
and decided the only way she could get her hands on the
money was to kill her sister. The curtain was rung down
as she committed the murder in the final scene. Rose

thought the court scene particularly well-structured and felt overall it would be a good vehicle for the girls.

When they read the script the twins were at first amused that Willard had unknowingly taken their own lives as children and built a similar if much exaggerated story around them. Just how close he had come to the matter of them being threatened he would never know.

"Perhaps he saw we were always in competition," Daisy said.

"Yes, but never to this sort of level, thank goodness – at least not so far," Mari was mockingly menacing. They both laughed.

"There's just one thing…." Daisy said.

"What, only one?"

"I don't really like this ending, with the murder."

"You always were too soft-hearted," Mari said, "Why do you have a problem with that?"

"It's just that, by the third act it seems Hester is starting to show some signs of remorse. I mean, she comes to see Hannah when she hears she's ill."

"That could have been just for show."

"Perhaps, but I felt she was having second thoughts. Do you really think she was going to be able to kill her own flesh and blood?"

"Well, there have been times…" Marigold was still laughing.

"Be serious. I would like to get Rose's opinion."

Rose was interested and pleased that they were now showing a more analytical approach to whatever was given them to read.Her response was, "You say you disapprove of the conclusion Daisy. So how would you bring the play to a close? Remember it must be a strong ending".

"Well, at the last minute she'd be unable to kill her sister and there would be a reconciliation."

"Much too tame," from Mari.

"Not necessarily. Right until the very last moment the audience must feel she is going to do it and then the whole thing is turned on its head. And let's face it, most of us like a happy ending."

"Well," said Rose, "I'm afraid it's not really a question of what *we* like. This after all is not our play and I think Willard Jones might have something to say, something quite rude, if you suggested altering his script. Now, the thing is do you both agree that you should both take part? Clearly it's been written with you in mind."

"Definitely" and "Of course" settled the matter.

"Now to other matters," Rose continued, "You realise Mari that we are now on a countdown to the date when I must comply with my father's wager. I've had a word with my solicitor and as no date was specified within the period of the fifth year, we have the whole of your nineteenth year in which to meet the challenge. So…we must plan the next months carefully.

"Between now and your birthdays I want you both to have some on-stage musical experience, probably in the Music Hall. A second time for you Mari and a first time for Daisy. We'll work with Estelle on that. Willard's play will start in the provinces, play for six to eight weeks, then if it's well received it would be considered for London next year, our critical year.

"There are auditions soon for two Shaw plays, 'Major Barbara' and 'Pygmalion', both going into the provinces this summer with a view to being moved into the West End as soon as Christmas productions come to an end.

I would like you both to read for the lead roles in these. Should Mari be lucky, then it would give she and I two possible strings to our bow with regard to the wager. Should you Daisy, land one of these plum roles it will be a wonderful bonus for us all. Should there be any clash of commitments we'll worry about it when the time comes. A bird in the hand etc., etc."

The girls were excited. So much in the pipeline. Estelle was currently playing in Pinero's 'The Second Mrs. Tanqueray' at the Aldwych, so the music would have to be put on hold for a while, but there was nothing to stop them looking at some of the Music Hall numbers and finding items they thought might suit them. Estelle approved that idea, suggesting they earmark six numbers, so as to have more material ready if it should be needed. Adding "It's always wise to do this. After all you will not know until you arrive at a rehearsal perhaps two days prior to the show, whether you have selected the same number as someone else on the bill. If that happened, you, as the junior performers would certainly have to make any alterations necessary." As this was such an important performance for them, she intended booking the services of a choreographer who would plan their routines and dance steps in detail. Armed with sheet music and notepads, the girls happily went away to start their planning.

"Bless them, I know they're excited, but I did so want to get you on my own for a while. We haven't seemed to have really talked since that last awful business with the glass. I saw Monty again yesterday. You know Rose, it's not really like a romance, at least I don't see it as that, but I am very fond of him and I just have this feeling that he might think we have a future together. I mean supposing he were to propose, what do I do? I love him to bits in one sense, but intimacy? That's another thing altogether. I love the thought of being taken care of. Not having to worry about finance, that sort of thing."

Rose's voice was sharp, "When have you ever had to worry about finance? I've tried to ensure you were always comfortable and had no monetary problems."

"Oh and you have! Don't get me wrong. But I'm a grown woman and I can't go on sponging on you for ever."

"It hurts me to hear you use the word 'sponging', you're my God-daughter for heavens' sake and very dear to me. There is no shortage of money here for whatever you need."

Rose's mind was in a turmoil. Was this the time? To do this now would certainly provoke adverse publicity at a time when she least needed it and when it might affect her future plans.

"Rose darling, the last thing in the world I want to do is hurt you. You've been everything to me, my rock and my lifeline, like a parent in every way possible.

"Thanks to you and your counselling over all these years, I have a rewarding career which I enjoy; but I am getting older and I do sometimes wonder what it would be like to share my life with someone else. And realistically, my biological clock will soon have run its course. I'd probably make a lousy mother, but occasionally I think how wonderful it would be to hold a baby, my own flesh and blood." Then, laughing, "I panic and think I would probably hate having to consider someone else's whims and fancies and being at the beck and call of an infant, which only makes me realise just how selfish I am and how embedded in my comfortable existence."

Rose felt relief. The crisis had passed but only temporarily. Soon, very soon it would have to be faced.

Rose's doctor was not pleased. She was not obeying his instructions and opting for a quiet life, on the contrary her blood pressure was high and she seemed uncharacteristically nervy. Again he suggested a holiday.

"My dear Miss Reece, you must get out of London and its environs for a time. Here there are far too many calls on you, too many commitments. I'm afraid everyone wants a part of you. You must go somewhere else, anywhere, pastures new and all that. I will not be responsible for the consequences if you do not do so."

Thinking about what he had said, she did some serious self-appraising. That stupid wager had developed in her a sort of tunnel vision, everything focused on its success. The young girls in her care had worked hard, one of them for almost four years. Because her own life had been steeped in all things theatrical, she had assumed an interest in them such as there had been in Estelle. But much of the world of theatre was a façade, a pretence. Life in all its facets was built on fact and experience. She picked up her diary. There was just time now before the pace quickened, to broaden the girls' horizons, let them learn some history in situ and for all of them to have a complete break. Estelle's play was due to close in two days' time, so hopefully they could all go together as before.

Her own childhood had been Bohemian, her father seeking out gambling houses throughout the world, on the pretext of studying and painting in dissimilar areas. Yes, he'd been a gambler and had cheated on her mother repeatedly, but he'd always managed to instil fun into almost any situation. Before his paintings were in demand, when money was tight, he had managed to make even the most difficult situations bearable. She recalled sitting in a dacha on the outskirts of Moscow. There was no furniture, but using a packing case as a table, Sebastian had with a flourish served them with caviar, a gift from a fellow artist. The accompanying bread had been stale and they were all chilled to the bone, but still they had been able to smile at his antics. On the Trans-Continental express they had alternately frozen and then almost fried in the heat, but the sights and sounds of the experiences were burned in her brain and she valued them. Yes, it was definitely time to introduce a little magic into these young girls' lives. And, it's a wicked thought I know, but if it removes Estelle from Monty's orbit for a while and allows me a little breathing space, then I'm grateful for small mercies.

Three whole weeks abroad. The girls were ecstatic. Rose explained laughingly, "It's a sort of miniature version of what the Victorians used to call the Grand Tour. We'll go to Paris first and spend about a week there, there's so much to see, then Switzerland and Austria, Germany, Baden Baden and the Black Forest and finally the beautiful old city of Bruges."

Rose's agent for many years was happy to assist with the organisation, he too was becoming worried about his most famous client and anything which was good for her was to be welcomed. Biddy would not accompany them this time, as Rose said, they would be moving from one hotel to another, where there would be adequate assistance with laundry, packing etc.

Paris in the late spring was a dream come true. Strolling down the Champs Elysees, the view from the Eiffel Tower, drinking citron pressé or coffee on one of the boulevards, the flowers in Montmartre and listening spellbound to the angelic voices of the choir in Notre Dame, they loved it all. Leaving Versailles in a glorious haze of fountains, gardens and chandeliers, they said goodbye to the beautiful Seine and moved on. Switzerland next and the mountain sides were in colourful bloom. But the majesty of the Eiger and the Matterhorn dominated all and the girls loved it. Staying at a hotel in the small town of Grindelwald, high in the Alps, Marigold said "I just feel I can reach out from our balcony and touch the Eiger, it's amazing," whilst Daisy kept repeating "It's the air, so clear and crisp, it's like drinking a glass of wine."

From Switzerland to Austria and inevitably here there were reminders of the bitter war which had not long been over, but the residents anxious to restore economic stability to their areas and restore the tourist trade welcomed them warmly. In Vienna they drank coffee and sampled the famous Sacher Torte, the cake which had originated in the very restaurant in which they we sitting. In the Viennese Opera House they sat in the orchestra stalls one morning and watched as the stage team prepared the set for grand opera. The girls draped themselves nonchalantly over the great staircase there and tried to imagine themselves in evening dress arriving for such an occasion.

In Germany they went straight to the Black Forest and relaxed in brilliant sunshine, sampling different foods, listened to folk music and swam in the hotel's heated pool.

Rose had lost her strained look and watching her two most recent protégées felt an upsurge of pride. They were now elegant, beautiful young women, treating everyone with whom they came in contact with the same courtesy and, when the occasion demanded it, the same wit and good humour. It was in fact a joy to be in their company. I must have done something right, Rose thought. I know their parents laid the foundations, but over the last few years, I have played quite a large part in their development. They could have been in awe of me, or even hated me for all that gruelling tuition, yet we are all comfortable with each other. Long may that continue.

Following her strenuous few weeks on stage in a leading role, Estelle was also loving the freedom from routine, new experiences and the opportunity to read and relax. Covertly Rose examined her. At thirty-five she was a beautiful young woman. Her dark curling hair and dark eyes always attracted attention, but it was her extrovert personality which held it. Often, as she said herself, Estelle would rush in 'where angels fear to tread', but she rarely gave offence. She was doubly talented, a competent, expressive and amiable actress, with whom directors were always pleased to work and her vocal ability made her a popular selection for musical theatre.

Gilbert and Sullivan operettas were currently all the rage and Old Time Musical Halls were very popular, but keeping very much au fait with what was happening across the Atlantic, Rose felt that, as was happening with vaudeville in the States, they would inevitably run their course and the West End would soon, like Broadway, be awash with musicals. Then Estelle really would come into her own. Voices were known to improve with the years so that Estelle could hope for many years on the stage – if that was what she wanted! Hearing Daisy at the pool telling the world in general that she could never, ever, acquire a taste for either sauerkraut or salami, Rose decided that it was time for her to intervene before the war was re-ignited.

Their last move was to Belgium and the ancient city of Bruges. Rose had always loved its peaceful ambience and she was pleased to see the girls loved it too. Sailing down the river on one of the wide barges, they were able to see and appreciate its beauty from a distance. But time was running out. They would not be visiting Holland for, as Rose had said, they had this year missed the bulb fields in bloom.

"We'll do that next time," she promised them smiling.

Back at Greenacres Rose had another surprise for them, they were to have a further three days free to go and visit their family on the Isle of Wight, then, as Rose said

"It really will be noses to the grindstone".

"Why is it everything seems so much smaller?" Daisy asked as they approached the farmhouse.

"Because you idiot, we've grown, that's why," Mari as usual, not mincing her words. "Everything looks good though, even the outbuildings, so Dad must be in fine form."

And he was. Meg Griffin, like their surroundings seemed shrunken and rather pale, the small boys boisterous and needing constant attention. The biggest surprise was

Sue. In the midst of all this, Sue appeared the dominant figure and now apparently a permanent fixture in the household. The girls had been unaware of this new state of affairs and were astonished to find clothes handing in the wardrobe and her belongings scattered about. It was not until the visit was over and they were on the return journey that they expressed to each other a certain disquiet.

"She seems to have taken over," Mari said "It hardly seems like our home any more."

"I just can't believe the way Dad jumps to it whenever she suggests something needs doing, but what I hate is," and Daisy here pulled a face, "the way she seems to be directing Mum also. 'Isn't it time the boys were in bed?' all that sort of thing, in someone else's home!"

"There's another thing…"

"I know what you're going to say…"Daisy cut in. "I saw them as well."

"Dad's things in her room. Surely they can't be…?"

"I'm afraid I don't think there's any doubt about it. I know Mum's frail and absorbed with her boys, but I still can't believe they would, not right under her nose. It's disgusting."

"Perhaps…" Mari hesitated, "I know we're a couple of innocents as yet about all this, but perhaps after the birth and it was a difficult birth, she's no longer interested in…you know. Dad, after all's a red-blooded male and Sue's not only vigorous and lusty, but might well be lustful as well for all we know."

Daisy sighed, "The only thing is they all seem to be rubbing along together alright. I just wish Mum didn't look so frail."

"Daisy, there's absolutely nothing we can do about it. It's entirely their own affair. And that, I hasten to add, was not meant as a pun. Now I don't know about you but I've got a script to read, mark and inwardly digest!"

And with that Marigold opened her book and settled back against the cushioned seat.

Chapter 9

In their absence Rose had bought Estelle a car. Driving lessons had been arranged straight away and when Estelle protested at her generosity, Rose silenced her by saying that they could no longer always rely on public transport and that it would of course be of great advantage to her personally if Estelle was able to drive her.

Estelle with typical exuberance had accelerated the driving programme, all too anxious to be able to drive her own shining and quite beautiful new car.

Rose had decided that each twin was to read for each of the two show plays' leading roles. The auditions for 'St. Joan' and 'Pygmalion' were to be taken in tandem with both directors and their assistants present. This, on the assumption that the same individuals would be able to play the smaller roles on the two different evenings. It also allowed the directors more flexibility in their choice of more major roles.

The plays had to be read and with Rose's help, analysed. The structure had to be discussed in detail, together with what each character should bring to his or her own role to achieve maximum portrayal of the author's aims. Which was a 'big' scene and which were those of lesser importance, which was the climax of the play and had it achieved its intention? The two leading roles were of course very different. Joan, the girl from a small French village, hearing voices telling her to away and fight and Eliza, the Cockney flower seller trained to be a lady and speak and behave properly all as a result of a wager. This latter they found quite amusing.

As Marigold said, "It's all because of Miss Reece taking part in a wager that I've been taught to speak proper and know which knife and fork to use."

They all laughed at that and even more so when, on the fourth lesson together, Rose suddenly said, "I really can't stand this Joan of Arc.

Astonished the girls turned to look at her.

"Well, think about it. If you had a daughter of fifteen and she suddenly said she'd been told by God to put on a suit of armour and go away with an army consisting entirely of men and fight, in order to save a Prince of the Realm, in this case, the Dauphin, wouldn't you be ever so slightly worried that she wasn't quite...?"

As intended, this lightened the effect of their studies and, also as intended, ensured they never took anything at face value. "Question everything," she said to them repeatedly, "because it's in print doesn't make it fact."

The two characters they were being asked to portray did of course have one thing in common. Both were being required to make massive changes in their life-styles, to leave home and everything familiar and venture into the unknown. Joan's key speech was the one when she was told that she was to be sentenced to life imprisonment and tells her captors that she would prefer to die in the flames rather than spend years shut away from the sunlight and the beauty of nature. For Eliza, it was the one when returning from the ball she is ignored and rounds on her mentor for lacking the courtesies with which he has supposedly imbued her. These were rehearsed repeatedly, but together the twins also practised duologues involving other characters, from the two plays. Now the time they had spent with Derek Lane during the Peter Pan production paid off. Both girls were able to reproduce the Cockney dialect well and Rose had them reciting whole poems in this, to ensure they could do so without lapsing into 'received' English.

Any spare time was spent in putting together a programme for their Music Hall numbers. For the first half the 'Burlington Bertie' number they had sung at Rose's party was to be rehashed with a couple of extra verses. Daisy would then sing 'I was a good little girl 'til I met you' and Mari would respond with 'I'll be your sweetheart'. The final chorus they would sing together. In the second half they would appear as a couple of Cockney urchins singing 'We're following in Father's footsteps' then 'Two little girls in blue', Mari to remain on stage and sing 'Daddy wouldn't buy me a bow wow' whilst Daisy donned a girl's dress and returned with 'Joshua, Joshua, why don't you call and see Mama?' Together they would close with 'In the twi, twi, twilight', inviting the audience to join them in the final chorus.

Rose and Estelle approved their ideas. Estelle arranged for them to meet their choreographer, Meryl, at a church hall in Richmond the following week and Estelle would both drive them there and accompany them on the piano. It went well, but Estelle said at their next rehearsal they must wear a suggestion of the costumes which were planned, in this way they would be more prepared than donning an unfamiliar outfit at the last moment. "For instance, Bert would doff his top hat when he meets Gert and in the urchins' scene, it would be typical of one of you to have your hands in your pockets at least part of the time. I'll bring some things along to Greenacre and we'll try that out."

The twins never ceased to be amazed at the attention to detail. Nothing, absolutely nothing was left to chance or not previously rehearsed, but then as Rose constantly pointed out to them "This is what gives all of us the confidence to do what we do. We know it has worked in rehearsal and what others on stage expect of us. If anything does go wrong, we can all contribute to putting it right as quickly as possible, hopefully without the audience being aware of the fact. It's also a well-known fact that the most successful, supposedly ad lib joke lines, have in fact been very well rehearsed so that the timing is spot-on."

The auditions for 'Pygmalion' and 'St. Joan' were to be held in the same church hall in which Mari had watched her first audition with, the now to be avoided, Celia. On a warm summer's day it smelled musty and airless. There were, Daisy thought, about thirty people wanting to read and it transpired that there would be four contenders for each of the female leads, with four for the part of Professor Higgins. Looking at the young women who were to try for Joan and Eliza she hoped against hope that they were much too old!

Marigold agreed "Three of them I'm sure are pushing thirty, but you never can tell, as Rose says it's possible to lose ten to fifteen years on stage, as far as the audience is concerned that is."

It was a long sticky, nerve-wracking afternoon and they left feeling deflated. Had they shown enough energy, had they shown enough pathos, had they picked up cues as quickly as they had been taught, at the same time throwing their voices to the rear of the hall?

"I don't know why we're putting ourselves through all this," said Daisy tongue in cheek, "after all we could be serving afternoon tea to the gentry somewhere quiet in the country without all this hassle."

"You know exactly why we're doing it, because we love it, that's why. Is there anything to beat that feeling on stage when you can hear a pin drop and you know the audience is hanging on every word? It gives me goose flesh just thinking about it."

"Couldn't agree more, big sister. Now going off completely at a tangent, do you know what I would rather like to try next?"

"No idea, but I'm sure you're going to tell me".

"I'd like to have a go at Gilbert and Sullivan. Wouldn't it be fun if we could be in one of those together? 'The Mikado' for instance; we could be two of the three little maids from school."

"Daisy, can you please allow us to get through the next few months, without leaping ahead, there's a lot of water to go under the bridge before we can even contemplate that."

Then, grinning, "But yes, it would be fun!"

It was two nail-biting, agonising days before they heard and it was splendid news. Marigold was to play Eliza Doolittle and Daisy, Joan of Arc. Rose announced immediately that they must have a party to celebrate and Monty and the usual group of 'luvvies' appeared, including young Ivor Novello. Now the twins fell in love again, hopelessly, and, when he played the piano, rapturously. But, as Estelle pointed out to them it was a lost cause, his taste was in other directions. Rose was, meanwhile, making discreet enquiries about Celia, who had apparently sold the family home and taken a flat in the Whitton area. Rose's heart sank when she heard; this was too close, much too close for comfort.

The two plays were being staged in Bath, running for four weeks from the end of September, so rehearsals started immediately. Rose warned the girls there would then be no respite at the closure, with rehearsals for Willard's play to be performed in Richmond for two weeks at the beginning of December. Then a short, very short breather, before the Music Hall at the Adelphi over the Christmas period. It was lovely that the girls would be working in Richmond for a time, which meant they could come home each evening. The only reservation Rose had was that of Celia's proximity.

If there had been whispers that the Isle of Wight twins were receiving preferential treatment these quickly ceased when their respective casts saw them in action. Here were two young girls who could act most people off the stage. In fact as one wag said,

"It used to be 'Never work with animals or children,' I think they should add the Golden Girls to that list!" It was tiring, demanding work and Rose was careful to see that they had plenty of rest, at one point saying that for several weeks it would be better if they didn't share a bedroom, so as not to succumb to the temptation of chatting for half the night.

Rose was pleased that the allocation of roles had fitted in with her plans. Shaw's plays were not terribly popular, but 'Pygmalion' was the exception and would certainly go into the West End in Mari's nineteenth year and, God willing, with her in the lead. When that happened, Rose's part in the wager would be home and dry. Yes, Daisy was losing out in all this but, she reminded herself, it was Marigold with whom the wager was started and Daisy was sufficiently talented to quickly catch her sister up with all the time in the world to do so.

The critics true to form, did not enthuse about 'St. Joan' but as Rose said they merely reflected the general public's feelings that Shaw could be rather heavy-going. If they objected to the playwright they clearly in no way objected to the performers. Simon Power who had played Professor Higgins, Marigold and Daisy were all singled out for special mention. Of Daisy it was said, 'Daisy Gold captures exactly the idealism and religious fervour of a young inexperienced girl on a mission, it was a first-rate performance.' And of Mari, 'Marigold's Cockney accent and her facial expressions as Eliza, were a joy and her transformation into a refined, well articulating young lady was a delight.'

And a further comment, 'The Golden Girls are appearing in a new play by Willard Jones, 'Double Trouble' at the Richmond Theatre early in December. Individually, their performances are a joy, to see them in a play together should prove a real theatrical treat.'

Rarely did Daisy and Mari get the opportunity to wander around the London shops together, but one precious day between the Shavian plays closing and rehearsals starting for 'Double Trouble' found them doing just that. Wandering down one side street, where there were jewellers' shops and art galleries Mari suddenly stopped dead. "What is it?" Daisy asked and then saw that her sister was staring into the window of an art gallery. In its centre was just one picture on display, a painting by Sebastian Reece.

"I don't understand it", Mari said, "I once asked Rose what had happened to all his work and she said the majority of it was in museums, but that she had several packed away until she had really made up her mind what to do about them. She also said they were her 'nest-egg' just in case she went bankrupt."

"I hardly think that's likely," Daisy retorted, "but I agree it's odd, perhaps we should go inside and ask about it."

They were greeted by a handsome young man with hair almost as blonde as their own and a complexion which suggested he either lived or had just returned from the tropics.

"We wondered about the painting in the window," Mari said. "We actually thought all his paintings were in museums."

"Hardly," the young man said, laughing, "look around". To their amazement they saw that the walls were lined with at least twenty other impressionist paintings by Sebastian Reece.

"We know Rosalie Reece quite well," Mari said tentatively, "I think she would be interested to see how many of her father's paintings are here."

"Miss Reece, his only daughter? You know her...? Oh please bring her along I would so love to meet her." The young man had produced his business card and said if they wouldn't mind telephoning in advance, he would then ensure that the gallery was open and that he could meet Miss Reece in person.

Rose was equally intrigued when told about it. Batches of her father's work were held in three different museums and she had a further ten packed away.

"But my father travelled the world and I certainly wouldn't have put it past him, if he were short of ready cash at any time to use the painting he had just finished as his way of paying a bill. All the same I will certainly make contact with this young man," and looking at the card, "Richard Keble. I'll telephone tomorrow and if Estelle can drive me, we'll pay him a visit."

Arriving home after the rehearsal the next day, the twins were surprised and concerned to find Rose looking rather pale, with Estelle fussing around her with tea and the tablets the doctor had prescribed.

"Don't be alarmed my dears," Rose said, "Come and sit down. I'm just recovering from the shock of seeing that amazing array of paintings by my father. Paintings I'd never seen before." And in answer to their unspoken questions, "Richard's home is in South Africa, the Southern Cape. His parents own an art gallery in Cape Town and Sebastian lived in that area for about three years. Richard remembers as a child having Sebastian pointed out to him as a well-known artist. During that time he must have painted a lot, you'll see that there's quite a strong African influence in the paintings, the Masai and Zulu cultures, that sort of thing. Obviously at some point Sebastian was totally out of funds, had probably been on the gaming tables for weeks on end. He kept selling Richard's father odd paintings and when he finally decided it was time to move on and needed the money for travelling expenses, offered Mr. Keble the rest of what he had painted in South Africa.

"That young man Richard is very sensible and when he saw that there didn't seem a great deal of future for him over there, he suggested to his parents that he came here with the paintings to try and make a new life for himself. They were happy for him to do that and…well, here he is! He's quite realistic about things, says he won't be able to buy himself a decent property until he's made some sales.

"I'm seriously considering whether I should offer to buy the whole collection. In that event I would have all my father's works in this country, which I know he would have wished. However I've decided, on Estelle's advice, not to do anything in a hurry, after all, as she has pointed out, I have first to prove their authenticity. I think the next step would be to get to know this young man a little better and I propose inviting him to dinner as soon as possible, that is, whilst all of us are at liberty to be present."

It was all too obvious from the faces of the twins that this met with their whole-hearted approval and with that in mind, they were despatched the next day to issue an invitation for the following week.

Willard Jones was overjoyed that his play was to be performed in Richmond. To have acquired the Golden Girls to enact the parts he had written for them was another bonus. They were now considered to be 'hot property' in the theatrical world and he had always been afraid another offer would prove more tempting.

He was glad that after a great deal of heart-searching he had changed his original working title. The surprised, uncertain looks he had received earlier when he had announced it was to be called 'Doppelganger' had been enough to tell him that an insufficient number of people were familiar with the word, so he'd played for safety and settled for something which to everyone would be both recognisable and signify some sort of conflict, 'Double Trouble'. He sighed with pleasure. 'Darling Lou' had been merely a case of dipping his toe in the water and he was all too aware of its many imperfections. With this play he felt he'd got it right, hoped he'd made huge strides with the dialogue and that the critics instead of baying for his blood would love it. Especially the court scene! Rose Reece had already complimented him on that and her judgement was second to none. It would be a long time, if ever, before he could be up there with the Congreves and Pineros, but he would keep working at it. The girls were brilliant and even now when rehearsals were barely off the ground, they seemed to be getting just the right sort of brittle edginess, which would later in the play develop into serious antagonism. No, it was all going well and was very, very satisfying.

A week after meeting Richard Keble, Rose looked at the faces of her two young resident guests and wondered if she had done the right thing in inviting him to dinner. Both girls appeared to be hanging on his every word and anxious to be the one to pass the cruet, the vegetables, anything in fact which would draw his attention in their direction. They were so alike! It would, she felt, be very difficult for any young man to select one of them in preference to the other and that could be a real cause for jealousy. I just hope, she thought, that nothing happens to cause a real separation between them. Their minor spats have to date been just that, minor, but if there were to be real conflict I would be saddened to see either of them hurt.

Daisy had decided. Richard Keble was the man for her. He was probably only late twenties but had lived abroad, was obviously well travelled and acted and sounded like a man of the world. Marigold also knew she had met the love of her life. He was so handsome with his blonde hair and blue eyes, talked so knowledgably about art, was amusing about his life in the Cape and the new experience of living in London, what more could a girl want? Estelle covertly observed the pair of them. Oh dear Rose, what have you done? I swear if I were a few years younger I would want him too. I wonder if he prefers the older woman? But there's something…Can't quite put my finger on it, but…

With regard to the provenance of the paintings, this seemed to present no problem. Richard said that in his possession were letters and receipts which Sebastian had given to his father, to ensure that there was no question about the author's origin. These would be handed over when any transaction took place. In view of this, Rose expressed her wish to visit his gallery again, taking with her one of the Tate art experts, whom she knew. He, she felt, would be able to fairly estimate the paintings' value before any sale was agreed. Richard seemed more than happy with this arrangement.

Before he left, Richard asked if the girls might join him the next Sunday afternoon in a visit to Hyde Park. There was to be a band concert there and they could perhaps follow that with tea somewhere. The girls accepted with glee, each inwardly regretting that the invitation was not for her alone. Were they always to be considered in tandem? That was beginning to prove very annoying. The afternoon was pleasant enough and it was not until they were having tea that they both became alarmed.

Once again they had returned to the topic of Sebastian Reece and when Richard said 'He used to sit at the table with his long hair flopping about all over the place. I don't think my mother liked that,' both the girls felt a frisson of shock. Neither commented on this, but later alone at Greenacres it was the main topic of conversation.

"I thought he said earlier that he vaguely remembered having Sebastian pointed out to him as a child."

"Exactly. Yet this memory of him sitting at a table seemed pretty vivid to me. To begin with it sounded as if Sebastian was sitting at their own table, that is Richard's parents' table and 'he used to sit' sounds to me as if he did it often."

"Sounds a bit fishy to me. I'm afraid we're going to have to tell Rose. Everything might not be what it seems."

And everything was certainly not what it had seemed. Rose did make her visit with the art expert to Richard's gallery, feeling it essential that she determined the paintings' value; this done she remained behind and spoke to Richard at some length. Eventually the whole story emerged.

"Sebastian stayed in the Cape for three years and during that time fathered a son, Richard's father. There was no art gallery and when Sebastian had financial difficulties and had to move on he left the paintings so that his mistress and her son would always have some way of raising money if necessary. He did send money at fairly regular intervals to Richard's grandmother, so this didn't prove necessary and when Richard eventually decided to try and carve out a new life for himself abroad it was suggested he used the paintings as collateral. The rest of the story seems true enough, other than the fact that in South Africa he is known by the surname Keble-Reece. He says he didn't use that in London, as it might have inhibited any sales he could make. This doesn't allow for the fact that he told us a lot of lies, which had we known the truth, might have inhibited our attitude towards him right from the start. So, I have a new nephew, there is another stack of paintings which I may or may not purchase and possibly another serious problem ahead."

Daisy spoke first. "So all that rubbish about Richard barely knowing Sebastian was, well, rubbish. This was his grandfather he was talking about, someone who obviously returned at some point and stayed with them, that is if we are to believe Richard's comments about seeing him sitting at their table."

Now it was Mari's turn, "The trouble is, once someone starts to feed you lies, from then on, you don't know what to believe."

"But why would he lie about this? Why couldn't he have said from the outset who he was. It isn't as if he or his family have done anything wrong." Daisy was sounding more and more indignant.

"I'm afraid there may be more to it than we thought and this is the problem that I said would now be looming. I should have listened to Estelle…"

"Why, what did she say?"

"She said he was handsome, charming, but perhaps a little too ingratiating. Now of course we can all see why. I telephoned her just now to say what had transpired and she immediately asked if I had considered the will."

"The will?" Daisy was surprised.

"Sebastian's will. Estelle is concerned that this is some sort of ploy to challenge that will. As she points out, we now know that Sebastian had a son and a grandson and there are a great many valuable paintings at stake. I think she may be right. In any event I've now asked my solicitor to come over as quickly as possible so that we might discuss it in detail."

Returning upstairs the girls were loud in their disapproval.

"He seemed so nice, I can hardly believe he's fed us such a pack of lies."

"Perhaps we're incredibly gullible. We don't seem to know a great deal about men."

"Oh come on, it wasn't just us. Rose and Estelle both lapped it up too. And," Daisy laughed, "there was I thinking I could happily spend the rest of my life with him."

Mari also burst out laughing, "Just as well this happened then, because I had decided he was the one for me, and that might have caused complications!"

"We could have a serious problem in that respect you know," Daisy was now serious. "If someone targets us just for our looks, they might not know which one of us is which, if you see what I mean and, even worse, they might not care."

"I think there's a possibility that might happen initially, but if they really get to know us, they'll realise we are two very different people," Mari, tongue in cheek, "You're the serious Miss Goody Two-Shoes, always have been, and I'm the lively, witty, good-to-be-with elder sister."

"You'd better watch out big sister, this Goody Two-Shoes is about to box your pretty little ears."

"You know, Daisy, it's just occurred to me that if we had really come to blows over Mr. Richard Keble-Reece, we could have been running almost a parallel story to the one we're playing in. Just watch out you don't cast your eyes on any more of the young men I fancy, always remember that I'm going to be the one wielding the paper-knife!"

Rose had invited Estelle over to hear what her solicitor had to say and it was good news. Afterwards she told the girls what had transpired.

"An artist he may have been and feckless with it, but my father made no mistake whatsoever about the wording of his will. I think he may well have been aware that he could have left a trail of fatherless children all the way from Russia to the Canadian Rockies and decided to guard against any eventuality. He makes it clear that any transactions he made with paintings are conclusive, according to the letters and receipts handed over and that no further demands may be made on him with regard to descendants of whom he knew, or those of whom he was unaware. Mr. Stokes, my solicitor had this codicil in a sealed envelope, which was only to be opened if an occurrence such as this arose. I think old Stokes was quite shocked to read it, but I personally found it not only a relief but absolutely typical of my father. I could almost hear him saying it to himself as he wrote it.

"So, the paintings do belong to Richard's parents, but if he has their written permission to sell them then, providing my Tate's man approves, I will probably purchase the lot. However girls," Rose smiled at them wryly," I think if you don't mind, we won't be extending any further invitations to Richard Keble. His family did intend contesting the will in some way and his role was to ingratiate himself here and find out as much as he could about the will's terms. Your unexpected visit to the gallery merely accelerated things for him. Thankfully, we now know they have no case whatsoever. My nephew he probably is, but I think you'll agree that stringing us all along with a lot of lies is not the best way to introduce himself as a member of my family, or to win a young girl's heart."

At this the girls blushed simultaneously, but nodded their heads in full agreement.

"In any event, I feel that once the paintings are sold and the terms of the will are officially made clear to him then we shall soon see young Richard departing our shores. Oh and I almost forgot, there was something else in the envelope, about which I knew nothing. Sebastian not only loved wagers, he loved puzzles, so goodness knows what's in store now. He says that amongst my own paintings is one called 'Beginners Please' and inside its lining, on the reverse, I will find a message."

The girls were hopeful that this might be found straight away and they could be part of the excitement in learning what the message was, but a signal from Estelle indicated that she felt Rose had dealt with quite enough difficult situations for one day. Taking the hint they made their excuses and left Rose and Estelle to drink their pre-dinner sherry in peace.

Next day it required the services of the gardener to assist in retrieving the paintings from their storage place in the loft. Then each had to be unwrapped from their protective covers until finally the 'Beginners Please' painting emerged. It was in the artist's usual impressionist style and depicted two artistes waiting in the wings ready to go onto the set, a garden with arbours and flowers. The stage and set was Victorian with the old style flame footlights, which added to the slightly blurred effect of the figures and fitments. Very different from the strident colours of the South African paintings, it was delicately executed and as one, they all declared it a delight. A further few minutes passed before they returned to their original task and the message was found. Another envelope! Tactfully leaving Rose to read her father's message alone, Mari and Daisy withdrew. Inside the envelope Rose found a folded letter from her father and a key.

My lovely Rose,

I don't know how your mother and you put up with me all those years, but you did so and for that I am eternally grateful. Even unreliable and often unscrupulous artists do need some sort of anchor in their lives and you certainly provided that. I have no doubt whatsoever, that you will win the wager I set for you. You are, after all, your father's daughter. It may surprise you to know that I do possess some business acumen – and before you fall about laughing, the key you should now be holding is an example of this. I know I always made light of all things theatrical, but I do want you to know how very proud I am of your success. There have been many occasions when I have watched you on stage, without your knowledge. (I was the man lurking at the back of the orchestra stalls.) Artists are allowed to be maudlin on occasion, it's part of their creative nature, so you may, or may not, be surprised to learn that your Katherine of Aragon pleading for Henry VIII's mercy, sent me home with tears streaming down my face.

Now to other matters… I have always known about Estelle and as I'm sure you have already surmised, this was another reason why I ensured you were well provided for. When she is eventually told of her parentage, please tell her that I have watched her progress from delightful child to beautiful woman, with pride and joy. Give her a kiss from me.

Now back to my business acumen – war is imminent and people are already moving to places in the country and closing down businesses. I have found, my love, a theatre for you, a theatre of your very own. It is paid for of course, lock stock and barrel as they say, and in a reasonable state of repair. However, it is closed at the moment and depending how long the war lasts, may suffer from neglect. In the envelope you will find the address of my own solicitor who has made all the arrangements for regular inspections. It is not in Shaftesbury Avenue, but close enough to come under the classification of the West End, which I know carries a great deal of weight with the 'luvvies'. You might want to open a private theatre club or turn your hand to commercial theatre, but whatever you decide, I wish you every happiness with your venture and every success. I have a small sadness that I will not be there to applaud you, but my life has been full of wonderful things and you, the most precious of all.

Your loving Father,

Sebastian Reece

P.S. If the wager is not yet accomplished, the girl is not to top the bill in your own theatre, that would be cheating!!

Rose laughed and cried at the same time. The postscript was so typical, her father determined to have the last word. But the warmth of the heavy brass key in her hand, his loving words, brought her back to reality. This carefully thought out gift, only to be disclosed if other factors made it necessary, made her realise just how much he had cared. And Estelle. Now it was time… there was much to tell and it could no longer be delayed. A phone call and Estelle was on her way, slightly alarmed at what sounded like an urgent request. Within minutes she was on the doorstep.

"What is it Rose, did you find the message, is it something awful?"

"No, my dear, please sit down".

"Goodness, that sounds very formal. Am I on the carpet? Have I done something wrong?"

"On the contrary, I'm afraid it is *I* who have done something wrong, very wrong, and it is for that I must ask your forgiveness."

Estelle looked at her in amazement, "Rose, you never do anything wrong. What on earth are you talking about?"

"Let me perhaps start by saying that when I first discussed with Celia her antagonism towards the twins she replied, without actually admitting anything, and I have repeated this to no-one else, that she was jealous of Mari living here, because this was her place."

"Her place, Rose? What on earth did she mean?"

"She is convinced that she is my daughter and that Mari has usurped her position."

Estelle looked and sounded astonished, "What? Why on earth should she…?"

"You remember me telling you that her parents were my best friends and that I was her Godmother? Following Celia's birth, Gillian, her mother went from severe post-natal depression into a peculiar mental state and when it reached a point that the medics felt she might be a danger to the baby she was put in a home. There her condition deteriorated and it became necessary to have her sectioned and placed in a mental institution on a permanent basis."

"Oh Lord."

"Because Celia has no recollection of her mother and years later found references to me amongst her mother's things, together with mementoes of herself as a baby, she began to think the people around her had been lying to her and that she was the result of a liaison between myself and Charles, her father."

"But surely…?"

"There's more. She started to explore her theory further and found, as she believed, further evidence in the fact that I was absent from the stage about that time for a period of some months."

"Even so…"

"I tried to convince her that Gillian was indeed her mother, but as time has gone on I'm terribly afraid that not only was I unsuccessful, but that we haven't yet heard the last of her persecution of the twins."

"Surely not, it's already been horrific."

"I'm afraid there's more, much more. You see although she's totally wrong in thinking that she is my daughter, she was in fact very close to the truth," Rose hesitated, "The facts are that I was not on the stage for six months and that during that time I did have a child, a daughter someone who was and is, very dear to me..." She looked steadily at Estelle, "I had you."

"Me...? But that's not what you and Biddy told me, what I've always believed. You said..."

"Dearest Estelle, I know. I said a lot of things. Things for which I can never forgive myself."

"But, if that's the case, why haven't I lived with you all these years, instead of with Biddy? You said my parents died abroad in a car crash...It's inconceivable that I should be hearing all this now at thirty-five years of age, which begs the question what has changed? Why now suddenly? Why now?"

Rose again hesitated, "Why now? I suppose if I'm honest, it's because I'm frightened. Frightened that I might not live long enough to explain it to you myself, frightened of what Celia in her half-crazed state might do next and a need to share that fear with someone. The only thing I can say in mitigation, is that today's social climate is very, very different from that of thirty five years ago. I was just starting out on my career, being hailed as a possible future star and..."

"So my happiness had to be sacrificed because of your ambition and, suddenly, it's convenient for me to know, because of your fears for the future."

"It's not quite so simplistic as that. At that time I also had fears for you. You would have had to bear the stigma of being a bastard child and I couldn't have borne that. Once you started to show talent, talent in abundance, I knew that if it became general knowledge that you were an illegitimate child, then it would have put a stop to your budding career. How could I do that? And..." Rose hesitated.

"Yes, and…?"

"There was someone else I had to consider, your father."

"Of course, I'd forgotten there had to be someone else in this equation. Do I know him?"

"Yes my dear, it is from him you get your musical ability. You know Monty very well."

For a moment Estelle was stunned into silence. "Monty…? Of course, that fling all those years ago."

Rose went on, "When I knew I was pregnant I decided to tell him. That evening, quite out of the blue, he started to say how pleased he was that both our careers were going so well and how it made sense for neither of us to form any lasting relationships for some years, until we were really established performers. Quite clearly he was pre-empting any suggestions of anything serious. I couldn't bring myself to tell him. If I'd made an issue of it, both our careers would have been on the line, so I decided I would have to go ahead and make my own plans."

A horrified Estelle had just realised something else, "Monty? For God's sake Rose, I might have married him!"

"I wouldn't have allowed that to happen."

"And just how could you have stopped it? Two consenting adults. Supposing we'd eloped! It just doesn't bear thinking about."

"No, it doesn't. I know now that I should have told you when you were small and…"

A furious Estelle cut in, "But at that time it would have been inconvenient and it's only now when you're feeling ill and vulnerable that suddenly telling me has become an option. Oh yes, I do have memories of you when I was small, of a fragrant lady who came in and read me stories and brought me pretty things. But it was Biddy who fed me, bathed me and put me to bed. It was Biddy I cried out for if I had a bad dream, Biddy who picked me up after a fall and cuddled me until I felt better...Now I find out it could have been and should have been you." Estelle was crying now.

"I know, I know and I'm so, so sorry," the tears were sliding down Rose's cheeks.

Estelle tried to regain control. "How did you manage to keep it a secret?"

"As soon as I started to put on weight, I arranged to go to Brittany and rented a cottage there. Biddy came with me and was there at your birth. Together we worked out plans for our return. I managed to buy a cottage very close to my own, so that I could see you almost everyday. And I picked up the threads of my career, trying to make as much money as possible for all of us."

"But thirty-five years...Surely someone suspected?"

"My father was always suspicious. He often gave me handouts and I know now that's why he gave me enough to buy Greenacres."

"And what about Monty? Is he ever to be told?"

"Yes, Estelle, I will tell him, but I feel this is not the right time. I have no illusions about the three of us playing happy families. He has his own life to live. You have always been a very large part of my life and I hope and pray that will continue, if you can forgive me for what has past. You and I both love Monty dearly and I hope that eventually when he knows, he too will forgive me and we can all be comfortable with this knowledge."

For the first time there was a glimmer of a smile from Estelle, "So, you're not expecting me to call you Mummy, or anything like that?"

"I neither expect, nor want it, my darling. You and I have always been close and my dearest wish is we will continue to be so. Without being maudlin, when I go everything that I own will be yours, which is another reason I wanted to ensure you were aware of the truth. At the moment only Biddy and my solicitor know about this and for the time being I would prefer no-one else to know. Perhaps later when Monty has recovered from the shock, he and I might marry quietly, purely so that the three of us can present a united front. Knowing Monty, with or without that formality you will certainly inherit his fortune, so all your dreams of travelling to faraway places will be well within your grasp. You have such a capacity for life and love, my dearest wish is that you will meet someone with the same qualities, have a family of your own and unlike me, make the time to enjoy it."

Estelle was drying her eyes and trying to smile. "I do wish you'd stop talking about wills and all that 'leaving this mortal coil' nonsense, it's very depressing."

"I'm afraid the past few days have made me even more aware of the frailty of human life and then, this morning, reading my father's message..." Picking up Sebastian's letter, she offered it to Estelle, "You too had better read this, I think it will assist you in appreciating the type of man your grandfather was."

Again Estelle's handkerchief was in evidence, as she dried more tears. Then, there was an eruption of disbelief, "What? A theatre! Rose, how absolutely wonderful. What a lovely man and such a wicked sense of humour.

176

Goodness how exciting, I wonder what it's like? I mean, after several years unused, it could be a wreck."

"Comments like that are hardly likely to lift me out of my depressed state, dear daughter."

That last definitive word resulted first of all in a stunned silence, then an embarrassed half-smile, until at last the chuckles started to bubble up and finally, to Rose's relief and joy, they were able to laugh together, comfortably and without reservation.

As Rose had suggested, the information regarding Estelle's parentage was for the time being to be kept a secret and it was just as well, because it was soon obvious that there was a great deal to be done before 'Double Trouble' was ready for the stage.

Chapter 10

Going to seek out Rose's new theatre in the West End, had them all in a fever of anticipation. It was as Sebastian had said, in a side street off Shaftesbury Avenue, ideally situated for theatregoers to pick up taxicabs or obtain pre- or after-show meals. Rose had invited the girls to join herself and Estelle in this first visit and they were met at the theatre by Sebastian's solicitor, a Mr. George Lawson.

Sited on the corner of the road running parallel with Shaftesbury Avenue, the theatre's front entrance was relatively small. They were pleasantly surprised therefore to find that the foyer was large and the theatre could seat fifteen hundred. It did need refurbishing, but there was no sign of decay. George Lawson was horrified at the mere suggestion of this. "Certainly not, I had the strictest instructions from Mr. Reece that everything was to be kept in as good order as possible and he left money for that purpose. With your experience, Miss Reece, I am sure you will wish to make many changes, particularly back stage, the dressing rooms leave much to be desired.

My company will of course be happy to assist you in any way possible."

Helpful as he was trying to be, they were all quite relieved when he left them and they were able to just browse and discover things for themselves. Yes, the dressing rooms were pretty awful, and as for the toilets for the theatregoers to use, they were as Daisy said 'Ghastly'.

The stage curtains needed replacing and the whole place obviously needed rewiring and the plumbing brought up to today's standard. Estelle stood centre stage and sang and declared the acoustics first-rate and Rose sat in one of the boxes and waved her hand to the three of them in the familiar royal gesture of greeting. She was in fact stunned. This little theatre had so much potential. She could make it truly beautiful, transform it into a jewel. Bringing that to fruition would be such fun and now that Estelle knew all about ... she would surely be happy to help, be happy to be a part of all this. Rose knew her own career was inevitably waning with age and that the chance of further really good roles was diminishing with each passing year. This new venture would take the place of that and her own knowledge of all things theatrical, together with the many friends she had in the business should prove very, very useful.

Estelle's call, "You're day-dreaming up there, your Majesty," brought her back to reality and her second call "We peasants down here think it must be time for tea," had the desired result. A quick look at the 'Green Room' which Mari had found and was nothing more than a glorified dumping ground for odd bits of furniture and they set out for the nearest restaurant. Rose was already mentally redesigning the Green Room and turning it into a comfortable haven, a tranquil place where the players could relax. And there were so many other things to consider…The girls were fast reaching the stage when they would no longer require her coaching and it was going to be absolute bliss to have something really purposeful into which to sink her teeth. But for the time being, "I think I'll have one of those delicious chocolate éclairs," she said, "All this excitement has made me feel decidedly peckish."

Estelle had wondered if she would ever recover from yesterday's shock, wondered too if she could ever forgive Rose for keeping her in the dark for so many years. But she kept telling herself this was the person, who apart from Biddy, had been closest to her all her life and as she had reached maturity, had been close in a very different way. All her dreams and aspirations had been brought to Rose. Difficulties with work at school, arguments with other girls and details of first boy friends, it was with Rose these had been discussed and invariably problems had been solved. Estelle realised with a start that this had continued and she was still asking Rose for advice about difficult situations. It was why she had confessed to Rose that she didn't think she could seriously consider marrying Monty. In retrospect, the mere thought of this made her go hot and cold. And yet… if one had to have a father, surely Monty was just about the most ideal person in the world. And Rose hadn't just dumped her and then gone away somewhere, she had ensured that she was well cared for, with no shortage of money and more importantly had retained close contact throughout the years. Years in which Rose had reached the pinnacle of success. From time to time there had been offers to play outside the United Kingdom, certainly there were frequent requests from Broadway. Often Estelle had wondered why these had never been accepted. Only now did it occur to her that she herself, was probably the reason.

Yes, in those early years Rose had gone back to her career. As she had implied, someone had to pay the bills and that must have included Estelle's own private tuition, her music and dancing lessons. But Rose had often turned her back on commitments which would have taken her out of the country perhaps for months on end and Estelle suddenly knew without any doubt that this had been because of her. Whilst, of necessity, Rose had lived separately from her, it was from choice that she had sometimes refused very lucrative offers to play abroad, offers which would have brought her even greater fame and fortune.

Estelle sighed audibly and the others looked at her with surprise. What was done, was done. There was little point in ruining the present, because of what was now history. The waitress carefully placed the china and cutlery on the table and as she left, Estelle turned the handle of the teapot in Rose's direction and said with a brilliantly wicked smile, "Would you like to be mother?"

Tempting as it was to become immersed in what had to be done in the new theatre, Rose decided that until rehearsals were concluded for 'Double Trouble' and the show up and running, she did not want too many distractions at Greenacres, it being imperative that the girls were totally focussed on their acting roles.

The two sets were now completed, drawing room scenes for Acts 1 and 111 and the Court Room for Act11. In the penultimate week before opening the costumes arrived and during this period people were found wandering backstage in negligees, evening gowns and, most bizarre of all barristers in their gowns and wigs. The dress rehearsal went well and the Director was delighted. "Well done, all of you. Play as you've played tonight and the audience will love it. Those who've worked with me before know that I don't hold with all that 'good dress rehearsal, poor performance' rubbish. To my mind you need a good dress rehearsal to give everyone confidence. So, tomorrow's the night, full house and everyone firing on all cylinders please. Have a good night's sleep and thank you."

Unusually, Rose and Estelle had decided to attend the performance on both the opening and closing nights. Rose had kept telling herself not to be foolish, but couldn't rid herself of a feeling of unease that Celia should have come to live in Whitton, so close to this venue. Now at last, she was able to discuss her fears with Estelle.

"Rose, after what you said to her last time Celia knows if she tries anything else you will report her to the police and that's the last thing she'll want, after all she'd never work again."

"That's alright for you and for me to say, Estelle, but it doesn't take into account how disturbed I suspect she is. People who get this sort of fixation, don't behave rationally, probably don't even consider the consequences."

"The twins are not stupid. After what has happened in the past, however nervous they are, they're going to be quite watchful. I think you're worrying unnecessarily. Now let's get going. I doubt if they'll have a red carpet at Richmond, but I'm sure we can make an impressive entrance and let everyone know we're there to give maximum support to our girls."

Rose was looking forward to seeing the play. Willard had, she felt, achieved a nice balance between the three acts. The initial harmony and warmth between the two sisters disintegrating in the growing resentment of the younger sister's jealousy at no longer being included their ailing father's affections. His death and Hester's anger at being excluded from his will, resulting in the crisply executed court case. Then the gradual build up of Hester's resolve to seek retribution and the explosion of that in Hannah's murder at the final curtain. Daisy's alternative ending theory had been interesting and she had been able to put forward valid reasons for her suggestion. It was good to see that the girls were not just sponges absorbing information fed to them, but were able to analyse and then draw their own conclusions.

Rose had often mulled over their different characteristics. Daisy seemed to be more shrewd and brought more logic to bear when making decisions, whilst Mari was marginally the better actress at the moment, but had of course been longer in training.

Daisy was probably the better singer and Mari the better comic…It was difficult to differentiate. They were in fact typical identical twins, their two halves making a very complete and satisfying whole. But now the house lights were dimming, the fidgeting cease and the curtains parted.

The audience was loving it. When the twins were first seen in their respective roles there was a shock wave throughout the auditorium. They were so alike. Tonight their hair was dressed in chignons, gleaming silver blonde under the lights. The first act required smart day dresses. Marigold as Hester, the younger jealous sister, was in palest lemon and Daisy in a champagne coloured two piece. Against the Edwardian chaise longue and arm chairs covered in apricot velvet, they presented a charming picture. But as Rose knew only too well, on stage 'handsome is as handsome does' and members of the audience were listening and watching intently to see if the Golden Girls' performances could measure up to their advance publicity and the commendations they had received in the past. The two characters began to live as real people when the acrimony and bitchiness started to take over from their pleasing exteriors. Once Hannah, played by Daisy, had inherited the money, then the sparks began to fly and were a joy to watch.

As Rose had anticipated the court scene was excellent. "Audiences always love a good court scene and young Willard has excelled himself with this one." Then to the last act and the moments before the final curtain when Hester, intent on vengeance, enters the drawing room to find the ailing Hannah, lying in the armchair, a shawl across her knees, apparently sound asleep.

Mari walked onto the stage, regal in her evening dress and long white gloves, a sparkling circlet round her brow. She paused to survey the scene. A ripple of anticipation from the audience. What was she going to do? As if ensuring she would not be disturbed, Hester first looked around, then crossed to the desk. On it was the retractable paper-knife to be used for the murder and specially designed for this scene.

Under Daisy's dress was a padded corselette into which the harmless blade would lock, appearing to be embedded in her chest. The palm of Mari's left glove had been neatly split and under it was taped a sachet of stage blood, with one corner removed.

Any pressure on the palm would send the 'blood' oozing out.

Mari picked up the knife. Another murmur of anticipation from the audience. But something was wrong. Why did the knife feel heavier than usual and...? Reality hit her like a body-blow. It was real! This was not the prepared weapon. It might look identical, but this was not the retractable stage prop. This was a wicked looking sharp-bladed knife. A knife with which to kill.

Her mind racing, she walked slowly across the stage. ('Whatever happens you must always stay in character,' Rose's voice thundered in her ears). She pressed the knife between her palms as if undecided, trying to make up her mind, but allowing just sufficient pressure for the 'blood' to flow from the sac in her palm and make the audience believe in the sharpness of the deadly blade. There was a gasp of horror as the stage-blood started to drip from her hands.

Half turning, she walked slowly towards Daisy and raised the knife so that it glinted under the stage lights. Another gasp. She bent her head as if checking to see if Daisy was still asleep. With her back to the audience, she hissed under her breath, "It's *your* version." Then turning away she shuddered, as if unable to go ahead and flung the knife away from her, so that it skidded on the floor towards the wings. There the watching Director groaned to himself "What the devil is she playing at?" Then looking down at the knife only a yard away from him, he realised..."Oh my God, it's real! How the hell's she going to...?"

Daisy had heard her sister's whisper, but it was not until she heard the slight clatter as the knife hit the stage floor, that she fully appreciated what Mari had said and in that instant guessed what had happened. This was to have been Celia's final assault on them, one sister killing or seriously wounding the other. And the ironic twist was that it would have appeared to the world as if, as in Willard's play, they really were deadly enemies.

Mari crumpled to her knees, apparently sobbing, and laid her head on Daisy's lap, as if in penitence. Daisy stirred, opened her eyes and placing her hand on Marigold's head, gently stroked her hair, smiling down at her. And, at the Director's signal, the curtain slowly... very, very slowly came down.

For a moment time seemed suspended, then came the applause, loud, overwhelming. Behind the curtains, the girls for a brief moment cried together then, as the curtains opened, stood bowing and smiling before a rapturous audience. Rose's reaction was a mixture of horror and pride. The shock of what might have happened was already taking effect and Estelle was anxious to get her out of the theatre and home as quickly as possible. But there was pride too. Pride in her Golden Girls and particularly Mari for having rescued the play's ending so brilliantly in the most awful circumstances. Had she faltered on seeing the knife, had she panicked and run off the stage, the Stage Manager would have had no recourse but to ring down the curtain. As it was the audience, under the spell of the story-line, was blissfully unaware that there had been any problem. And Daisy had been right about the ending. It had been satisfying and realistic to see that the ties of blood and the happiness the sisters had earlier shared were sufficient to take precedence over any monetary rewards. At that final curtain, the audience just knew that the sisters were going to enjoy those rewards together.

Taking Rose's arm Estelle ushered her from the theatre. A message left in the foyer and the girls would understand.

One member of the audience was well aware of the scene's dramatic change. Willard was reeling under the impact of what he had just witnessed. Delighted throughout, he was shocked to the core, to see Marigold's change of moves in those last minutes. Anger welled up in him and he was ready to explode with fury that someone should have not only dared to tamper with his writing but had done so at a public viewing. Then he saw Hannah's loving gesture, her sister's penitent form and hearing the silence of suspended emotion, followed by tumultuous applause, he knew that whatever had changed, it was for the better.

Like Rose, the cast and back-stage team were awash with conflicting emotions of horror and pride. Someone remembered that a young man, whom they assumed to be a second assistant to the Stage Manager, had checked the props on stage between Acts 11 and 111. In the euphoria of the play's first public performance running so well, no-one had thought this unusual. Only now did they realise its significance. Front of House staff also remembered a young man going to the Box Office at the play's opening. On being told the theatre was fully booked, he had said he was quite prepared to stand at the rear of the orchestra stalls and they had allowed him to do so. Because of his quick disappearance, once the curtain had come down, they had joked about it 'Last in, first out'. No-one was laughing now. Clearly when Celia saw that her plan had not worked, her retreat had been swift.

It was the Director who called the police. Armed with the information he had culled together, he phoned Estelle at Greenacres and asked for the young woman's address, determined there should be no further attempts, not only to sabotage his production, but to cause serious injury. Finding Celia in a comatose state, the police called an ambulance and she was admitted to hospital. As she recovered from her overdose it was obvious that she had slipped further into her own world, which now merged reality and fiction. In no fit state to be prosecuted, she was admitted to an institution for further surveillance and assessment.

For the press, all this would have made a wonderful story, but from those involved came the unspoken decision to close ranks and allow the play and the author to be judged on their own merits without sensationalism. Amazingly it worked. When the facts of the story did start to filter through some weeks later, whilst raising eyebrows, it had lost its impact. The theatrical world had moved on.

The two at the heart of the drama were also in shock. Estelle's decision to stay overnight at Greenacres was to ensure that they and Rose slept late the next morning and that all had the most leisurely day possible, before the girls left for the theatre in the evening. A great believer in the efficacy of alcohol at times like these, Estelle ensured that a tablespoonful of whisky was added to the hot milk they were each given on retirement. It worked wonders and after a tumultuous evening, the occupants of Greenacres finally slept.

With Celia now removed from their orbit, the twins were able to relax and enjoy the remaining performances of 'Double Trouble'. There was a slightly awkward moment when they first met Willard, but the warmth of his embrace and his compliments on what they had overcome and achieved, told them all was well. As planned, Rose and Estelle, accompanied by Monty, attended the final performance. This, the first time Estelle had seen him since Rose's disclosure, could also have proved awkward, but Monty, oblivious to any undercurrent or concerns, was his usual amiable and courteous self and soon they relaxed. At the conclusion it was Monty's expressed wish to 'have words' with the young author that told Rose all she wished to know. Monty was obviously prepared to back this play and see it staged in the West End. Probably in the late summer with Mari in the lead, it would still be within the year for Rose's wager with Sebastian to be valid. Everything was going according to plan.

Almost seamlessly they moved from 'Double Trouble' to the preparation and polishing of their Music Hall numbers.

"I can understand now why actors say they almost take on the character of the role they're playing," Daisy was in one of her thoughtful moods. "Only a few days ago everything seemed sombre and rather gloomy because the play was a serious one and now we've started on our Music Hall stint, the numbers are such fun that suddenly we're all bright and cheerful."

"You speak for yourself. It's eight thirty in the morning and I personally would have liked to stay in bed for at least another hour, but no, we have to go chasing off to that awful musty room and try to appear jolly for goodness knows how long." Marigold was not impressed.

"Stop being such a sulk, you know you'll love it when you get there. That Burlington Bertie routine is right up your street and I know you're going to milk it for all its worth. Just don't steal my thunder that's all…"

"I see, so I have to play down my act, because you can't keep up. Hard cheese. And anyway, how does what you just said relate to the fact that comedians are often the most miserable people on earth?" Mari was determined to have the last word.

Their usual friendly banter continuing, they went down for breakfast.

With all that had been, and was about to happen, their eighteenth birthday promised to be fairly low-key, but Rose couldn't let their successes go uncelebrated. She had reserved a table for herself, Estelle and the girls at one of the regular, afternoon tea dances at the Savoy. It was a new experience for the twins. Now Daisy could put into practice the lessons Mari had given her. She thought herself quite adept at the usual ballroom dances, but longed to have a go at the Charleston where there was more room to manoeuvre and knew that however adept one felt in practice, having a partner might prove very different. There was a respectable sprinkling of young men there. Some obviously accompanying their mothers or aunts, or perhaps as Mari whispered to Daisy "They are those gigolos we keep hearing about!"

When the first young man came and stood in front of their table smiling, they were both too stunned to say or do anything. It was Estelle's "I don't think this young man has come to dance with me, but if one of you doesn't move quickly then I shall certainly join him," which galvanised Mari into action. Smiling sweetly she was on her feet and swept off at waltz tempo. Daisy was annoyed with herself, she had missed her moment, but before she could chastise herself too harshly, another smartly suited male appeared and she too was swept into the waltz. It was light-hearted fun, with Rose and Estelle both in turn being invited onto the floor. When the Charleston was played it was Estelle who shone and then was invited to dance the last waltz. Unusually she was very quiet when she returned to her seat, but the girls noticed that before they left she exchanged a surreptitious smile with her erstwhile dancing partner and that he raised his hand in farewell before leaving the restaurant.

Once in the theatre, the adrenalin started to flow again. Their own performances were to be half way up the bill in each of the two sections. "Going up in the world at last," said Mari, well aware just how significant their move from the bottom of the bill was. Their successes in the Shavian plays and in 'Double Trouble' had obviously been a great help. She was also aware there had to be careful selection of the acts in each half, in order to ensure a balanced programme with plenty of variety. There were, true to form, a juggler, two comedians, a contortionist, a balancing act, a troupe of dancers and a soloist ballet dancer. Topping the bill was a tenor, Lester Sinclair, who had been much acclaimed in recent months. The accommodation backstage was ludicrously small, so that they were forever juggling for the minimum of space in which to change and make-up. But everyone was good-tempered and the atmosphere out front was, as always, totally cheerful and responsive.

The twins found it was quite unnecessary to invite the members of the audience to join in the singing, they were longing to do so. The greater difficulty was keeping them quiet during some of the solo pieces. A nod to the conductor and the twins added an extra chorus to each number, so that everyone could sing along. Their own grins as they left the stage said it all, there was nothing to beat that feeling of carrying an audience with you. In their slot in the second half the welcome they received and the applause at the end of each number was tremendous. The requests for 'Encore' were deafening, but there were other acts to follow and a deadline for closure to meet.

"Better for them to go home wanting more, than for us to outstay our welcome and disappoint them with something substandard," this was Daisy in her logical mood.

"I hate it when you're in your 'pearls of wisdom' dropping mood," retorted Mari.

On the third evening Lester Sinclair asked if they would care to join him for a drink and a snack after the show. They accepted with alacrity. Oozing confidence on stage, he was rather quiet and self-effacing in private, but Mari's witticisms were more than able to handle this and he was soon relaxed and laughing with the pair of them at the anecdotes they had all acquired during rehearsals and shows.

He was not handsome in the usual sense. The girls decided that was because of his slightly Roman nose.

Twenty five and about five feet ten in height Daisy estimated, with dark auburn hair, stylishly cut. His eyes were a light hazel and she felt that although quiet, he missed very little of what was going on around him. Having trained as a chorister, the choir master had ensured that when Lester's voice broke he did no singing for two years until his tutor was satisfied that his vocal chords had recovered. Coaching had then been resumed and had of necessity included Italian and French lessons. Mari teased him by saying,

"You're quite slim at the moment Lester, I do hope you're not going to develop one of those barrel chests which so many male singers have."

His response was both surprisingly swift and funny. "I would never presume to comment on your chest, Miss Gold, other than to suggest that if you look after yours, then I most certainly will look after my own!"

The three youngsters enjoyed each other's company and at the end of the evening the twins felt they had made a good friend and one whom they would look forward to meeting on the theatrical circuit in the future. It was as they were leaving the restaurant that Mari spotted Estelle. Seated in one of the side, rather shadowy bays she was accompanied by the man with whom she had danced at the Savoy. She did not look in their direction and they felt it was politic to leave without making their presence felt.

Back in their bedroom Daisy said, "She's a dark horse. He must have asked her out the other afternoon."

"Sister dear, she's a big girl and under no obligation to discuss with us her romantic trysts."

"You're jumping the gun a bit aren't you? Romantic trysts? He's getting on a bit for that."

193

"For heavens' sake, he might, just, be forty, that's not exactly one foot in the grave is it. I mean Estelle's about thirty five and let's face it for a time she was seeing Monty quite regularly and he's much older."

"You're right Mari as always, and I do wonder what's gone wrong there. I thought they were ideally suited, they have mutual interests in music and theatre and they're both such lovely people."

"But Daisy sweetie, the paths of true love never did run smooth as you should know, now that you are so fully conversant with the works of Mr. Shakespeare and his famous 'Romeo and Juliet'."

"And sibling rivalry is an ever-present running sore, as you should know dear sister, being equally conversant with Mr. Shakespeare's 'King Lear'."

"One thing though... Monty and Estelle do seem to have remained friends, I mean he accompanied her and Rose to see us on stage at Richmond, so it can't have been anything very serious, it certainly hasn't caused a rift between the three of them."

"And Mari, there's another thing, that invitation from Monty for us to spend Christmas Day with him again at Claridges, Estelle's included in that as well, so either their fling wasn't very serious or whatever has brought it to a halt wasn't very serious either."

Having put the world to rights and their bedside lights extinguished, the twins slept.

The end of the Music Hall run saw them tired, but happy. All had gone well and they were becoming increasingly confident in both singing and acting roles. As far as the theatre critics were concerned, it seemed they could do no wrong and Rose felt that as soon as the venue for 'Pygmalion' with Mari in the lead was declared, she would be home and dry with regard to her wager. Monty had confirmed that 'Double Trouble' would indeed be coming into the West End but not until the Autumn, so both the girls now had a period of 'resting'. At the after-show party they bade a fond farewell to Lester who was leaving for Italy to consolidate his language training and gain more experience in the opera houses there. Complimenting the girls as they left, the Producer said that on future occasions he would ensure they had much more time allocated. "And," he hinted with a smile, "I think you might find yourself higher in the pecking order."

Just two days of peace and quiet at Greenacres and the twins were champing at the bit and discussing what they should do next. Envying their energy, Rose smiled at them over the breakfast table and said, "I think it's now time for us to put my theatre to rights and I'm going to need a great deal of help!"

Electricians and plumbers were needed first of all, and whilst they were working Rose and the girls made copious lists of what required repairing and what replacement items had to be purchased. Their greatest difficulty was determining the priority for both tasks and purchases. Rose had managed to hire a small warehouse very close to the theatre and they sent all scenery flats, stage furniture, stage props, and carpeting to be stored there. Washbasins and lavatories were bought ready for installation and everything in the existing dressing rooms and Green room was removed and collected as rubbish. New toilets for cast and backstage team were to be installed just behind the Stage Door entrance cubicle so that members of the cast already costumed would be able to go down that particular corridor at will, without being seen by members of the public.

Rose had been quite adamant about this, "Everyone wants to visit the toilet the very last thing before going on stage, especially if you know you're going to be on the set for an hour or more. It's quite ridiculous that there's often just one lavatory for about fifteen people. No, while we're about it we'll have at least four, then there should be no complaints. The most stupid thing I've ever seen is a theatre where the only toilets were in the public foyer, so that once in costume you either had to wait in agony or spoil the whole element of surprise, which is what the theatre's all about, by going into the foyer before curtain up and letting everyone see you in your stage wear. Only someone who's never been in a play could design a theatre like that!"

Mari imagining this, said "There must be some costumes which once on, make it almost impossible to go to the lavatory."

"No 'almost' about it. I once played a mermaid and had to have a long, rather beautiful tail strapped on. Once in position, there was no removing it for three hours," Rose smiled at their shocked expressions.

"Actually it wasn't as bad as it sounds. Once you're in character, you're too busy thinking about lines, moves and expressions to even give it a thought. Might be difficult if you had a gastric problem though." Again she laughed at their horrified faces. "Occasionally actors have to wear what we call 'a fat suit' which is specially designed to make you look really huge. There the problem is that in the course of the evening your system sweats inside it and you lose a lot of body water and salt. To counteract this you have to drink about two litres of water before you even put the suit on. But girls, I can't imagine either of you will be required to wear one of those for a very long time, so I shouldn't lose any sleep over it.

"Now come over here and look at what I've sketched out for the dressing rooms. They each need at least two wash-basins. I think, if the architect agrees, the Green room could be enlarged slightly and in one corner I'm, going to have a small section screened off, which will incorporate a shower and changing cubicle."

The girls had strict instructions from Estelle that they were to watch Rose carefully and if she appeared exhausted or stressed they were to return home at once. This was not always easy, but they did try to pace her work levels by suggesting now and again that they popped out to somewhere close by for a cup of tea or coffee. During these times, names were suggested for the new theatre... the Sebastian Reece, the Rose Reece but both the girls felt a theatre should have a single name and their preferred title was the Reece Theatre.

"It's got to be that", Daisy said, "it pays tribute to your father and reminds them of his fame as an artist, but equally, as he would have wished, it pays tribute to your contribution to the theatre."

Mari agreed, "I don't think you'll better that, unless you go for something totally unrelated to either of you, like the Empire, the Victoria or something similar. No, I think your father would have loved this idea."

It was obvious that Rose, too, liked it, but said she felt she should discuss it further with Estelle, silently thinking 'She is after all the most important person in my life and one day this will all be hers'. It was time too to tell Monty about Estelle, he must be wondering why Estelle had turned down his last few invitations out. Her mind racing ahead, she decided it must be done this week and then she would be able to delight in showing him her latest acquisition. With his shrewd business acumen she had no doubt whatsoever that he would have many ideas as to what when it was completed was her best way forward. Her mind made up, on her return to Greenacres she rang to invite him to dinner on the following evening. There would, she told him, be just herself and the girls present, as Estelle was busy rehearsing. His acceptance and the enormity of what lay ahead was enough to make her feel very nervous indeed.

Dinner over, as arranged, the girls made their excuses and departed to their own small sitting room. Rose suggested to Monty that they move in to the drawing room, and once the maid had brought coffee and brandy they were left alone. Monty settled himself comfortably in an armchair and said, "I can't remember when we last did this, Rose, all too often you're surrounded by other people. The girls are wonderful company, but it's so nice for we two 'oldies' to be on our own and wander down memory lane. Or have you perhaps something serious to discuss with me? I've been hearing ripples about a new theatre, is that really something to do with you?"

"I'll come to that later, but yes, I do want to go down memory lane and yes, I do have something very serious to discuss."

"Sounds ominous, but fire ahead."

"I have a confession to make Monty and when I've finished you may hate me…"

"Hate you? For heavens' sake Rose, how could I ever do that? You've been my best friend for as long as I can remember some, what thirty five years isn't it?"

"Thirty six."

"Alright, thirty six…" he waited.

"Do you recall all those years ago that I disappeared from view for a time?"

"Disappeared? Ah yes, you went to France to visit friends. Never could understand you doing that, with so much going on. We both had offers starting to come in, some from quite unexpected and interesting quarters…"

"There was a very real reason why I left at that time".

"Don't tell me it was a love affair, you were considered to be my girl at that time. I can't recall there being anyone else around."

"In a way it was a love affair…with you".

"Sorry, you've lost me. With me? So why go?"

"I went away to have my child – *our* child – a beautiful daughter, who is now an equally beautiful young woman of thirty five years of age."

"Oh my God…not… of course…Estelle."

"Yes, Estelle."

"But why didn't you tell me? If not then, later. You must have needed help and money… Rose, how on earth did you manage?"

"I didn't tell you because on that evening you expounded at some length how important it was for us both at our age not to be distracted by serious love affairs.

In effect you warned me off. It was obvious that for you and, as you believed for me, our careers must come first. And later, well so many times, I've been on the brink of disclosure, but it never ever seemed to be the right time."

"Does Estelle know?"

"Yes, but only a very short while ago."

"So that explains her attitude at the moment. I thought I'd upset her in some way. How did she take it?"

"At first I thought she'd never forgive me and I'd lost her. But, like you, she has a loving generous heart and I think, I hope, that now all is going to be well."

"Good grief Rose, you knew I was attracted to her, your silence might have…" a stunned silence.

"I know and I'm sorry. It's only now that things have come to light re my father's will that I've realised the fragility of life and that matters between those who love each other must be transparent and on a proper footing."

"I don't quite see what your father's will has got to do with all this."

"It galvanised me into action. I won't go into details but some of his paintings appeared in London, brought, would you believe, by a grandson we didn't know existed. Clearly the boy's family wanted to make some claim on Sebastian's estate. He had pre-empted claims by them, or any of the other wild oats he might have sown, by tying things up legally in the tightest possible way. He'd also guessed at Estelle's parentage and ensured she and I would always be financially solvent. But with regard to your earlier question, he left me something else in addition to paintings and money and this bizarre wager. He left me a theatre!"

"So the rumours were true…But where..?"

"Monty, it needs oodles of work doing to it, but I know I can turn it into a little jewel and I absolutely love it." The words spilled out and as the reaction of her confession hit her, tears slid down her face.

"Darling Rose, please don't cry, I'm so happy for you. Yes, you can give me all the details later, so that together we can wallow in them. But for now, what do *you* want me to do about Estelle?"

"I would suggest that I phone her in the morning and tell her that you know. Wait until after lunch and then call her. I'm sure she'll probably see you in the afternoon. I do feel you two should be alone when you discuss this. Monty, it's such a relief that you both now know, it was making me quite ill worrying about it."

"Rose, you're the bravest person I know. I can't believe that the stupid idealistic ramblings of a twenty two year old persuaded you to go away and shoulder all the burden of having a child miles away from home. I'll never forgive myself for that."

His arms went round her and she cried on his shoulder.

"And what about you, Rose? Once Estelle knows, what do you feel is the next step for all of us?"

"I don't know. I think we all need time to reflect. We are each of us people who have been accustomed to running our own lives and having our own space for many years. I see no necessity to change that unless…"

"Yes unless…?"

"My own will ensures that Estelle will of course inherit everything of mine, but you might also want to make some proviso."

"Proviso! That's the understatement of the year surely? She's my child, my only child. Of course she must receive everything I've got. I wouldn't wish it any other way. And now my dear, all this emotion is very draining and you look quite exhausted. In a moment I'm going to call your maid and make sure you take your medication and retire."

He kissed her. "You are and always will be my own darling Rose and very brave. I've loved you for as long as I can remember," and seeing her smile, "and certainly for over thirty six years. And in different ways. Passionately, admiringly, comfortably. You're the one person in the world with whom I feel completely and utterly at ease. That is never ever going to change. Now off to bed with you."

Another kiss on her forehead and he went in search of her maid.

Phone calls were made and received the next morning and at teatime, a still tearful Estelle phoned to say that she and Monty had met, laughed and cried and, "I think now we're ready to get on with our lives."

Replacing the phone Rose felt again an overwhelming sense of relief. Now she too could get on with her life. Enjoy showing Monty her new beautiful possession, enjoy seeing Mari win that wager and most of all enjoy seeing

Estelle, meeting her eyes in the shared, secret knowledge of their relationship.

The girls knew that something serious had been afoot. Just what it had all been about was a source of animated discussion.

"It's what we first thought," Daisy said, "Monty and Estelle had a row and Rose was brought in as a sort of mediator to pour oil on trouble waters."

Mari responded, "So why, when all this was going on did they visit the theatre to see us? They weren't exactly spitting blood that evening, it was all sweetness and light".

"That's because of the sort of people they are – too polite to let everyone know their business and certainly too polite to let their feelings show."

"Hmm", Mari wasn't convinced. "I'm not so sure. I think Rose has been deeply upset by all this. She'd obviously been crying last night and the day Estelle was here, her hanky was soaking. I can't believe all that was the result of sorting out a lovers' tiff."

"One thing's for sure, they're not going to tell us until they're good and ready and that might not be for a very long time. Back to work I think. I've been meaning to ask if you've got those ghastly theatre cherubs on your list for replacement."

"Too right I have. Three of them have broken noses and the others with noses look as if they have nasty smells underneath them. It will be great to have some wholesome looking, angelic little people looking down on us for a change. The whole of the proscenium arch needs remoulding and painting of course, and I think Rose has finally decided on traditional gold."

"Good. That dear little theatre has such a lovely period feel about it and apart from updating the plumbing and other essential services I'm hoping she'll keep it that way."

"No doubt of it. I think she'd like Estelle and Monty to give their approval to her choices, but she's set her heart on royal blue velvet seats and curtains, with gold on the boxes and the mouldings on the two circles."

"Sounds lovely. Mari, there's something I'd really like to do sometime, but I don't know if it's going to be possible…"

"Just about anything's possible. Tell me."

"You know I had that letter from Mrs. Barton on the Island and she said perhaps sometime they might try and come and see us on the stage here in London. I wondered if we might be able to try and arrange that, perhaps when 'Double Trouble' comes into London."

"Daisy, let's do it. We'll try and organise a group to come up, Mum and Dad and your friends from Farncombe Manor. They'd love it and it would be a way of saying thanks to Mum and Dad for making sure we had a decent education, that sort of thing."

"Why don't we go down and see them for a few days? There's not much left for us to do here. The lists are completed, Estelle and Monty are both coming to see the theatre, which means there's someone to keep an eye on Rose. I'm sure she'd be happy to spare us. And now that we've at last earned some money, we could afford it!"

There were no obstacles, in fact Rose was rather pleased, it meant that there would be just herself, Monty and Estelle together for a while, a time for readjustment with regard to their different roles. She could show

Monty her lovely gift and discuss with the two of them her colour schemes and plans for alterations. Monty's business acumen and his success as an entrepreneur were going to prove very, very useful. The next few days were going to be very special

The Isle of Wight visit was not a success. Sue clearly did not approve of the short notice given of their visit and Sue's approval or disapproval appeared to be the major factor in determining whether all at the farm were happy or not. Meg Griffin looked even more cowed and frail. Her skin had a transparency which alarmed the girls, but when they questioned their father about her health, it was Sue who answered,

"She won't eat, that's her trouble. Says she's not hungry, always. Yes, we've asked the doctor about it, but he says she's still suffering from that post-natal stress. I ask you! It's nearly three years since those boys were born and with me here to do most of the work, how stressed can she be?"

Throughout this their father looked embarrassed, but remained silent. The girls took Meg for a ride in the old trap, but always she seemed distrait, as if not really with them. The boys by contrast were sturdy and it was Sue who said proudly that they could now recognise their letters and that they talked non-stop. It was to Sue they turned for approval of a drawing or a clean plate at meal-times, it was almost as if their mother no longer existed.

The feelings of unease which the girls experienced resulted in a change of plan. Two days at the farm were going to prove ample. Tearfully they embraced their mother's now skeletal figure and said their farewells to their father, Sue and the boys. They had walked for some distance towards Ashey station before they broke their silence.

Daisy was the first to erupt, "It's horrible. We've lost her. She's not our Mum any more..."

Mari was equally furious and upset, "And as for that Sue. I'm not saying she had a master-plan from the start, but..."

"But she's getting things just the way she wanted. She's in charge and no-one, not even Dad, dares to question her authority."

"I can't bear thinking about it," Daisy was almost crying again. "A few short years ago Mum was so excited about being pregnant and she looked young and pretty and now..."

"Yes and those little boys seem to regard Sue as their Mum, that's something I find very hard to stomach". Mari thought for a while, "But I don't know what more we can do if they say the doctor has seen her. Any interference from us would probably make life more difficult both for Mum and Dad and that's the last thing we want."

"I think those plans I had for bringing them to London will have to be shelved. Mum's not fit enough for one thing and I'm certainly not having Sue coming up and taking her place even there."

"That's not a viable option. No, we'll just have to wait and see what the next few months bring. Now shall we look out for a paper at Ryde, we ought to see who and what the theatre critics have got it in for at the moment and whether their comments are as acerbic as usual."

"Except of course when they're commenting on the Golden Girls."

"Point taken. There are of course, exceptions to every rule."

Chapter 11

From the girls' expressions, Rose guessed that the visit had not been all that they had hoped for. In answer to her enquiries, she was told that their mother looked ill and that the girls were concerned about her, but there was no other elaboration of the situation offered and she did not enquire further.

"Well I do have some good news to cheer you up. I've just been informed that 'Pygmalion' goes into Drury Lane Theatre Royal with Mari in the lead at the beginning of August for a period of two months. And you know what this means Mari? My father's wager will be won. You will top the bill in a West End production in the fifth year since you came to me. That will certainly be worth celebrating. Just one change from your original cast, Lenny, Colonel Pickering, has had quite a nasty accident and will be out of the circuit for some months. 'Double Trouble' is now scheduled to come into London to the Wyndham's also for two months and, surprise, surprise, you are both cast in your original roles.

"And here's another date for your diaries. Mark in as a query, the dates the twelfth to the seventeenth of December which is about the time when theatres are changing over to their Christmas shows. *My* theatre", laughing she paused for effect, "I love saying that! My theatre will, God willing, be completed at that time, and I intend launching it in style during that change-over period, when hopefully all our friends and the people I've worked with over the years will be free to attend.

"Now come with me you two, you look as if you could both do with some tea and sympathy."

Estelle was in need of neither. The knowledge imparted in the past days had added a new spring to her step. Why was that, she wondered? Rose was the person to whom she had always been closest, this new knowledge had merely cemented that fact, but Estelle had to admit, it had made a difference. Repeatedly she watched Rose and noted gestures, expressions, which she knew to be her own. She studied Rose's hands, her stance, the way she walked and talked and compared them with her own mannerisms. Her own dark hair and eyes Estelle knew to be inherited from her father, together with his musical ability and, hopefully, his charm.

How fortunate she was to have parents who were not only talented artistically, but had generous warm natures. Both comfortable with people from all walks of life, they made no differentiation between the rich and the poor. Their talents had raised them in their own particular spheres, but fame had not coarsened them or changed their inherent kindness.

But perhaps this spring in her step was for an entirely different reason. The new man in her life. It was her secret. She had told no-one, not even Rose. Clive Mason was forty and a stockbroker with Lloyd's, his type of work so far removed from her own that they were able to laugh about it. They laughed a lot and she liked that. He openly admired her, always complimented her on her dress and made special efforts to meet her quite late in the evenings when she had been busy rehearsing. They laughed about Estelle's inability to cope with quite simple sums, whilst his mind had a built-in calculator which coped with stocks and shares routinely. Her own work routine was non-existent, rehearsals spilling over into evenings and weekends, whilst his own hours were fairly regular with the exception of occasionally entertaining business guests. He was now suggesting she might like to join him in this, but to date she had held back. Wouldn't it indicate to others that if she donned the mantle of hostess she was one step away from becoming his wife? Not that this had been suggested, yet....

Twice now she knew she had stopped him at that crucial moment. The indecision was entirely her own. Was she really ready to have someone share her life?

She was not a virgin, not afraid of intimacy. In fact there had been many times before she met Clive when the thought of going into old age without that loving closeness had been terrifying. The two affairs in her twenties had been with young men with little or no experience of life, people with whom she would not now consider it possible to have an intelligent conversation. She had moved on, wanted more, and expected more from a relationship. Clive seemed able to offer that. He was so very different, a man of the world, experienced, knowledgeable and fun.

She would tell Rose and Monty about him very soon.

The phone call informing the girls of Meg Griffin's death came on a Tuesday evening, just six days after their return from the Isle of Wight. Whilst shocked, they were not overly surprised. Both had felt that the parting from their mother had had a sense of finality about it. The message came from Mrs. Murray-Rogers of Southfield House who had been informed that Meg had died within a few hours of suffering a severe stroke and asked to tell the girls as soon as possible. Sympathising with them on their loss, she gave them details of the funeral which was to be on the following Friday at two o'clock at the Swanmore village church.

Possessing nothing in black, it was to Estelle the twins turned for assistance in acquiring suitable wearing apparel for the occasion. She accompanied them into London and directed them towards the best outlets for ready-made clothes and at her suggestion they purchased identical two piece outfits, which consisted of mid-calf length straight black dresses with matching hip length jackets and three quarter length sleeves. The linings of the jackets were of a striped black and white silk and this motif was carried out in the long jacket collar and its cuffs and in the belted waistline. With the suits they were to wear cloche type hats, white gloves, plain black court shoes and carry small purse shaped bags. The suits were elegant and as Estelle pointed out whilst right for the occasion, they were not overtly funereal and would be highly suitable for other occasions.

"Wear your hair up of course, at eighteen years you really should no longer wear it down, except on casual or perhaps evening occasions."

She added, "You are now quite well known in theatrical circles, some of that will have probably reached other parts of the country, even perhaps as far as the Isle of Wight. What I'm trying to say is this, there has now come a time when because of that, you will be expected to measure up to a certain standard, particularly on special occasions.

"I'm quite sure your fame *will* have spread to the Island and sad though this day will be for you personally, some of the people there will be quite excited at the prospect of seeing the Golden Girls in the flesh. Some, I'm afraid to say, may have come for that reason only." At their horrified looks, she added "This is something you will have to learn to accept. Watch Rose, she is adept at weaving her way through hosts of people who have only come along just to see her. She never offends, continues to smile sweetly, but if it's not convenient she moves on. It's an acquired art."

Blissfully unaware of it before, they knew even as they boarded the train at Waterloo, that Estelle was right. They noticed now that people looked at one of them, saw the other and registered surprise, a split second would elapse before they realised who the girls were and inevitably made a whispered comment to the person nearest them. Mari and Daisy became accustomed to it. Only when the staring became intrusive to the point they felt normal behaviour and conversation were impossible did they resent it. At such times when seats were available elsewhere they moved.

Mrs. Murray-Rogers had kindly offered to arrange for them to be met at Ryde and suggested they might prefer to change at Southfield,before being take to the farm to join their father in accompanying the hearse to the church. Refreshments for after the service were being provided at the farm and she could also arrange for them to be collected from there the following morning and taken back to Ryde. Gratefully they accepted all her offers of assistance and duly arrived at the farm at one o'clock on the Friday afternoon. The boys had been despatched to a neighbour's house for the day and everything was ready to receive visitors later, with two of the village ladies in attendance. A somewhat smug Sue asked if they did not think everything looked splendid and just what their mother would have wished.

Their father was a broken man. Repeatedly Sue admonished him 'Do this…' or 'Fetch that…' he obeying like an automaton. To the girls, their father appeared shrunken, whilst by contrast Sue seemed larger and more energetic than ever. The flowers helped. Their mother's favourite flowers, yellow and white roses had been chosen by the girls and their wreath together with one from their father and brothers were in pride of place on the coffin.

Everyone was kind, said all the right things and if eyebrows were slightly raised at Sue's overbearing prominence at the proceedings, no comment was made. Covertly the villagers eyed the two elegant young ladies who had left them as schoolgirls and were now being talked about in the national press. They approved what they saw and their behaviour. No side, no putting on airs, greeting old friends warmly. Yes, they would do and the community which had earlier nurtured them, wished them well. As their young voices soared in the singing of their mother's favourite hymns this feeling of being welcomed home was heart-warmingly reassuring and helped to cushion this, their first experience of death. When the time came for the final goodbye at the graveside, each clasped the other's hand tightly for support and together they cried.

The twins felt they had got through the day better than expected. That illusion was dispelled back at the farm, when Sue slipped off her jacket to officiously assist with serving tea. To the girls' astonishment and mounting anger, they saw pinned to her blouse their Mother's cameo brooch. Remembering how, whilst shopping in Newport, their Mother had admired it, they had in their twelfth year painstakingly saved their pocket money and done extra jobs for money around the farm, until they had collected enough to buy it for her next birthday. As soon as the guests had left and Sue was out of the way, they tackled their father.

Daisy first of all, "Dad, Sue is wearing Mum's brooch, the one we bought her. What's going on?"

He blustered in reply, "Well…she's been so good to us, done such a lot and she's always liked it, so when she asked me…"

Now Marigold, "I can't believe it. We, her daughters expected to have something of hers to keep, a memento. We would have been happy to share that between us. It was her very favourite thing."

Sue appeared from the kitchen, cross at missing something, "What's all this?"

Daisy, "We're asking Dad about Mum's brooch, the one you're wearing".

Sue bridled, "Yes, he gave it to me for all I'd done."

"There were other things you could have had," Mari retorted sharply.

Sue, "Like what? This place isn't exactly awash with jewellery."

Daisy, "But… you must have known that brooch was very special to Mum and to us."

Sue tossed her head, "I know all sorts of things can be special, as long as you're miles away from the problems and living the life of Riley. I've earned this and don't you forget it."

The door slammed as their father, unable to face any more of this and incapable of participating in any helpful way, left the house.

"We're not quite sure what's been going on here, Sue, since you took up residence," Daisy's tone was more controlled, but laden with anger, "but you seem to have poisoned our mother's life."

"Poison? I hope you're not suggesting…"

"No, I'm not suggesting food or drink or anything like that. What I am saying is that you systematically squeezed every bit of joy out of her life, making her feel it was impossible to go on."

Marigold now, "She must have known about you and Dad. How could you, under her own roof and so soon too, after the boys were born? Every day you made her feel incompetent, incapable and worthless, until eventually she just gave up trying."

"You stole from her the boys' love and," Daisy added, "our father's love."

By now Sue was red in the face with anger, "I don't have to stay and listen to this."

"No you don't", Daisy replied, "and we certainly are not prepared to stay here with someone who has taken something which was rightfully ours and someone who, as surely as if you had put a bullet to her head, killed our mother. We're leaving." And gathering up their overnight bags they set off for Southfield House.

A sympathetic Mrs. Murray-Rogers made them welcome. There had been a disagreement they told her, nothing more, but they had felt it was best to leave. The twins were obviously exhausted and had been crying. Their mother Meg had been a pleasure to have in the house and so proud of her girls and she would have been especially proud if she could have seen them today. Mrs. Murray-Rogers was well aware of the rumours circulating in the village and had a personal sense of guilt at having originally sent Sue to the farm. However, what was done was done and now her main objective was to see these unhappy young girls were made comfortable and had a good night's sleep.

On their return to Greenacres, still subdued, the girls found an ebullient Rose waiting to greet them. Delighted with her theatre's progress, she had now decided they all needed something to cheer them up.

"The weather's good and I think we should make the most of it. We're going to hold a garden party. So, make a list of the people you'd like to invite. I think we'll make the total figure of about eighty maximum. I've already booked some outside caterers, a marquee, tables and chairs and warned the gardener to find some more help so that everything looks really attractive. What do you think?"

Before they could even begin to answer, she was in full flow once again telling them that Estelle and Monty had both thought the Reece Theatre was the ideal name, an artist had already sketched out the new proscenium arch, complete with cherubs, cheerful ones this time and that the electricians had nearly completed their work.

Her enthusiasm had the desired effect and soon the girls were busily working out just who should feature on their own guest list. Lester, the tenor of course, if he was back from Italy, Tessa Rainer, who'd been in 'Hamlet', the young man Derek Laine, who'd helped so much with their Cockney accent and most of the cast of 'Double Trouble'.

"We don't really know many people of our own age, more's the pity. Perhaps this is one occasion when we might get to meet some. On the other hand if Noel and Ivor are invited I don't mind a bit spending the whole afternoon with either one of them, even if there's no romantic involvement at the end of it," as always thinking of the handsome Ivor, Marigold had a faraway look in her eyes.

"*If* they're invited and I think that's highly possible, there is absolutely no way that I would countenance your hogging the company of either one, or both of them for the whole afternoon, so don't even consider it," this was Daisy in her mock belligerent mood.

Estelle was also in the process of making out her own invitation list and had decided that now was the time when she must introduce Clive Mason to her 'friends', Rose and Monty. Clive had heard her speak many times of Rose, but Monty she had never mentioned and Clive seemed curious to know more about him. She explained that he was an old friend of Rose and she had known him all her life, that he was very wealthy and something of an entrepreneur.

"So how did he make his money?" Clive wanted to know.

"Well like us he was on the stage, a singer and pianist and very much the top of the tree, so he was quite well off, but his real influx of money came from the unexpected death of his wife some years ago."

"What happened?"

"She was drowned. Disappeared from a yacht they were on, a sailing party in the Greek Islands I think. It was all very unpleasant, but of course Monty did inherit all her estate and a great deal of money."

"Lucky man," Clive said drily.

"Yes, I suppose… but it was all very distressing and not really the ideal way for anyone to come into a fortune."

"I'll look forward to meeting him, as I'll look forward to meeting all your friends. Now isn't it time we went in to dinner?"

Saturday the seventh of July, and cloudless skies for the garden party. The marquee and extra furniture had been put in place the day before, the gardens were immaculate and the view down the Thames valley at its stunning best. The ladies in their chiffons, silks and mousselines fluttered around like pastel shaded butterflies, their hats a sublime mixture of flowers and feathers on delicate straw. It was on occasions such as these, that Daisy thought back to her arrival at Slade Manor and that initial instruction from Mrs. Carstairs 'No feathers and no flowers'. Just what Mrs. Carstairs would make of the pale lavender Daisy was wearing today, she couldn't imagine. It was so pretty she felt even the bees and butterflies were deceived. Marigold wore the palest of pinks and with Rose in her favourite deep rose pink and Estelle in lemon, Mari's comment

"We look like a set of sherbert sweets" whilst not very flattering, was probably somewhere near the truth.

Clive was duly introduced to Rose and Monty, the latter having expressed real interest in the fact that Clive was a stockbroker at Lloyds. Deep in conversation the two men wandered off and as Estelle laughingly said to Rose "They're probably talking in figures, hundreds and thousands that is, if I know Clive. The trouble is I'm so hopeless at arithmetic I can't keep up with it. It's nice for him to be able to converse with someone who understands what he's talking about."

"Well, I'm not sure Monty does understand that much about stocks and shares, but I'm sure he's quite happy to be talking finance with someone who does."

Ivor and Noel had both attracted their usual coterie of admirers and the twins were more than happy when the former broke away from one group and made his way towards them saying, "Here are my favourite girls, the Golden ones. One day I really must write a musical with you two in mind. Today my darlings, you look good enough to eat."

"And on the subject of eating, Ivor," Daisy took one arm and Marigold the other, "we can offer you strawberries and cream, meringues, banana splits…"

"Too rich for my taste, my lovelies."

"Then how about salmon and cucumber sandwiches, ham and mustard, egg and cress?"

"Ah much more to my liking. Lay on McDuff."

Relinquishing him later to others anxious to meet him, the twins had much to discuss.

"What about Estelle's new beau?" Mari asked.

"Mm, she looks like a cat that's swallowed the cream. I'm not sure about him…"

"You can't be serious. He's handsome, articulate, obliviously loaded and hangs on her every word, I mean what more can a girl want?"

Daisy hesitated, "There's just something –is he perhaps a little too ingratitating, too anxious to please."

"Surely that's absolutely normal, if you're meeting the girl-friend's whole bevy of friends, people she's known for ages – of course you'd be anxious to please."

Daisy was still not convinced, "I suppose…"

"Did you meet those friends of Estelle from the D'Oyly Carte Opera Company?"

"Yes. Liked the young man, Chris Manning, who's just won a contract with them. He's only nineteen, must be good. And that girl Lisa, lovely. Stunning auburn hair and those eyes, so green. They made a handsome pair."

"But they're not, are they?"

"Not what?"

"A pair, stupid."

"How on earth would I know? I've only just met them. But stop right there, don't tell me little sister, you've fallen in love…again!"

"I'm not telling *you* anything, at least not until there's something to tell," then

Daisy quite obviously changing the subject, "We should go and see if Rose wants any help. Only a few stragglers left and they seem on the point of departure."

"Looks as if Estelle is having difficulty prising Clive away from Monty, he's stuck to him like glue for most of the afternoon."

"'Twas ever thus' when men are talking shop, perhaps a little chivvying from us might help."

That evening, the marquee gone and the grounds returned to their normal tranquil beauty, Rose relaxed and she too, reflected on the afternoon. Had Estelle at last found the man she'd hoped for? Clive seemed to fill all the criteria and he and Monty had obviously got along famously. The latter had been quite complimentary,

"Knows his stuff that young man. Seemed keen to encourage me to form a limited company and started to explain how very much I'd benefit from it. I'm not sure… but I'll probably discuss it further with my own solicitor. He seemed the right sort for Estelle though, didn't you think? Sound job, intelligent and seems to adore her."

He'd been as always observant of Rose's own needs, commenting "You, my love, have been doing your hostess bit all afternoon and doing it successfully. I think it's time now for us to go inside and watch the world go by over a gin and tonic."

Rehearsals were due to start for 'Pygmalion' the following week. Whilst the rest of the cast would need only 'warm up' rehearsals, accustoming themselves to the changed venue and ambience, the new Colonel Pickering joining them had not only to be rehearsed but had importantly, to bond with the rest of the team, particularly Professor Higgins and Eliza. Marigold and the two men were therefore on call for a great deal of time, whilst others were excused.

"I don't mind at all", Mari said, "I'm just so thrilled at playing at Drury Lane. I suppose it's every actor's dream and Dennis Soames is so grateful for every bit of support we can give him, it is after all his first West End role."

Daisy also loved Drury Lane and regularly accompanied Mari, either watching from the stalls or on odd occasions going into Covent Garden and enjoying the bustle of the city, such a far cry from life on the Isle of Wight. It was on one such occasion that she met Chris Manning, the new D'Óyly Carte recruit and happily agreed to his suggestion that they find a Lyons Corner House and go and have some tea. He too was a long way from his home in Wales and having only just joined the company felt homesick. They arranged to meet two days later and again the following week. On that day she took him into the theatre to watch Mari rehearsing and he laughed when he saw her mouthing her sister's words on stage, even as she spoke them. "Just how much of her part do you know?" he asked and stared in amazement at her reply, "All of it."

"You can't mean that."

"But I do. Mari and I have always helped each other learn lines in the first instance, and don't forget I've seen her rehearse and play this role before, when it was in the provinces. I just love it. For what it's worth, yes I know it all."

And it did in fact become worth a great deal. With just ten days to go before the opening, Mari started to feel ill. She had had no cold or cough, but suddenly complained of a tightness in her chest. A quick check showed that her temperature was well above normal. Further checks by Rose's doctor ruled out glandular fever and meningitis, but he insisted that he wanted her moved into hospital straight away and put in an oxygen tent. It was there that pneumonia was diagnosed.

There was panic on all sides. Primarily of course for Mari's safety, but also for her major commitment at Drury Lane. No understudy had been rehearsed, it was too late to get another experienced performer who might substitute, tickets had been sold and a full house promised for at least the first two weeks. Panic, until Rose suggested Daisy. The Director was dubious, yes he had seen Daisy on stage in 'St. Joan', she was not totally inexperienced, but this was Drury Lane! Rose was persuasive and at last he agreed to Daisy being taken to the theatre and rehearsing on set the principal scenes with Professor Higgins and Colonel Pickering. He was impressed. The whole cast was brought in and on one exhausting day the play was run through three times. The cast also were impressed. It was decided. A few minor adjustments to costumes and Daisy was after all, to play the lead at Drury Lane.

At first Mari was too ill to be told and when the news was finally broken she cried, tears of weakness and frustration that fate should have dealt her this cruel blow. But the doctor was encouraging. They had caught the illness in time and she had been given the correct drugs and treatment. After one week in hospital and one week's complete rest he would consider whether she might be allowed to complete the run herself. With that she had to be satisfied.

For Rose it presented another dilemma, if a less important one. Although Mari's name featured on all the publicity, on bills and programmes, if she did not in fact play the lead, the wager would be invalid, leaving only a second run of 'Double Trouble' with Mari in the lead, to enable it to be won. They were getting very close to the deadline. But...Mari's health must come first and she, Estelle and Monty, between them would not only watch over her, but also give Daisy the support she would undoubtedly need.

Chris, watching the curtain rise on Daisy's performance, was full of admiration for her bravery. It was one thing to rehearse a performance until you knew the play upside down and inside out, knew the other players well enough to be aware if they were not well and to 'cover' if they stumbled, but to take on a major role virtually 'cold' and in a theatre whose reputation was second to none, that really took some courage. She was a very plucky girl. Watching her, he found it difficult to relate the flamboyant delightful character of Eliza to the rather self-effacing girl, who had sat opposite him in Lyons drinking tea.

She was an absolute delight and his biggest worry was that someone else would snap her up before he had time to do so, and before she became so famous that she removed herself from his orbit. Enthusiastically applauding, he took in every graceful movement of the transformed Eliza. This 'Cinderella' type story was such a joy, everyone loved it. Perhaps someone one day would look at it more carefully, add music to it and produce a musical to enthral. Who knows, he thought, in a couple of decades if I'm still around, I could be singing the role of Professor Higgins.

Daisy felt guilty. Everyone tried to persuade her that she had saved a great many people a lot of inconvenience and money, but she was still unable to rid herself of the feeling that it was not right that she should be having such an amazing time, playing a wonderful role in this famous theatre, whilst Mari was ill. Clive had been an absolute brick. On the evenings when Estelle could not accompany her he had collected Daisy after the show and ensured she was safely ensconced in a taxi and on her way home to Richmond. If there were times when he sometimes seemed a little too inquisitive about them all, she felt it was a small price to pay for being looked after, late at night in London, when a young girl on her own inevitably felt vulnerable.

It took her a long time to settle each evening after the show. As she had been warned, the adrenalin pumped into her system during a performance was not easily dispelled, and often it was two o'clock in the morning before she could finally settle and sleep. Another small price to pay, she kept telling herself. Mari was recovering steadily and, as the doctor had promised, within one week had been sent home to rest. "Plenty of red meat, liver would be particularly good, fresh vegetables and lots of fruit and go sparingly for the moment on dairy products." The doctor's recommendations were being strictly adhered to and Mari was now able to sit each day in an arm chair looking down the beautiful view of the Thames valley. Another few days, Daisy thought, then there'll be a Sunday rehearsal for Mari's benefit and I'll be out. A 'has-been'.

If the critics had been expecting a low-key performance from someone who had until recently been seriously ill, they were rocked back on their heels by the verve with which Mari's Eliza burst onto the Drury Lane stage. Members of the press left the theatre stunned that two sisters could look so much alike and possess an equal amount of talent. Try as they might to separate the two in terms of ability, they could not. The twins' voices, gestures, expressions of emotion all were superb. "But", as one critic wrote, "be under no illusion that these performances are stereotypes. They have been trained by one of our greatest actresses, whose tuition has gone far beyond the rudiments of speech and stagecraft. From her they have learned the essence of acting, the creation of believable, living characters with whom the audience can both laugh and cry. We thought we would never see Rose Reece's like again; how fortunate our generation is to see not one, but two such performers."

They cried when they read it, first Rose, then the twins, then Estelle and Monty. What a tribute. How could they possibly live up to it? Rose shrewdly pointed out that they had not yet either of them been called upon to play the 'big' roles, Hedda Gabler etc., which could not happen until they were older, also that every play would not be of the same calibre as Shaw or Shakespeare, but that the more astute critics would realise this and know that any actor's performance must be limited by the material with which he or she was working.

"And this, without appearing disparaging of Willard's play, must apply to the one you will next be re-rehearsing, 'Double Trouble'. All I would ask is that you always give of your best, as indeed you have done to date. Thanks to you Mari, I have won my father's wager and my thanks to you too, Daisy, for Mari will agree that this could not have been achieved without your full co-operation. Now before we get emotional again I just want to ask you all to keep next Saturday evening free. I think a celebration is called for, so I'm going to suggest we assemble here for a pre-dinner drink and I will book a table for us. Girls, I think in view of your outstanding success, you should select the venue. Now, take your pick…the Ritz, Savoy,

Claridges, the Grosvenor, you name it." And name it they did.

In the ensuing few days Rose first of all called upon her solicitor and explained that the requirements of the wager had now been fulfilled and would be doubly so in November when Mari would be playing the lead in 'Double Trouble', also in the West End. His response was enthusiastic.

"My congratulations, Miss Reece, to you and to your protégées. I am of course, not surprised, it would be difficult not to be aware of their outstanding success. Your claim to winning cannot be disputed in view of the number of people who have seen Miss Mari Gold in her leading role, and of course, the many hundreds, possibly thousands who have read about it. If it is convenient I shall call upon you tomorrow and personally hand over your winnings!"

A few days later, assembling as planned for their dinner engagement, they formed an elegant group. Rose wore silver grey lace, Estelle palest green chiffon and the twins were in pale gold mousseline, their dresses in the latest 'flapper' style, with dropped waistlines and scalloped hemlines. The dapper Monty, surveying them declared, "I do feel I should be paying someone for the privilege of escorting such a bevy of beautiful females."

"On the subject of payment", Rose began, "I've asked you to join me here in a drink so that I could not only thank Mari and Daisy again, but do so in a more practical way," with this she handed each of them an envelope.

"You are responsible for winning me the wager and I know that Estelle and Monty agree with me that you should therefore receive some recompense, other than the plaudits which have already come your way. This money is a 'cushion'. There will certainly be times when you either want to do something special or dream of somewhere you long to visit, this should help."

Their protestations that it was Rose's generosity which had been keeping them in food and clothes for the past few years and that her tuition was beyond price, were all smilingly rebutted, the money was theirs and there could be no refusal. They were stunned, two thousand pounds each! More than many people earned in years.

Rose had not quite finished her dissertation, "There are two other things I have decided to do with some of this wager money. I am going to award three scholarships for Drama, Art and Music respectively. In this way I feel we will all have contributed to the creative arts and enabled someone with talent to further their skills. Now, that's the business part of the evening over, let's see what the Ritz has to offer."

What the Ritz offered were stunning flower arrangements, pristine napery, glittering crystal and exquisitely presented, delicious food, their own entrance causing quite a sensation and ripples of applause. The Maitre D. smiled a welcome, his staff were deferential but not unctuous and to everyone's delight the music from the grand piano changed suddenly from Strauss to 'Two little girls in blue'.

After dinner there was dancing and Mari found her first would-be partner was one of the consultants from the hospital where she had been treated. Stephen Vickers away from the hospital environment took on a completely different persona. He remarked that she appeared to be fully recovered, but from then on the conversation was strictly confined to trivia! He complimented her on her dress, congratulated her on her recent success and said that he hoped to see her in a few weeks in 'Double Trouble'. He also asked her about the progress of Miss Reece's new theatre, the development of which was by now common knowledge in the City. Returning to their table he was introduced to the others and invited Daisy to dance and then Estelle before rejoining his own family party, celebrating the birthday of a cousin. His return to ask Mari for the last waltz and to invite her to dinner the following week, was met with nods of approval from Rose and Monty.

Daisy was also pleased, she had not said too much to Mari about Chris, and the fact that they were still in contact. Again it had seemed somehow not quite the thing to be enjoying herself whilst her sister was ill. Now she would be able to tell Mari all about him, the fact that his contract with D' Oyly Carte was going well and that there were two quite strong roles for him in the pipeline.

Back at Greenacres after Rose had retired, they sat in their own little sitting room and for a short time discussed their good fortune.

"We can't always stay here Mari", Daisy said. "I know every time it's mentioned Rose brushes on one side the possibility of our looking for a place elsewhere. Before today it really wasn't possible, but I do think that now we have some money, we should talk to her again about our moving out."

"I agree. I know she says she enjoys our company, but there are times when I'm sure she'd prefer to have breakfast alone or have dinner with either Estelle or Monty on their own. As soon as there's a suitable moment, we'll mention it again."

Such a moment presented itself a few days later. Rose did not on this occasion brush aside their reasoning, but what she did say was, "I appreciate that you've given this some thought girls. What I am going to suggest is that we leave the matter in abeyance, at least until after Christmas. By then your nineteenth birthday will have passed, including other important dates on the calendar, 'Double Trouble' and the opening of the new theatre. I think you'll agree that is enough upheaval for the next few weeks, but when things quieten down we'll discuss it again in detail."

They were more than satisfied with her response. Rehearsals had started for the play and each of them was now being pressed by their new-found friends to meet now and again. At thirty three Stephen Vickers was young for a consultant, but considerably older than Mari. She rather liked that. In the past she'd been accused of being headstrong and wilful, but Stephen saw this as vivacity and working in an environment which could prove sombre and at times disheartening, he welcomed her ebullient nature. It mattered little to him that she might, as she warned him, 'drop the occasional brick', her company was stimulating and often challenging. She was beautiful and intelligent and she was beginning to play a large part in his life.

'Double Trouble' played for the planned four weeks without a hitch. To the delight of Mrs. Barton,

Alice and Michael, Daisy and Mari invited them to one of the performances and arranged their overnight accommodation. Mr. and Mrs. Carstairs and Mrs. Murray-Rogers also declared their intention of coming to see the show and staying with friends. Meeting them all after the show was, Daisy said, like stepping back in time. Mr. Richard was courteous as ever and had arranged transport for everyone. Mrs. B was her same warm, cuddly self and the young couple were obviously very happy together. For their part the Island group were astonished at the professional performances given by the girls. They were astonished too at the recognition the twins received on the London streets. As Mrs. B. said "To think that our two little girls from the Island should have come this far!" Willard's play had been carefully examined by the critics and all felt that the court room scene in particular augured well for his future as an established playwright. Then, almost without warning, the threat of a different court room scene entered their lives.

Estelle's stockbroker friend Clive, had spent the morning with her and on his departure she asked if he would be kind enough to call at Greenacres and leave with Rose a script for her to read. On his arrival there, he found Monty having just finished coffee, also about to leave. At that moment Rose asked if they would be kind enough to put in the garden shed several potted plants the gardener had overlooked. "They're nice plants and if we have a frost, I'll loose the lot. Please let yourself out, I'm going up to the study, I've a stack of letters to deal with."

The plant-pots duly delivered to the shed, Monty turned to leave to see Clive locking the door.

"What on earth are you doing?" he asked.

"I think it's time you and I had a talk, a long one and I don't want us to be interrupted."

Monty was annoyed, "If this is about those stocks and shares…"

Clive was dismissive, "I don't think so."

"Then, whatever it's about, I think your behaviour is unacceptable. If you wished to speak to me privately, you should have said so and arranged it in a civilised way."

"Strangely enough, I don't feel particularly civilised. I want to talk to you about Lydia."

"Lydia?" Monty's voice registered amazement. "You mean Lydia my wife who drowned."

"Slight correction necessary there I think… who we were *told* was drowned."

"Not that again," Monty sighed, "I don't know why you should be interested, but the police went into all that…thoroughly."

"Not thoroughly enough, I suspect. The police are not always as careful as they might be with the wealthy and famous. But that's beside the point, I happen to have some new evidence, evidence that you are not going to like, but which the police will be delighted to have in their possession."

"Well, I'll believe that when I see it, but I'll ask you again just how and why does this concern you? *I* don't know you. To my knowledge Lydia didn't know you."

"Wrong again old boy, not only was she my cousin, but she knew me alright, you might say, intimately. We were lovers for several years before you appeared on the scene. I *was* going to marry her. Didn't love her of course, but that way I would have got the girl, the estate and probably a title. I can't think of any other Warrens in the pipeline."

"So, I beat you to it in the marriage stakes, but ...?"

"But we continued to be lovers. I think you were from the start, rather old for her taste. The trouble was she could never resist fame and as she already had the fortune...I now have a witness who overheard you and Lydia having a violent quarrel in your cabin on the afternoon just before they all went ashore, leaving the two of you alone on board. You're not denying that?"

"No, I'm not," Monty was by now furious. "I didn't tell the police that and I imagined your friends didn't either, because it made Lydia look like what she was, a cheap two-timing little tart. She'd told me about your long affair but said it was all over and that you wouldn't be coming to the wedding so there would be no embarrassment. Then a friend of mine saw the two of you booking in at a hotel somewhere and that afternoon when we were in the cabin I tackled her with it...Oh, Lydia admitted it alright, was quite brazen about it. When the others had left she suddenly went quiet, started saying how sorry she was and that she wouldn't be seeing you again. She even mixed me a drink, a sort of peace offering. Afterwards I realised how gullible I'd been. I wasn't even suspicious until much later when I realised that after I'd returned to the cabin to read the papers, I could hardly keep my eyes open and very quickly fell asleep. You know the rest."

"I know what you've tried to make everyone believe. I now have a letter which convinces me otherwise."

Monty was puzzled, "A letter from whom?"

"Lydia." Monty's face registered disbelief.

Clive continued, "I own a cottage in Honfleur, Northern France. An agent handles it for me and I rent it out from time to time. It's several years since I visited it myself, until a few months ago. There was a note waiting for me to say that something was being held for me in the Poste Restante and would I collect it. It was a letter from Lydia saying you'd found out about us and knew that she was pregnant with my child. She said she'd been ill before leaving for Greece, was suspicious that you'd tried to poison her and was now afraid for her life."

"And this letter is where?" Monty's voice was cold.

"Where you can't see it."

"And now you're going to show it to the police?"

"At last…you're beginning to get my drift. Of course I'll be showing it to them, although several years in a metal mail box has somewhat impaired its condition."

"You'll be wasting your time."

"I think not."

"Perhaps it would interest you to know, Mr. Evans, or Warren, or whatever you're calling yourself today, that having slept with Lydia the night before her disappearance and shared a small rather cramped cabin with her, I happen to know she was not pregnant. She was in fact menstruating. There was no sex that night and there was blood on the sheets."

"Difficult to prove, several years on!"

"Just what would you hope to gain from my being convicted of this so-called crime?"

"Painfully obvious I would have thought, old boy. I did consider one or two ways in which I might bring you down, just for the fun of it. The stocks and shares thing was a possibility, but then I reminded myself that if you lost all your money, some of which is rightfully mine, then I would lose out too. No, this way seemed the most foolproof."

"And you plan to do what?"

"Inform the police, produce the witness to repeat what she heard and show them my letter."

"And Lydia is?"

"Dead of course," Clive was emphatic.

"You seem very sure of that."

"Oh, I am, very sure."

"And if the police believe your story?"

"No *if* about it dear Monty. They were dubious before and time may have moved on, but this is just the evidence they need to reopen the case and have you convicted. The others on board knew you were always at each other's throats and it was an open secret that you wanted 'out' of the performing arts business so that you could set yourself up as an entrepreneur. Dear Lydia wasn't having that at any price and certainly wasn't prepared to stump up any money to start you off, so you had every reason for wanting her out of the way for good."

"There's no body. It'll be 'murder not proven' without one."

"Oh, I'll settle for seeing you get a lengthy prison sentence."

"And then?"

"Well I'm certainly not in this from any deep seated conviction to get justice for Lydia, God rest her sweet fickle-hearted soul. No, once you're safely tucked away, I can then set the wheels in motion to claim the money I should have inherited on her death and probably contest any claims to my family's titles whilst I'm about it."

Monty looked at him with contempt, "Then by all means go right ahead."

At this quicker than expected capitulation, Clive registered surprise. Then unlocking the door, he threw the key on to the floor and walked away without a backward glance.

Monty's first point of contact was Estelle. It was imperative she was made aware of her so called friend's treachery. Finding it difficult to comprehend that the Clive to whom she had been so close had plotted and schemed against Monty, it was some moments before realisation dawned that that very closeness had been merely a ploy to enable Clive to learn as much as possible about Monty. At last she was able to rouse herself from her own bitterness and disappointment to deal with his more serious problem.

"This letter he speaks of ?"

"Probably a forgery."

"And the witness?"

"Oh I don't doubt the truth of what she heard. Lydia and I did have a blinding row, not uncommon I might add. The friend who heard us might have kept quiet to protect Lydia's image, quite a tall order. What I think is more likely is that she was paid to maintain silence. You see Clive's name would have been mentioned in our argument, quite a lot, as I recall. I can't remember if his surname was used, if so it would have been his real name, Clive Warren. I think he wouldn't have wanted either his Christian or surname to be in the police domain, it might have been sufficient to start them thinking. No, I think it's most likely what whilst enquiries were being made he paid his witness to keep quiet, not wanting to be drawn into the investigation in any way."

Estelle looked puzzled, "But he couldn't have been involved, he wasn't there."

A terse reply from Monty, "So he says. Listen my dear, I want him to make all the next moves. I'm going home now so that the police will not have to search for me and I want you to alert your mother. It's important that she should not be alarmed and I would like to think you were with her. I may or may not be arrested, but in any event please remember and tell Rose this also, there will soon be a murder trial, but it will not be mine."

As anticipated, Monty was taken in by the police for interrogation and after twenty four hours was released. The following day Clive Warren was arrested and charged with suspected murder and perverting the course of justice. The evidence against him was overwhelming. At the time of Lydia's disappearance Monty had kept his own dossier of events and had done his own police work for as he explained to Rose and Estelle afterwards, "I always felt that some day, somewhere, someone would crawl out of the woodwork and we would finally learn the truth. And Clive has done just that.

"Following Lydia's disappearance once the police had cleared me, I stayed on in Greece for several days. Fortunately for me, the crew had not been able to get about their usual chores whilst the investigation was going on, so they were still on board and the first thing I did when the police left, was to speak to our steward. I asked if there was anything about the cabin Lydia and I had occupied, which might have made him suspicious. He said that when he'd gathered up the glasses for washing he'd found that one required more careful cleaning than usual It appeared to have a filmy encrustation at the base, as if someone had used a dispersible tablet which hadn't completely dissolved in the liquid. He also said without prompting, that the morning of Lydia's disappearance he'd had to change the cabin sheets as they were blood-stained, which confirms my story and knocks on the head the thrust of the letter, which Clive claims to have. I asked the steward to accompany me to the notary's office where under oath, he confirmed everything he'd said to me.

"Next I made enquiries about people hiring out small boats in the area and I was directed to a small fishing village called Kastos. I was taken to meet Evagoras Limni, a fisherman, and I could see at once, that he and his wife were very worried about something. At first we could only communicate by signs, but there was one man in the village who could speak English, if not fluently, reasonably well, and on my return he accompanied me. Through him I learned that Evagoras had hired out a boat on the day in question to a young man from England. Before he took the boat out the couple were surprised to see this man gather several quite large rocks and put them in the boat, together with his haversack and jacket . When the boat was returned to them the rocks had gone and in the bottom of the boat, there was a coil of rope from which a length had been cut. They also found and produced them for me to see, a pair of ladies' sunglasses. They were Lydia's. I assured them that they were not in any sort of trouble, but that I would be bringing someone back with me, a Greek notary, who would ask them to sign a document stating what they had seen and they were to hand over the sunglasses to him.

"They were frightened of course, but I tried to explain that in the unlikely event of them having to attend a trial, then I would personally see that they were well looked after and compensated. The one thing I didn't have of course, was a picture of Clive, but one has now been sent to the Greek notary by the police, and the fisherman has already confirmed that this is the young man who hired their boat."

"What on earth could Clive have said to Lydia to persuade her that it was alright to accompany him that day?"

"I think he would have told her to spike my drink, probably with a sleeping pill and that then the two of them could have a cosy afternoon somewhere, preferably on a small deserted beach. The poor girl could have had no idea what he really had in mind."

Out of all his plotting and scheming, the one thing which Clive had got right was the fact that without a body, a conviction of murder was extremely doubtful. However the judge left no doubt in the minds of the jurors that he expected them to bring in a verdict of guilty on the charge of suspected murder and also on the charge of perjury. Clive was found guilty on both counts and sentenced to fifteen years imprisonment.

For all of them, the relief that all the case was behind them was tremendous. Monty confessed that over the years he had still felt people were looking at him rather sceptically, as if pondering whether he had or had not disposed of his wife. Now the real culprit was behind bars and they could get on with their lives.

Chapter 12

After the verdict, almost the first thing which Rose did was to talk to Estelle about 'their' girls. Estelle, she knew, had been deeply disturbed by the whole Clive episode, blaming herself for being gullible and that she had not at some time realised he was just too good to be true. Now Rose had a new proposition to put to her.

"Would you consider coming to live here with me at Greenacres... and Biddy too of course? The girls will soon be nineteen and I feel it is time they branched out on their own. I wondered if you might consider their moving into your cottage and you coming here. I don't want you to think I'm looking for an unpaid nurse to see me through my dotage, there will be Biddy as well and if we do need extra help for either of us, then we will get it. We need not be always in each other's hair either, there is now the sitting room I had made for the girls and there are plenty of rooms if you wish to create another study. What I don't want you to feel is that you are in any way giving up your independence." Rose almost held her breath, was all this much, much too late? How would Estelle react?

"Rose, that's a wonderful idea. You and I have so much in common," then laughing, "quite apart from the blood ties that is. There's so much space here, there's no chance of our getting in each other's way and you're too unselfish to intrude on anyone's independence. My cottage is just right for Mari and Daisy, I think they'll love that too. They'll be able to do their own entertaining and they're getting to the age when that is important. I'm not sure about Biddy, I just have a feeling that once she knows you and I are together, she might decide to go and live with Lily, her sister. She lives near Hampton Court so it wouldn't be very far for us to visit them now and again. I'll put it to her right away and see what she says."

"We'll wait before saying anything at all, until we know what she wants to do," Rose was thinking it through, "and then plan accordingly. If you agree, I'm going to suggest we make this move immediately after Christmas. In fact, on second thoughts, it might be better if you came to stay here for the holiday, with or without Biddy. That would give us time to have any redecorating done, any necessary alterations, before the girls move in. I'm sure they'll want to choose their own colour schemes. Meanwhile you should be considering which rooms you want upstairs and it's time we had another bathroom installed there too, and possibly a shower room."

Estelle laughed, "All this work at your theatre has got you all fired up about new plumbing, but yes, my own bathroom here would be lovely and the girls will certainly need another at the cottage. A couple of the windows need replacing and I'm afraid of late, the garden has been neglected."

Rose was full of enthusiasm, "We'll get as much of it done before the girls move in, although it's not exactly the right time of the year for gardening. But not a word to them before it's all settled. I'm quite looking forward to seeing their reaction."

Within twenty four hours Estelle had phoned to say that Biddy had said that much as she loved them both she would now be very happy to 'spend the rest of my days with my sister'.

Now it was time to tell the girls. They looked slightly apprehensive on entering the drawing room and seeing Rose and Estelle waiting for them expectantly. At Rose's opening gambit, "You did mention the possibility of looking for somewhere to live elsewhere and we decided to discuss it later. Well now's the time." their faces fell.

They were going to have to leave this beautiful house where they'd spent such happy times. Rose continued, "Estelle is going to come and live here," so that was it, they were going to have to make room for her, "and we wondered if you might like to take over her cottage. It is, as you know only a few hundred yards from here. What do you think?"

Their faces said it all. It was a pretty little house, here in the area with which they were now so familiar. Close to London, where they would hope to find most of their work, and most importantly, close to their benefactor and dear friend, Rose. With Estelle still on hand as well, it all seemed too good to be true. They made their plans. Estelle would move into Greenacres before Christmas enabling work to be carried out at the cottage, before the twins transferred to their new home.

"It's occurred to me," Rose was still trying to tie up a great many loose ends, "you girls are going to need some sort of assistance at the cottage. I'm sure you're both very domesticated," at this Mari pulled a wry face, "but if for instance, you are both tied up with a play, rehearsing or performing, the last thing you want is to have to worry about food on your return home. And there's cleaning, laundry and some gardening… The latter can be handled by my own gardener, but I think we must make some enquiries about a live-in housekeeper, cum maid-of-all-work, someone who really is prepared to turn her hand to anything and can cook as well! I think you'd better leave that with me. The very next thing we must do is let people see my theatre."

The Reece Theatre was launched on Friday, 14th December. Invitations had been sent, as Monty said, 'to the great and the good', asking them to assemble outside the theatre at six o'clock promptly. Floodlights were in place and the brief ceremony of Rose naming the theatre and cutting the tape into the foyer was, in view of the time of the year, conducted as quickly as possible. As the crowd surged into the foyer, they exclaimed at the walls covered with paintings by Sebastian Reece, reproductions of course. The attractive vibrant colours were a talking point and for a while there was animated conversation whilst champagne cocktails were distributed and drunk. Then it was on to the main bar. More exclamations of delight to find the walls full of pictures, both photographs and paintings, of Rose in her many different roles. The bar displayed a rich variety of buffet-type food and an abundance of wine and spirits, guests admired the new fitments and décor everywhere and congratulations flowed in Rose's direction.

At seven o'clock the doors to the auditorium were opened so that people could wander at will. And they did just that. They loved the smaller VIP bar, the corridors with their paintings of old London, even the new toilets! In the auditorium itself the full effect of the deep royal blue velvet seats and stage curtains and the touches of gold everywhere were striking and elegant. And flanking the stage on each side was a veritable mountain of bouquets sent by people to mark this special occasion. At seven thirty promptly everyone was seated as the orchestra filed in.

Rose was to make the introductions and everyone stood and applauded when the curtains parted and the diminutive figure in her favourite deep rose colour appeared, her diamonds sending shafts of light in all directions. The plan had been for a short and light-hearted concert and if it proved longer than intended, that was because the audience loved each item so much they asked for more.

The D'Oyly Carte company had provided six of their soloists to sing numbers from various Gilbert and Sullivan shows. One of the singers selected was, to Daisy's delight, her friend Chris and when Ivor Novello asked if Chris would also like to sing a number drafted for one of his future shows he was ecstatic. The song was 'Rose of England', and its significance was not lost on the audience. Estelle, accompanied by Monty, sang another of Ivor's songs, and Noel almost brought the house down with 'And her Mother came too'. It was Noel too who at the final curtain congratulated Rose and wished the Reece Theatre a long and successful existence. More flowers and it was all over.

Back at Greenacres they mulled over the events of the evening and decided that if any mistakes had been made, they could not have been too serious, as their guests had all left for home, giving the appearance of being very happy. Ten days now to Christmas. As was anticipated, Biddy had decided to go to her sister's and Estelle was moving in. The twins were doing some preliminary packing and Greenacres had to be decorated before the festival. Everyone helped. There were sorties out to the borders of the garden and into the pastureland on the river banks. Soon there was a vast pile of greenery and holly and yards of scarlet ribbon ready to be hung. The tree was carried in and decorated with scarlet candles and bows, the vases filled with sweet scented narcissi from the Scilly Isles and from the kitchen the odours of Christmas started to seep into other rooms. Monty was to stay with them for the two days over Christmas which meant that the house was almost full for the first time since the girls had made it their home.

A card had arrived from the Isle of Wight signed 'Ted and Sue Griffin'. Their father had scribbled a message underneath to say that they were all well and hoped the girls were too. At first upset, the twins tried to be realistic.

"At least now they've made it legal," Daisy said, "which is certainly better for the boys."

"I just can't rid myself of the feeling that that woman has got what she planned right from the start and I can never forgive her for the way she treated Mum."

"Nor me, but you know, we're no longer involved. Yes, we'll send things for the boys' birthdays and Christmas presents, as we've already done this year, but I can't see us ever going to stay at the farm again, not while she's there."

"No possibility of that. Sad as it seems, if and when we do go back to the Island, it will have to be the briefest of visits just to see Dad and the boys and we'll arrange to stay elsewhere."

"Right, let's put it behind us now, we can't walk around with long faces all day, it is Christmas after all."

Amongst the other cards received, those from Chris and Stephen were displayed prominently in the girls' bedrooms and there was a particular pleasure when Lester's card arrived with its Italian postmark and a note to say his Italian was now fluent and he would hope to see them during January.

Amidst flurries of snow alternating with crisp pale primrose sunshine, Greenacres was a warm and glowing haven in all its Christmas finery. They ate too much, tried to walk it off down on the river bank, played silly games and exclaimed over their lovely gifts. The girls each received from Rose and Monty sets of beautiful luggage with smiles and assurances that this was something they would undoubtedly need in the not too distant future, and from Estelle there were Leichner theatrical make-up cases containing every conceivable colour and shade of grease-paint. A treasure hunt around the house revealed further small gifts, photograph frames, tortoiseshell backed hair brushes, chocolates and perfume. Never had Daisy and Marigold been the recipients of such a treasure trove of lovely gifts.

Managing to secure a few moments alone with Rose, they broached the subject of the cottage and the finances involved. Her reply was firm and to the point,

"The property is mine and you are to have it rent free until your twenty-fifth birthdays, by which time I am hopeful you will be earning reasonable sums of money. You will pay for your own food, light and heating of course. I've arranged for a lady called Sarah Brent to work for you. She's forty, a young widow, and since her husband's death has had to give up the tied cottage they were in. Her husband was a farm labourer on the Rushford estate; I know Lord Rushford, and Sarah comes with excellent testimonials. He tells me she worked in Rushford Hall for some years and is pleasant, conscientious and, very important from your point of view, a good cook. Again, I shall pay her wages until your twenty-fifth birthdays. My own gardener will look after the cottage garden for the time being, but if either of you feel you have 'green fingers' and want to do anything special just talk to him about it."

"But Miss Reece the money you gave us…we could now afford to pay our way, we can't continue to let you provide for us."

"Two things, one I've been meaning to say for some time. I think you might now start to call me Rose, as everyone else does. I'm not saying the teacher-pupil situation has come to an end, because I still feel there's much I can do to help you, but you are now nineteen and I know you well enough to feel we can dispense with the formality. Secondly, you left your home to come and live here with me, that in itself was an enormous step, but you have both worked long and hard to achieve the goals I set, and I think it's time you reaped the rewards of that." Then, laughing, "But don't think the hard work is over, I can assure you I have other challenges in mind."

Back in their own sitting room the girls discussed what Rose had said and started to make plans about their new home.

"We'll be able to invite Chris and Stephen over for dinner and in the summer we can sit in the garden and have a picnic lunch, always supposing of course, that Chris isn't touring with the Doylys somewhere up country, or even worse, overseas, and that Stephen isn't up to his elbows in gore in the operating theatre."

"Ugh! Mari, what a horrible thing to say."

"Daisy, my little one, I know what he does for a living, there's absolutely no point whatever in being squeamish about it."

"You don't think Estelle will mind?"

"Mind what?"

"Well, our having boy friends. It was rotten for her finding out what a villain Clive was, just when we all thought and she seemed to think, that she'd found someone really nice."

"Daisy I've always said you were much too soft-hearted for your own good. What we have to do sister dear, is delve into any murkiness which might be lurking in the pasts of our own gentlemen friends, before they get too serious. I suppose Chris didn't have a wife who drowned at sea in mysterious circumstances?"

"Don't be ridiculous! What is far more likely is that your Stephen has been plying his trade somewhere other than the operating theatre."

"Ugh, we'd better stop this, now I *am* beginning to feel rather squeamish."

The day before they moved in, the twins called to see Sarah who was now installed and doing what she called a 'post-builders' clean. Dwarfing the twins by about four inches, she was large-boned with large hands and, as she laughingly pointed out, large feet to match. Easy to talk to, she expressed her delight at the cottage, which almost matched their own. There were now four bedrooms, each with washing facilities, two bathrooms and a shower room. Downstairs was the sitting room, overlooking the garden, a small dining room, study and large kitchen. Sarah had her own annexe with bedroom, bathroom and tiny sitting room.

"We keep calling it a cottage," Mari said, "which implies somewhere small, but it's really quite large."

"It's gorgeous and I'm so glad we settled for that cream and pale copper colour in the dining room, it gives it such a warm welcoming feeling."

Sitting in the kitchen of their new home, drinking coffee with Sarah, they discussed their particular loves and hates with regard to food and by the time they left for Greenacres were enthusiastic about everything they'd seen and especially about Sarah.

"I was quite worried, someone living in the same house with us…I suppose I was afraid she might just treat us as a couple of youngsters, but she's lovely, easy to talk to. You know, Daisy,I think we're going to be really happy there. And with Rose just a stone's throw away…"

The night before they left Greenacres Rose had some other startling news to divulge. With Estelle at her side she told them, "I've waited for some time to tell you this, but it's right now that you should know. Estelle is my daughter." There was no comment from the girls, just wide-eyed amazement. "Yes, really. I was not married at her birth, have never been married and to avoid scandal she was born overseas in France. I'm sure you'll understand that now seems the right time for us to live together. None of this is common knowledge, but you girls have become like members of our family, so we feel you should know. I'm sure your next question would probably be regarding her father, who is Monty, of course. I'm sure you'll understand and comply with our wishes that for the foreseeable future we continue as we are, with the three of us caring for each other as we have always done."

They were shocked, of course, but felt privileged to have been confided in and touched that they should be regarded as 'members of the family'.

"Why would they not have married?" Daisy mused, "They're obviously devoted to each other."

"Well, they'd have only been early twenties, not much older than us, perhaps it was the career thing."

"All the same, if Estelle's only just found out – a bit hard on her surely."

"Daisy, it's their lives, their business. We've now read enough English Lit., to know life is not easy, straight forward or predictable. We've all got enough to cope with dealing with our own lives, without worrying too much about what others are doing with theirs."

"Touché."

So for two blissful weeks after Christmas they enjoyed settling into their new home.

"What about a house-warming?" Mari asked one day.

"Not a brilliant time of the year" was Daisy's response, "Starting next week we've got a lot to think about. I'd prefer to wait a while, it would be nice to have it in the Spring so that hopefully we can spill out onto the garden."

"Don't like the sound of that 'spill out' bit, you're not planning to invite a couple of hundred I hope."

"Don't be silly. It's just that these rooms are not the size of those at Greenacres and now that Rose's agent has managed to get us a short-term contract with the Doylys we'll have quite a lot of work to do before March. I just felt it would be lovely if we were not under any pressure and don't forget there would be the bonus of the spring flowers being out."

"Right, I'm quite happy to go along with that. If something crops up and we have to change our plans, so be it. I suppose there's not another reason?"

"Such as?"

"Being under pressure planning a house-warming, might leave you less time to spend with one particular Doyly, Chris by name."

"You know what you said just now dear sister, about meddling in other people's lives. Time you took heed of your own advice."

The contract they had received from the Doylys and set up by Rose's agent, was for six months only. During that time they were to be in the chorus of 'Yeomen of the Guard' and 'Patience' and then, if considered ready, sing the roles of the wives of the gondolieri in 'The Gondoliers'. Three mornings each week were now spent in rehearsing with Estelle, singing scales, reading music, learning libretti. On two mornings, under Rose's supervision, they were familiarising themselves with the classics. To Sarah's amusement and delight, she would hear them moving about the cottage singing solos and duets and reciting long passages from Shakespeare. As she said to the gardener "There's never a dull moment, it's so lovely to be in the house with youngsters, they're so full of life."

Towards the end of January during one of Estelle's lessons with the girls and without saying where she was going, Rose succumbed to a wave of guilt that her God-daughter was locked away and unloved and decided to visit Celia. The home was sited close to Hampton Court and it being a cold, but bright day, she decided en route to walk through the Palace grounds. She loved the Palace gardens. Now dormant, in a few short weeks they would be a blaze of colour, with daffodils as far as the eye could see. The grounds of Shawcross House were in the same winter sleep with only snowdrops and a few brave aconites visible.

Rose, instantly recognised by a smiling maid, was shown into a sitting room where there were four young women, obviously inmates, and two attendants. As the door opened and seeing Rose, Celia jumped to her feet saying excitedly in a loud voice to everyone, "It's my mother, my mother's come to see me," and to the nurse "I told you she would come". The nurse looked at Rose, raising her eyebrows as if to say "We indulge her fantasies" and then seated her with Celia, a little apart from the others.

Rose went through the pleasantries, asked Celia how she was, what the food was like, did they walk in the gardens each day? Celia's responses were erratic and she produced just one reciprocal question "May I come and stay with you, at your house?"

After a few minutes one of the other inmates came across and placing her hand on Rose's shoulder said, "Hello, who are you?"

Celia leapt to her feet, viciously pushing the girl away and knocking over a table and coffee cups in the process. "That's *my* mother", she shouted, "don't you dare touch her." The attendants reacted swiftly. One went to separate the girls, whilst the other escorted Rose from the room, behind her were howls of protest from Celia on realising that she had gone. The nurse apologised, "I'm sorry, Miss Reece, but once they are disturbed in any way, it is likely to escalate and sometimes spreads to the other inmates."

Rose, shaken by the incident, said she would like to sit down for a moment before making her return journey. "I'll bring you some coffee, Miss Reece", the nurse was concerned by her pallor, "and here's the Superintendent, she'd obviously like to have a word with you."

A brief rest and then at the Superintendent's insistence, Rose was put in a taxi for the return journey home.

Determined to put the disturbing visit behind her, Rose asked Monty to call, with a view to looking at future bookings for the Reece Theatre. Monty had been impressed with a play by a new Welsh author, when he'd seen it performed by a repertory company in Bath and at his suggestion they booked it for the whole of March. As he pointed out, this would enable them to 'run in' the theatre and ensure that everything was in place for a 'bigger venture'. The bigger venture he had in mind was a successful Broadway musical, due to close at the end of the winter season. The cast would be available from mid-April and he recommended that the production was booked in its entirety, again to give them breathing space in which to ensure they could deal with all the problems of staging quite a large musical.

"The cast will all be totally familiar with what they are doing, which will assist our back-stage teams tremendously. We'll put it on for an indefinite run. Once we've tried out different types of show like this, we will know, I hope, just what works for the Reece and what doesn't."

Rose was quite happy to let him have a large say in the theatre's future plans. She knew him to be a shrewd business man and a good administrator. Everything he was saying made sound sense.

"We *must* talk to Ivor and Noel, they've both got material in the pipeline. The pair of them are hugely talented and it would pay us to get our hands on whatever they write just as soon as it becomes available. If I were a betting man, I'd lay heavy odds on Ivor's music and Noel's plays being popular for a good many years. We'll book Music Hall for next Christmas, say for a three week run just to cover our backs and," he hesitated, "I think that's about as much as we can do at the moment." At last, Rose thought, it looks as though the Reece theatre is really in business. Fingers crossed, Dad.

Daisy had come to the conclusion that actors and actresses seemed to be constantly changing partners and usually the preference was for the one with whom they were currently acting. It now seemed to her perfectly obvious that this was because it was the person they saw more frequently. Trying to arrange trysts with Chris was no easy matter. When he was free, she was rehearsing and vice versa. Yet, she was glad they shared the same profession, it meant they had much in common. If he had been impressed with her performance in 'Pygmalion' when substituting for Mari, she was equally impressed at seeing him in 'Pirates'. She was glad too that his career had gravitated towards operettas and musicals rather than classical opera, reasoning that if he had opted for the latter, he would have probably been out of the country for months on end.

As a family the Griffins had not been tactile, in retrospect she realised there had been a dearth of kisses and hugs and only rarely a loving caress. Now when Chris put his arms round her and held her close, she felt safe, and loved. His kisses were becoming bolder as she responded to him and there had been occasions when she had wanted to take that closeness much, much further and throw her inhibitions to the wind. But she resisted. Whilst having no personal experience of sexual contact, her explorations in English Lit., had taught her this was an area fraught with danger. The work of D. H. Lawrence was causing a stir throughout the literary fraternity, these were books which hid nothing from their readers, said it all out loud, as it were, but the resultant situations never seemed particularly happy ones. And, Daisy reminded herself, in Rose there was a classic example on their doorstep, of a love affair which had taken a wrong turning. For whatever reason Monty and Rose had not lived together with Estelle their daughter and enjoyed a happy family life. Yes, they had had wonderful careers all of them, but perhaps it was impossible to have both. And she did so want to succeed. Performing in Drury Lane had been the most wonderful experience of her life and she wanted it to happen again and again. And she wanted Chris too. Oh dear, life was so very, very complicated.

Mari was also finding it difficult to handle her emotions. She was beginning to wonder if she was, after all, much too young for Stephen Vickers. It surely wasn't her imagination that whenever Estelle was present, Steve seemed to gravitate towards her. Of course Estelle was about his age, had a great deal more experience of the world than Mari and in addition she was darkly pretty, vivacious and dressed elegantly. It was going to be some time before Marigold could measure up to all that. When Stephen did kiss her it was in a rather decorous, 'big brother' sort of way. Perhaps he didn't trust himself, was afraid he'd become too passionate and then again, perhaps he still thought of her as a silly young girl who just wasn't ready for anything more than polite kisses. If she dispelled that illusion, what would happen, would she be able to handle the situation? Life was so complicated.

Estelle, warm and comfortable in the sitting room of Greenacres, surveyed the cold and damp scene of a February afternoon in the Thames valley. Rose was resting, the twins were entertaining their two male friends to afternoon tea at the cottage and she was enjoying a quiet period of being on her own and doing absolutely nothing. Suddenly her peace was shattered. She jumped up startled as the door was flung open. She was even more startled to see Celia, bedraggled and wet, bearing down upon her.

"What are you doing here?" Celia demanded, "Where's my mother? What have you done with her?"

For a few moments Estelle couldn't understand. Then remembering Rose telling her about Celia's fixation about her parentage, she moved towards the door. "She's out at the moment, but I'll ring and try and reach her." Quickly she went out into the hall, picked up the phone and got as far as, "Number 3829, Shawcross House please," when the phone was ripped from her grasp and she was flung bodily across the foyer, striking the opposite wall with such force that she slid down the wall into an agonised heap.

"You scheming, lying bitch, you're calling those bastards where I live, I'll make you sorry you did that."

Ripping the phone from its socket, she hurled the instrument at Estelle, hitting her hard on the cheekbone. Now she advanced towards Estelle, who cowered in pain, awaiting the next onslaught. At that moment calm, measured tones came from the top of the staircase, "Celia my dear, how nice, I wasn't expecting you on such a miserable day." Steadily Rose moved down the stairs. "Come over here and let me take off that damp coat and then we must sit down and talk." Quietly her voice murmured on and on, reassuringly, and Celia without hesitation, walked towards her. Gently the coat was removed. "There, that's better, now sit beside me," and carefully she drew Celia down beside her onto the stairs. The girl seemed to relax, placed her head on Rose's shoulder and started to weep silently. "Estelle can get us a hot drink, then you will feel much better." Eyebrows raised, the merest inclination of the head and Estelle knew she had to force herself to get up and go into the kitchen where Milly and Mrs. Knight would be.

They had, of course, heard the raised voices, but assumed that this was some sort of family quarrel, none of their business. Seeing Estelle with blood now pouring down her cheek they sprang into action. Milly was directed to the cottage with the message that someone must ring Shawcross House at once and explain where Celia was, whilst the others were to get to Greenacres as quickly as possible. Mrs. Knight was already boiling the kettle and had produced antiseptic, lint and cotton-wool.

Stephen was the first to arrive and using Mari's key, let himself into the foyer. In a matter of seconds he had sized up the situation. Then, spoke quietly, "Good afternoon Rose. Ah, I see you have a visitor, I'm not disturbing you I hope?"

"Not at all Stephen. This is Celia."

"How do you do?" he extended his hand. His movement with the syringe was imperceptible. Celia collapsed like a puppet and he swept her up in his arms and carried her into the girls' sitting room. In the ensuing silence Daisy and Mari and Chris burst into the hall. "Daisy, I want blankets from upstairs first, cover Celia and stay with her until staff from Shawcross arrive, Mari and Chris take Rose upstairs. I want her to lie on the bed, she can remain fully clothed, but cover her too, with blankets. Stay with her Mari. Chris, phone her doctor, you'll have to do it from the cottage, the number will be on the pad here. Tell him either to come right away or say exactly what action he would like me to take. Now where's our other patient?"

Never had Estelle been so glad to see anyone. Stephen had taken control and everyone knew what they were doing. He was a tower of strength. Examining her cheekbone, he decided stitching would not be necessary and complimented Mrs. Knight on ensuring it was a clean, sterilised wound. However, he said he would tomorrow like an X-ray to make sure there were no hairline fractures. Estelle's back was another matter. He suggested Mrs. Knight accompany her upstairs and that

Estelle undressed to 'brassiere and knickers'. At her look of horror he exploded "For heavens' sake girl, I'm a surgeon, not a lounge lizard. I've seen it all. Now do you want me to see if there's anything wrong or not?"

Meekly, Estelle nodded her head.

"Can you manage the stairs, or is your back too painful?"

"I think I can manage."

"Good, in that case there shouldn't be any broken bones. No nausea, dizziness?"

"No."

"Good again. I'll be up in a moment."

Having examined Estelle's back, with Mrs. Knight discreetly averting her eyes and looking as if she wished herself anywhere but where she was, Stephen said there would certainly be severe bruising which would take several days to appear. Estelle would feel stiff and sore for quite a while. He could find no evidence of fractures, nevertheless he felt it advisable that she should have two X-rays taken, on the back and her cheekbone, to make absolutely sure as he said, that there were 'no hidden nasties'.

Minutes later and the Shawcross House team arrived. Estelle's angry query as to how Celia could have left the House and arrived here produced both apologies and explanations. Many of the inmates had been outside in the grounds that afternoon and when it was time for visitors to leave Celia had walked alongside one couple down the drive. Unaware that she was from the House, when they reached their car and rain was starting they had offered her a lift and taken her to the road where she said she lived, very close to Greenacres. Staff had not noticed her absence for an hour and had then notified the police, who had been searching since that time. In view of what had happened the Superintendent would certainly be recommending that she be placed in a more secure unit.

"Amen to that," Estelle said, as they left carrying the still heavily sedated Celia.

"What amazes me," Stephen said, "is how, when she'd injured you, you managed to get her quiet again. That can prove very, very difficult."

"Oh, that was Rose. She walked down the stairs as if nothing had happened. Spoke to Celia as if she had just dropped in for tea and suddenly Celia quietened down. It was amazing."

"It is amazing. *I* know how to deal with someone in those circumstances, but I'm a medic. How on earth did Rose manage it? She must have been frightened, especially when she could see you on the floor injured and bleeding."

"She managed it, Stephen, because above everything else, she is a consummate actress. Terrified she might have been, but letting her audience, Celia in this case, see that...Not on your life!"

Rose's doctor suggested that Stephen give her a dose of the sedative already in her possession and advised a minimum of twenty four hours rest. Rose had been very distressed by the incident and by Estelle's injuries but, as Stephen pointed out, things could have been much worse. Her own calm handling of what was a very precarious situation had tipped the balance in the right direction and, he added, "You're a very clever lady. Now it's time you do what *your* doctor and *this* doctor says, take your medicine, have a good night's sleep followed by a quiet day and you will be absolutely fine. Good-night."

"Good-night Stephen and thank you".

What a pity Estelle didn't meet him before Mari, Rose thought as her eyelids closed, he's so sensible and nice with it.

Mari too, was still pondering on that. Stephen had seen Estelle in her brassiere and knickers, in fact he'd seen lots of women in similar attire, or less! How do surgeons feel about making love to their own wives, when they've seen so many others naked?

And what about when you're turned forty and starting to lose your figure, how will it feel to know your husband is still gazing at beautifully formed young ladies in the peak of condition? I don't know if I'll be able to handle that. I think I want a man who only sees *me* stripped off, not one who's going to be constantly making comparisons with all the others he's seen.. Perhaps if I push him in Estelle's direction and turn down a few of his invitations he might get the message. He's a lovely, lovely man, but not the one for me.

In fact, Mari had to do little or no pushing. Stephen Vickers made sure that he was around the very next day, when Estelle was taken to the hospital for her X-rays. Afterwards he bought her coffee and insisted he take her home so that 'he could check up on Rose'. At the end of the day, neither he nor Estelle was under any doubt that there had been a spark between them which was worth exploring further. Out of courtesy he waited for Mari to tell him that it might be a good idea if they didn't meet so often, as she 'was going to be very busy rehearsing', which they both knew to be a euphemism for 'this relationship is not working'. Afterwards Mari heaved a sigh of relief; she was only nineteen after all, there was plenty of time!

Chapter 13

Within a few short days the twins decided that working with the Doylys, in their own theatre, the Savoy, was fun. For the first time they were part of a large cast, forty in all, and the opportunity presented itself to meet and make new friends of all ages.

They learned how important chorus grouping was on stage to obtain maximum benefit from voices singing in the same musical range and the careful planning needed to get thirty people on and off stage without it looking regimental. In the wings, space was inevitably limited and such a large number of people had to be well disciplined, with no talking which might be picked up on microphones and careful attention to the singers on stage, whilst awaiting their own cues for entrance. On stage they learned again that reaction to the events being played out before them was an essential ingredient of their role and loved being a part of the delicious melody when the entire chorus sang in harmony. They made mental notes of which gestures the soloists used worked best and how, in costume, they dealt with voluminous skirts and anything which might impede their performances.

Daisy's boyfriend, Chris, was by now a regular, his contract having been extended for a further two years and for Daisy it was an added bonus that, whilst he would have numerous soloist rehearsals, they would at least be working in the same production for some weeks. Mari, meanwhile, had reneged on her earlier decision. She was now slightly worried that, although only nineteen, she could not risk being left 'on the shelf', so there would be no harm in looking around and immediately set about doing just that!

Chris seemed to be exceptional in the D'Oyly Carte company, in that most of the males were aged between twenty eight and fifty. After the Stephen episode Mari had ruled out anything over thirty, however attractive, and this considerably narrowed down the field. Very soon she was having a glass of wine with Trevor, Norman or James and trying to decide which appealed to her the most. Daisy was quite acid on the subject.

"You seem to be determined to find someone whatever the cost. Why don't you just let Nature take its course? Someone will come along."

"I'm not prepared to wait until I'm thirty-five for that to happen. I want to look around and see what appeals and what definitely does not. Don't worry about me, I'm quite happy about the way my research is going, but I should warn you that it might take some time and there might be a great deal of trials and a good many errors along the way."

"As long as you don't get hurt along that way."

"Little sister! I do believe you're worried about me."

Between Mari's search for the 'right man', Daisy's steady courtship with Chris and their busy rehearsal and performance schedule, they seized what opportunity they could for relaxing in their new home. Weather permitting they would walk in the Thames Valley or to the Hampton Court Gardens. It was on one of these expeditions that they discussed the viability of buying a car.

"We can afford it, that's why Rose gave us the money to make our lives easier. As it is we are constantly trekking around on public transport, having to wait ages for trains or buses or being totally reliant on the good nature of people travelling in the same direction as ourselves. Daisy, you know it makes sense."

"Couldn't agree more that it would be wonderfully convenient, but there's just one small hurdle before we get that far..."

"I know! We've got to learn to drive. But that's not insurmountable. It can't be *that* difficult, after all *men* do it."

"Right, I'm convinced. We'll start straight away. But not until we're given the go-ahead, do we buy a car."

Without more ado their lessons started and by the end of April both had qualified. A small dark blue Ford car was purchased and for two weeks they drove each other on every possible occasion, in and around the Richmond area. As anticipated, it transformed their lives. No longer faced with journeys which seemed interminable, they had in fact more leisure to enjoy. The only problem as far as Daisy was concerned was that Mari's constant presence in the car did not allow her and Chris any attempt at furthering their intimacy - it was, as she protested to Mari,

"Like having one of those Spanish duennas, a permanent chaperone."

"Quite right too," was Mari's response. "Don't forget I'm the eldest and who better to watch over you and your morals."

When the weather was suitable and if Estelle was busy rehearsing, they would often ring Rose and suggest they pick her up and take her for a drive. On one such morning in Spring they had arranged to take her to walk in the Hampton Court gardens, knowing that they would all enjoy seeing the carpet of daffodils and the banks of azaleas and rhododendrons. Waiting in the foyer for her to put on her hat and coat they saw the postman arrive and hand her a letter for which she had to sign. The next moment they both registered alarm, her face had drained of colour and then suddenly flushed. Thinking she was about to faint, or worse, they each took an arm and started to propel her towards the sitting room, asking where her medication was kept. To their surprise she suddenly laughed out loud and said, "Darlings I'm not ill, just overwhelmed. Do look at what has arrived." The letter was from the Lord Chancellor's office and stated,

'His Majesty George V has graciously decided to bestow upon Miss Rosalie Reece the honour of Dame of the British Empire in recognition of her services to the theatre. Should you be unwilling to accept this honour it would be appreciated if this office could be notified at the earliest possible date. Please note that until the official announcement of His Majesty's Birthday Honours List, this information should be considered confidential. Further information will be sent to you regarding dates, investiture timings, dress etc. Congratulations.'

Confidential the news might have been, but the three of them decided they must celebrate straight away. As Daisy said, "We don't have to tell anyone just what it is we're celebrating." So, plans for walking in Hampton Court were put on hold, the girls hurried home to change, leaving Rose to do the same and together the three of them set out for champagne and lobster at 'Le Jardin', a newly opened restaurant in Richmond.

Back at Greenacres there were discreet, but ecstatic calls to Estelle at the Wyndham's theatre and to Monty in a meeting somewhere in the city and then, replete, they sat in Rose's sitting room and talked non-stop about this wonderful future event.

"An elegant new outfit for you of course Rose, and for Estelle."

"You'll be allowed to have two people with you I think..." Daisy hesitated

"Oh, Monty of course." No hesitation whatsoever from Rose. On this, one of the most important days of her life the two people in the world who mattered most to her must be present. The many people who had not known of her relationship with Estelle and Monty would surely after this occasion be in no doubt whatsoever. The press too, would be tricky, but no matter, the time was now right. This accolade would quash any snide comments and mentally sending a quick thank you to her Maker for extricating her from what had been a long-standing problem she knew she was going to enjoy every moment both of the anticipation and the event itself.

The attraction between Estelle and Stephen quickly developed into a more permanent and loving relationship. There was little point in waiting, they decided. Both turned thirty and eager to put down roots and start a family, discussion started to take place as to where and when they should be married and, most important of all, where they should live. Stephen, familiar with the story of Estelle's birth and the fact that she had only just moved in with Rose, was sensitive to the fact that this might prove a stumbling block. He possessed a two bed-roomed flat in London, which had to date been sufficient for his needs but knew this would no longer prove viable as a family house. Tentatively he suggested that for the time being he moved into Greenacres and that they retain the flat in London for convenience, on the occasions when either he or Estelle was working late. Sighs of relief all round. Rose insisted that the small sitting room was perfectly adequate for her requirements, that they should make the larger room their own and that, of course, they regard Greenacres as their own home, inviting people to dinner as and when they wished.

As Estelle said to Stephen later, "With anyone else I don't think I could have agreed to such an arrangement, but Rose, being Rose, is so sensitive to other people's needs, that I don't think we need have any qualms about being under the same roof."

"And, realistically, my darling, although it's sad to contemplate such a situation, Rose will not always be with us. The only problems I can foresee is if and when we start a family and Rose becomes more frail, then it might all be too much for her."

"Let's cross that bridge when we come to it. There's so much space here, we could always build another annexe just for the children to play in, somewhere they can shout and scream to their heart's content without disturbing anyone."

"Estelle my love, I am sure that any children we produce will be models of propriety and never, ever, shout and scream."

"So, not only are you handsome and skilful, but a wishful thinker!"

The wedding, they agreed, should be as soon after the June investiture as possible.

"We can't have it before, it might just steal something of Rose's thunder and that's the last thing we want," Stephen was quite emphatic. "Besides which, just in case she has any reaction to the excitement, I would like to be around for at least a week afterwards."

And so, the third week in July was decided upon, the venue, St. Margaret's Church in Richmond. Stephen's parents were both now in their sixties and lived in a small village in Somerset , where his father, now retired, had been the local doctor for many years. His sister, her husband and two small children lived close to them. It was agreed that the eldest child, a boy aged five should be asked to be a pageboy and that the twins act as Estelle's bridesmaids. Monty would, of course, give the bride away. The reception would be at Greenacres, with a marquee for the wedding banquet and, as at the garden party, everything else would be brought in. Soon there were lists everywhere. Jobs already dealt with. Jobs still to be done. Invitations, guest lists, seating plans, flowers, food, wedding cars, choir, honeymoon arrangements, it was endless. With regard to the honeymoon Stephen was maintaining the strictest secrecy. Since they met, he had known that Estelle shared with him a love of visiting new places and exploring unfamiliar cultures, she also loved travelling by sea and he had accordingly booked their passages on one of the new P&O steamers plying between Cape Town and U.K. They would stay in Cape Town for two weeks before making the long journey home.

The majority of the arrangements made, they were able to concentrate on Rose's big day. Rose had chosen cream lace with ropes of pearls, a hat made entirely of swansdown with a pearl flower to one side, cream shoes and gloves and would carry a small cream lace purse studded with pearls. Estelle's choice was apricot silk with matching hat, gloves and shoes. Monty would of course wear morning dress. It was decided that when it was all over they would go to Claridges for a celebratory lunch and to this the twins were invited.

The morning of the investiture and it was warm and bright as they assembled in their finery at Greenacres, where Rose had arranged for a professional photographer to capture the moment 'for posterity' as she said. The twins, Milly and her new husband and Mrs. Knight were all there to see this momentous occasion and their departure, then a leisurely cup of coffee in the cottage garden and the twins, not to be totally eclipsed by their luncheon companions, changed into their own finery and set out for Claridges. Mari had agreed to drive and all went well until they entered Knightsbridge. Suddenly from a slip road a large car turned into the main stream of traffic, Mari braked hard but it was no use, the bigger car clipped the front wing, spinning them round and leaving them stranded in the middle of the busy road and facing the wrong way. Both girls were badly shaken and remained in their seats struggling for composure. They saw that the car responsible had continued on its way and were now both shocked and angry.

A tap on the window roused them. To their amazement it was the tenor Lester, who had appeared with them in the Music Hall and obviously, if his tanned face was anything to go by, just returned from abroad.

"Are you alright girls?" then realisation, "oh, my goodness it's my Golden Girls, Daisy, Mari, are you hurt?"

"No, I don't think so, but we're very cross that any idiot would do what that one did and then just drive away and leave us!" Mari was clearly furious.

"Don't worry, I've got his registration and there's another chap over there who made a note of it. We'll make sure he has to pay for the damage. Someone has gone to call the police, they'll stop the traffic so that we can turn your car round. From a quick look it appears as if it will be alright to drive but I don't think either of you should be driving for a while, you must be quite shaken. Where exactly are you going?"

Daisy explained.

"Then I think this is what we should do. My apartment is only a hundred yards away, in the close there, I'm going to suggest that once we've got you safely out of the car, you stay in my flat for a few minutes whilst I sort out the paperwork here for you. As soon as that is done we'll move your car into the close and I will drive you to Claridges."

They were more shocked than they had realised and having someone take over the details was a relief for which they were thankful, and impressed. In Lester's absence Daisy remarked on the amazing coincidence of having been rescued by a familiar face, adding, "Not that it was all that familiar, I mean to say, what a gorgeous tan!"

The tan had apparently been acquired in both Italy and, latterly, in Australia. There he'd actually met Nellie Melba who'd been made a Dame in nineteen eighteen. He added, laughing, "Just think, I shall be able to tell my children and grandchildren that I had the privilege of singing with one of the great divas, Dame Nellie Melba."

At Claridges, Rose and the others had arrived and were beginning to be slightly concerned that the girls were late. The story of the errant driver was related and relief expressed that the outcome had not been more serious. Monty insisted that Lester join them for lunch and after protesting that he was not really dressed for such a smart occasion, Lester finally succumbed, was handed a drink and sat down. He proved to be an easy conversationalist, first of all congratulating Rose on receiving such a great honour. He added, "I've just been telling Daisy and Mari that I would be able to tell my children that I actually sang with Dame Nellie Melba, I'll now be able to add to that and say I've had the privilege of eating lunch with Dame Rosalie Reece." Estelle he already knew and his travels and musical experiences abroad proved entertaining and a delight.

Rose's pink cheeks denoted the fact that she was still bursting with the thrill of speaking to the King at the investiture. To her delight and surprise Queen Mary had also appeared in one of the reception areas and had made a point of asking that Rose be presented to her. The Queen had said that she had seen Rose in several of her major dramatic roles and complimented her on the pleasure she had given to so many people. The ribboned award and accompanying testimonial Rose had received were duly displayed to the girls and Lester, and were much admired.

Lester's travels had now come to a halt and his next engagement was at Covent Garden in September. He, in turn, was interested to learn of the twins' activities. Previously unaware of the wager, he was staggered to learn what had been achieved in a relatively short time and asked if there were any more such wagers in the pipeline.

"Not at the moment," Rose replied, "but I'm working on it!"

The girls looked at her astonished. What did she mean? Was she serious? It was a happy, lively occasion, with everyone contributing to the conversation.

On returning to Knightsbridge, the girls thanked Lester profusely for all his help. He told them that the police had said the car was perfectly safe to drive, but of course the bodywork would require some attention once they had time. Before leaving they invited him to visit them at their cottage and on his ready acceptance a date was decided upon.

Later that night, Mari solemnly told Daisy that she had fallen in love.

Daisy was not impressed, "What... again?"

Early morning, Saturday, 21st July, saw the heat mist blanketing the Thames Valley, beginning to disperse. Greenacres seemed to be holding its breath ready for a momentous day. The marquee and its furniture were ready in position, tables being laid and flowers starting to arrive, pedestals awaited the cascades of pastel-shaded arrangements and vases the posies for each table. Outside every shrub had been pampered and trimmed, every border weeded within an inch of its life and lawns cut to manicured perfection.

The twins arrived at ten o'clock to assist where required, to help Estelle and Rose dress and to change into their own dresses. Estelle was wearing a white silk dropped waist dress with a fine lace veil and the girls wore pale aqua satin, also with the fashionable dropped waist-lines. The small page-boy was being delivered to the house at eleven and would wear an aqua satin shirt and matching long trousers. Rose and the bridal attendants would leave for the church at eleven thirty, with Monty and Estelle following at 11.50 for the mid-day service. There were the usual minor problems. Stephen's nephew, Eric, decided he did not like the suit in which he'd been dressed and only the promise of a great deal of jelly and ice cream after the service persuaded him to continue taking part in what he obviously considered 'silly'.

Estelle held her breath when the minister asked 'If anyone has just cause..." and then reproached herself for being stupid. There would be no worms crawling out of this woodwork, Stephen was as straight as a die and the best thing that had ever happened to her. She might have waited a long time, but goodness he was certainly worth that wait. Incredibly it was her father Monty, standing at her elbow and her mother, Rose, just visible to her left. She had had to wait a long time for that also to become reality, but then how fortunate to have been blessed with two such wonderful parents.

Rose, watching her daughter and Monty, the man she had always loved, standing at the altar rails, felt herself becoming emotional. Following her investiture, there had been one or two ripples of speculation in the press about the relationship between herself and Estelle, but nothing unpleasant. Now seeing Monty in his role today, they would in all probability draw their own conclusions. She was no longer worried. The press had been kind to her in the past and she felt they would treat her gently. Today was for enjoyment and the happiness of seeing her dear daughter married to someone of strong character and kindly nature.

Daisy, meanwhile, was keeping a close eye on Eric. Tired of watching this boring man with a white skirt round his neck and listening to him droning on, she noticed that Eric had been edging closer and closer to the front to see if the view was any more exciting from there. Now he had found the kneeling cushions in front of the altar rails and in one swift movement lay down on them. The slightest murmur rippled through the congregation and then smiles all round as Eric closed his eyes and went to sleep. The minister used to the unpredictable behaviour of small children on these occasions proceeded without faltering. Vows and rings were exchanged, the marriage register signed and, following a quick prod to Eric from his mother, the bridal procession left the church.

At Greenacres the champagne flowed, as did the tears from the Bride's and Groom's mothers during the speeches. Suddenly the newly-weds were in the taxi taking them to Southampton for embarkation and it was all over. Only the wilting flowers, crumpled napkins, some tired looking canapes and one jelly and an ice-cream stained aqua blue satin suit remained.

The wedding behind them, it was back to work as usual for Daisy and Mari and the first items on the agenda their two auditions. Mari was to read for Desdemona in a Stratford production of 'Othello' and Daisy for the lead in a new thriller to be produced first of all in Guildford and then hopefully transferred to the West End. Mari secured her role and accompanied Daisy to her audition the following day.

To their amazement when they arrived at the church hall there was only one man present, a Mr. Finlay, the Director. Assuming they were early and that others would soon start to arrive they seated themselves and waited.

"Miss Gold, here is the script. Would you please look at Act I, Scene II and be prepared to read in a few minutes."

"But…are we too early? Where are the others?"

"The others?"

"Yes, others reading for the part of Meriel."

"There are no others reading."

"What do you mean?"

"There are no others reading for that part, no-one except you."

"Why not? I don't understand…"

"It's just that Mr. Seymour said…"

"Mr. Seymour, what has he got to do with this?"

Mr. Finlay, reluctant to go further, hesitated, "Well Mr. Seymour, Monty, said that if you got the part, he would ensure that this play goes into the West End."

"He said what?" Daisy looked at Mr. Finlay and at her sister in amazement.

"Well that was the… arrangement."

"You're telling me that it was all pre-arranged that if you cast me in the lead in this play, then Mr. Seymour would ensure it went the West End?" Daisy turned to her sister and said, "Mari get your things together, we're leaving."

Finlay blustered, "But, you haven't read yet and…"

"Mr. Finlay I have not read yet and I have no intention of doing so. If I cannot be awarded a role on merit, then I do not wish to acquire it any other way. If Mr. Seymour gave you any other impression then you were misled and I apologise. I am sure you will be in touch with Mr. Seymour and I shall certainly be making contact with him. I think there's nothing more to be said. Good day."

Stunned silence from Mari as she got into the driving seat and then "Wow! You certainly told him." To her consternation Daisy burst into tears. "I can't believe Monty would do that. I know Rose occasionally eased our passage with a word here and there, but we always had to show our mettle by reading for the part and showing we were capable of handling it. This way…it was so humiliating."

"I agree. What now?"

"Now, I'm afraid I have to give Monty a blast he won't forget in a hurry and then see what else there is on the table suitable for me to do."

Back at the cottage Daisy phoned Monty. He had, as she had expected, already been contacted by a concerned Mr. Finlay.

"Monty, what on earth made you think I could accept a part under those circumstances?"

"My dear Daisy, it happens all the time."

"Not to me it doesn't. If someone came to me, as indeed Willard Jones did and said, 'I've written this part for you, will you do it?' That would be entirely different. But bargaining with roles and theatre availability, sorry I don't want to be any part of that. I felt so humiliated."

"I'm sorry Daisy. I didn't see it like that. You were right for the part, the fellow wanted to get into the West End, it just seemed the logical thing to do."

"Not for me, if I can't win a part by merit alone, then I'm afraid I'm not interested."

"Please accept my apologies, it was not my intention to offend you in any way and I'm truly sorry."

Rose had to know, and following the call to Monty, Daisy went to Greenacres. Rose's attitude was prosaic. "It happens all the time I'm afraid, which doesn't excuse Monty from his part in this. What you will have to expect, is that the more well known you become and the more your talent is witnessed by people in the business, then they will make assumptions about your capability of playing a role they have in mind. In that case, as has happened to me often, I have been offered a part before others have been even consulted. I agree that this was slightly different and it is the question of bartering which has offended you. I am quite sure that Monty did not mean to do so and," with a twinkle in her eye, "would not dream of doing so again."

Later discussing it with Monty she said to him, "I always told you those two girls were quite highly principled. It must have taken Daisy quite some courage not only to speak up to the Director present and state her case, but to tell you, whom she knows so well, that she didn't want any sort of involvement in that sort of deal."

"So…I've learned my lesson. What is she going to do now?"

"She's going to read for 'The Shrew' at Stratford on Friday. There'll be plenty of stiff competition there to satisfy her, but fingers crossed."

Stiff competition there was, but Daisy was at her most dynamic. Fiery and energetic in the early scenes and then, reading as the married Kate, totally compliant, but with just the suggestion of hidden passion smouldering. She got the part.

The twins rejoiced on their way home. They would be at the Memorial Theatre in Stratford together, not on the same bill but playing alternate weeks. For Rose it was another major achievement. The girls were now each playing major roles at the most prestigious theatre in England. Surely the theatrical world was now their oyster.

The Cotswolds in late summer were a delight. On Sundays the girls would drive down to the canal-side, often taking a picnic. There they would watch the barges' slow progress, the horses on the tow-paths and the locks being regulated. After the heat of the theatre it was peaceful and relaxing. Each of them was conducting a long-distance relationship by letter. Lester was still in London, but Chris was somewhere on tour in the North. As Mari said, "If absence makes the heart grow fonder, then the four of us must be very fond of each other indeed."

The roles they were playing were exhausting, added to which Mari did not feel comfortable with the man playing Othello. As she said to Daisy, "Iago might be the villain of this particular piece, but if I had to choose between him and Othello, my money would be on Iago every time."

"I'm going to say to you exactly what Rose would say if she were here. It's like families, you can't pick and choose them, you're stuck with what you've got, so make the most of it. After all he wouldn't have been given the part if he was not a very good actor."

"I didn't say he wasn't a good actor. Far from it, he's excellent. But oh my goodness does he play on that fact. Thinks he should be treated like royalty. He's forever swanning around in his silk dressing gown smoking a Havana cigar. He's just so self-important, I can't stand him."

"Somewhat different from Rose then. She's ultra famous and so unassuming with it."

"Don't mention them in the same breath. There's another thing…"

"Yes?"

"Well in the dying scene, you know when Othello's killed me because Iago's planted it in his mind that I'm having an affair, well I always want to giggle."

"What, when you're supposed to be dying?"

"Yes and that's the point, I keep passing out and every time the audience is convinced that's it, she's gone, I seem to pop up and say something else."

Daisy laughing, "You're exaggerating. I've watched it, don't forget. It's very dramatic, it doesn't come across like that at all."

"You're being kind. Oh and there's something else. All that black make-up Othello has to wear. His face comes so close to mine and every night some of it rubs off on me. If we're not careful we're going to end up looking like coloured minstrels."

By contrast, Daisy was full of praise for her leading man Petruchio, played by a dashing young man who hailed from Kent.

"He's a very generous actor, never hogs the stage and somehow gives me every opportunity to play at my best. Our Director, Sam, is amazing, he's a really mercurial character, seems to be in half a dozen places at the same time and never misses a thing. His attention to detail is really formidable."

Mari had been thinking, "It seems to me in the long run it's a lot more fun playing a wicked character like Iago, or someone volatile like your Kate the shrew. Much more exciting than playing a wilting reed like Desdemona."

"You know what else Rose would say, if she were here?"

"No, but I'm sure you're going to tell me..."

" 'Always' and I quote, 'accept the role you don't think you can play. That's when you will dig deepest into your reserves and probably achieve your best performance ever'."

"That's far too many homilies for one day. I'm going to have forty winks."

"Sorry, I keep forgetting you're older than me."

Chapter 14

In Cape Town, Stephen and the new Mrs. Vickers were enjoying life to the full. The activity of the Waterfront area with its stunning backdrop of Table Mountain was an ongoing source of pleasure but it was the delight in each other which made it special. Estelle, Stephen found, bubbled over with enthusiasm for each new experience. She enjoyed talking to the people of different cultures and whilst he would not have instigated such conversations, he quickly found that not only did he learn a great deal from them but they were entertaining and stimulating. In one store selling gifts they were served by a delightful girl, her bearing singling her out as of the Masai tribe. She in turn introduced them to her half sister, a Zulu. The entire family, now born-again Christians, were courteous, happy people.

They visited the Medical School at the Cape Town University. Stephen was interested to learn that only English was spoken here and there was no shortage of students. Later, on a visit to Stellenbosch in vineyard country they found that at the university there, Afrikaans was the only language spoken. This area encircled by mountains with its lush vineyards and Dutch Colonial Mansions was like being in a different world from Cape

Town, now a thriving city. In quiet bays they saw dolphins leaping and laughed at the penguins waddling on the sand. At the Cape of Good Hope they kept their distance from the monkeys, wickedly intent on stealing anything which was edible or intriguing. They saw poverty and affluence and after a visit to the Cecil Rhodes museum, formed their own opinions about the way the country had developed.

At the end of the day, returning to their hotel and dinner, they discussed the day's events. Each gradually built up a more complete picture of the person they had married, learning their foibles and traits. And later still, each enjoyed what had first drawn them together, the other's physical attractiveness. Estelle had never been a shrinking violet and her attitude to sex was the same as to everything she did. There was to be no holding back, no forbidden territories. Life was to be explored fully and fully enjoyed. Loving and being loved, they bloomed.

The gentle journey home by sea enabled them to adjust to what lay ahead and to make plans. Some alterations were necessary at Stephen's flat.

"A new double bed is the first purchase," Estelle pointed out, "which will mean extra linen. I'll probably need to add one or two things, extra cutlery, that sort of thing, nothing major, it's a nice little flat."

"Darling, it's going to be a second little nest for us, buy whatever you think is necessary."

"Don't forget my work is irregular, when I'm 'resting' I'm not earning, so I shall be entirely dependent upon you, husband."

"I wouldn't want it any other way".

"If I become pregnant then I'll be 'resting' for a very long time."

"And I wouldn't want that any other way, either. The sooner the better is what I say. By the way are we settling for two? Another little dark eyed, dark haired girl and…"

"And another big fair-haired beautiful boy. Oh no, that's just the beginning. I think once we've got the hang of how to produce them, we ought to keep going."

"Perhaps it's time we had another practice." And they did.

Within three weeks of returning home Estelle found herself to be already glowingly pregnant, the happiness which she and Stephen exuded, embracing everyone with whom they came in contact. Her miscarriage at fourteen weeks was a devastating blow but as Stephen said it was not uncommon in the early weeks and at thirty six Estelle was not at an ideal age for child bearing. Tears were shed in private but their public faces showed them to be undeterred, with Stephen warning,

"Next time Mrs.Vickers, it will be feet up and behaviour strictly according to doctor's orders, *my* orders."

Monty had now, at Rose's request, taken over fully the administration of the Reece Theatre. She would accompany him there at least once a week. With a secretary in attendance, the afternoon would be spent in bringing all paperwork and accounts up to date, a walk-through inspection of the theatre, checking for any necessary work. This would be followed by an early dinner and then the theatre's evening performance.

Together Rose and Monty worried about Estelle, but were aware that giving voice to such worries would not help the situation. Often they had discussed Sebastian's paintings still housed at Greenacres and eventually decided, instead of sending them to another museum, they would open their own art gallery.

The idea had taken shape when they saw that a store with shop frontage had become vacant next to the theatre. The narrow front rooms opened into a large area at the rear, which Rose wanted to turn into a small restaurant.

"People coming to a matinee might want tea before starting on their journey home and equally people arriving for the evening performance, don't always want a full scale dinner, they need either a light meal before going into the theatre or when they leave. There's not enough room to provide that sort of facility in the theatre, this would be ideal."

"Right, I take your point, but can we please first of all decide about the paintings."

"The front rooms to be an art gallery with Sebastian's paintings taking pride of place. I think there are twelve in all and I am quite prepared to let four of those go as part of an opening attraction. The others, I think we should keep to entice people into the gallery, to have a look round."

"As always, you seem to have thought it through. Sounds good. I'm not sure whether up-market purchasers of paintings will mix terribly well with people popping in for coffee and cakes and you may find it is better to operate this in reverse, café at the front and gallery at the back, but we can only give it a try. Nothing to lose."

"Well I wouldn't say that exactly, the work will be quite expensive, but if all else fails we'll just enlarge it into a bigger restaurant, we're only round the corner from Shaftesbury Avenue after all, so the market is there."

The Reece theatre itself was not as yet showing a profit and Monty estimated that it would be at least one more year before it became established as a regular venue for London's theatre-goers. Monty had quickly made his peace with Daisy following the auditioning debacle and now said that he would like to have the girls in the December Music Hall at the Reece.

"Your Golden Girls have so much to give. This summer they will have worked hard at the classics, which let's face it are for a more rarefied audience. At the Reece not only will they be able to have fun but everyone else will enjoy participating in it."

"Strange isn't it? Just a few short years and now, well I just can't imagine life without them."

"I'm sure they probably say exactly the same about you...after all for several years now you've been there to advise, both as tutor and surrogate mother."

"I do sometimes wonder Monty, if I've been trying to compensate..."

"For what?"

"For not having Estelle with me when she was small."

"I thought we'd decided to leave all that in the past where it belongs. Come along my love, it's time to go home."

The end of the girls' contract in the Cotswolds and their cottage had never seemed so welcoming. Sarah made a fuss of them, allowing them to sleep late, undisturbed, for the first few days and then, when telephone calls became more and more insistent, decided that they must all get back into routine, with her delivering their tea trays at eight o'clock. Rose and Estelle had appeared well, though the twins thought they detected a slight sadness in the latter's eyes. Stephen they had not yet seen because of work commitments, nor Chris and Lester whose persistent phone calls had resulted in Sarah's back to normal regime. Both were invited for dinner on the fourth night, a Sunday, after the girls' homecoming.

It was a strange reunion. The weeks away, in spite of their exchanged letters, had broken the close bond, developed whilst they were meeting on a regular basis. For all of them, those weeks apart had been filled with new experiences, new acquaintances and it was going to be a while before they could feel as completely at ease together, as they had before. Chris had been singing the Minstrel role in 'Pirates' and Lester had been the soloist with a choir touring the cathedrals of the North, both demanding tasks and they too were exhausted.

Daisy shed a few tears that evening. "I won't say it was like meeting a stranger, but even his kisses were, well, not quite so intense. Do you think he's met someone else?"

"I doubt if he'd have been pestering Sarah with phone calls if he had. It's just well… Lester was the same. Goodness knows how those poor fellows managed who were separated from their families for three or four years during the last war, coming home must have been a nightmare for them and for the ones they'd left behind."

"I've had first hand experience of seeing a victim of that. Although of course the Major wasn't just separated from his family, he had been fighting in the trenches for much of that time, which must have been the most ghastly life imaginable."

"The only thing we can do, is just behave as normally as possible and I think things will gradually right themselves."

And right themselves they did. Very soon it was as if they had never been apart and as they were all currently 'resting', it was a rare opportunity for just enjoying themselves. Out of this was born the idea that the four of them might go on holiday together. Various venues were suggested and it was decided that it should be somewhere new for each one of them. The South of France fitted this requirement, was not too far away and fairly accessible, so Nice it was. Monty knew someone there.

"Of course," said Mari, "it's only what one would expect." He suggested that he make contact with his friends and if the foursome liked to book into a hotel for the first week, it might well be that they would receive an invitation to stay with his friends during the second week. He was, of course, absolutely right. Not only would the Sudberys be delighted to meet the Golden Girls and their young men, they would be more than happy to accommodate them for the whole period.

Daisy was rather reluctant. "It's not quite what we had in mind…"

"Never look a gift horse in the mouth. We're none of us so flush with money that we can afford to turn down an offer like this, at least I'm not, I don't know about the rest of you," was Chris's reply.

And so, on one blisteringly hot afternoon towards the end of the summer, they arrived at the home in Nice, of the Hon. Mr. Justin and Mrs. Lucinda Sudbery.

"It's a mansion!" Mari exclaimed.

"You didn't say we were staying with royalty," Lester retorted.

Daisy could only manage, "Oh, my!"

The opulence of the building, the magnificence of the gardens and the swimming pool, suggested a formality that was non-existent in its occupants. Lucinda was American and anyone less stuffy would be difficult to imagine. Completely unpredictable, her constant advice was "Relax, treat this as your home. If you want something please ask, it's really no trouble." Mid-forties, she was a large boned, full busted lady with blue-black hair and eyes as blue as the sea the house faced. The couple had been married for some ten years. Justin's business was…well, as Mari said rather vague. He seemed to have shares in transport, the Simplon-Orient Express frequently featured in his conversation, and also in the hotel industry, which was gathering momentum on the Cote d'Azur. There were two children who seemed to be almost entirely in the care of a nanny. Occasionally they were seen in the pool, or setting out for the beach, but never at meal times. The guests caught glimpses of a large staff, chauffeur, maidservants, chamber maids, barman even and gardeners.

Eating breakfast by the pool, reading in the shade, swimming and walking along the beach was a luxury that none of them had yet experienced, and in the face of such warm hospitality, they did just what was asked of them, enjoyed it. In the evenings Lucy, as she preferred to be known, and Justin joined them. They would have a drink in the gardens and then go into the cool elegant dining room to dine on French cuisine at its best. The Sudberys had on one occasion met Rose in London, were delighted at her newly won honour and amazed to learn of the wager and how it had been won.

"I can't believe, Mari, what you achieved in such a short time, I know Rose must be a wonderful coach, but all the same! And you Daisy, an even shorter time and now up there with the stars." The twins made self-deprecating noises. "No really, we have heard of you here in France, you know. I think it will not be much longer before someone is asking you to appear in Paris, if that happens we will drop everything and come and see you. Although of course we might visit London before that and see you there."

The boys were interested to learn from Justin the history of the Orient Express. His usual austere expression changed and his face lit up as he described the train to them, "It's such a beautiful thing. The dining cars and the saloon car are exquisite, everywhere you look there are bowls of flowers reflected in polished surfaces, there's even a grand piano. And the views through those big windows, especially travelling through Switzerland and Austria are unbelievably beautiful."

It was at this point that Chris decided that when he and Daisy got married, a journey on that train, would form a part of their honeymoon. Of course he hadn't actually asked her yet, but he just couldn't envisage her refusing him, they were so good together. And if he hadn't pressed her for intimacy it wasn't because he didn't want her, God no, it was because he respected her too much, didn't want to spoil things, wanted it to be the right place and the right occasion, and if that meant waiting until they got married, well a good many people did just that.

Lester was starting to feel rather desperate. When could he ever manage to provide Mari with this sort of luxurious lifestyle? Clearly she was loving every moment of it.

The money he earned from music would allow them to live in reasonable comfort but this... Today she and Daisy had accompanied Lucy to the fashionable shops she used. Mari had returned with underwear made, she said, in Paris, from triple ninon and appliquéd. From the glimpses of them which he was allowed, they appeared exquisite and had probably cost a small fortune. At the moment the twins were subsidised quite a bit by Rose Reece but even so, if this was how Mari expected to live...

"A far cry from living on the farm, isn't it, little sister?" this from Mari, in the middle of brushing her teeth.

"I always knew there was something missing there. Whatever happened to the swimming pool? And I never did get my private bathroom."

"This, dear Daisy is how the other half lives. I mean, we've always loved Greenacres, it's charming, but this is just amazing."

"It's also way out of our league."

"Why do you say that? Surely if you're ambitious the sky's the limit."

"I think if you dabble in stocks and shares you might be in the market for something like this and it sounds as if Lucy's American Pa is very well-heeled, but can you really imagine, on the sort of money we theatrical people get paid, that it would ever run to anything as palatial as this?"

"It looks as if I might have to have a drastic change of plan and start searching for a very rich man. I'm sure I'm cut out for this type of life-style."

"And I think you're getting too big for your boots again, as usual. Just be thankful you're currently seeing a handsome, talented young man who thinks the world of you and settle for that."

"Not starting to fancy him yourself are you?"

"*I* am quite satisfied with what I've got thank you. Good night!"

Nevertheless at the end of the fortnight, with the exception of Mari, they were all ready to return home. Sometimes, Lester felt, after lovely experiences, it's necessary to come up for air, to resume the routine which gives one a sense of reality and order. Perhaps we all need the discipline of that he decided, I certainly do. Goodness, I haven't done any serious singing or worked at my music for two weeks. I've got a Lieder concert in November and before then a lot more work to do on my German language skills. I'll have a lot to catch up on.

Chris had come to a momentous decision. As soon as he had some money saved up, he was going to write to Justin and ask if he could purchase some shares in the Orient Express. It was worth a try, after all he could only say no. If it was as good as Justin had said, and there was no reason to doubt his word, then it could be successful for years. Once Europe had recovered from the war, people would start travelling abroad much more and the Express could become even more popular. It would be worth trying to get in early and make sufficient money to allow him and Daisy to live in the style to which they might not yet be accustomed, but had certainly tasted and liked.

Daisy had enjoyed the break and revelled in the luxury provided, but like Lester, she missed the framework of a routinely ordered day and was now ready to work again. There was so much to learn! She and Mari had really only touched the fringe of the classics and, as yet, they hadn't taken part in the sort of musical which was just starting to filter through from New York. My tap dancing certainly isn't up to scratch for anything professional, so I think I'm going to ask for more lessons in both that and some elementary ballet routines. The latter will at least help me look graceful in those dream sequence numbers which now seem to be popping up all over the place. I've missed Rose too. She's become our rock, a reference point to which we're always able to turn. Every now and again I seem to think 'I must ask Rose about that'. What would we do without her?

Back at the cottage was an offer from Monty regarding the Christmas Music Hall at the Reece Theatre. He explained that he was inviting Lester and Chris to join them and the four of them would top the bill. They could then sing solo, duets and as Lester was a counter tenor he was sure the Musical Director would be able to adjust quartet pieces so that the four of them could sing together. As he said, there was a wide range of material to draw on in the Gilbert and Sullivan operettas, but the American musicals and songs by Ivor and Noel could, with their permission, also be used.

To the surprise of the others Lester declined. As he explained to the twins,

"I know I was playing Music Hall when we first met, but at that stage I needed to do everything possible to keep myself in the public eye. To be honest Music Hall is not my scene, I prefer the classical arena. I've now had an offer to sing the lead in 'Carmen' in Paris, about which I'm really excited. This is what I want to do.

So, I'm sorry girls, much as I would have enjoyed your company, the Music Hall's not for me."

Consternation all round. Suggestions from Rose, phone calls by Monty. At last after drawing several blanks, he decided, with apologies to Chris, to revert to his original idea of the Golden Girls topping the bill with Chris in second place, his profile not being quite so high as that of the girls, this in spite of the fact that he'd been longer on the circuit. And so their plans started to take shape. Several Gilbert & Sullivan items of course. Then with Noel at the piano a musical sketch, Daisy as the daughter and Mari the formidable mother in Noel's own song 'Don't put your daughter on the stage, Mrs. Worthington'.

At Rose's suggestion they put together a musical tribute to Marie Lloyd who had collapsed and died on the stage at the Alhambra theatre the previous October. Rose and Monty had been present on that evening and deeply affected by it. When Marie had first slipped to the floor they, and the audience, had at first thought it part of her comedy act. Several seconds elapsed before they all realised this was not the case. When the curtain came down and the announcement was made, the entire audience had been in tears.   Now Rose proposed, as a tribute, they perform a collection of Marie Lloyd numbers. This to include her two most famous songs, the one Mari had sung before, 'The Boy I love is up in the Gallery' and culminating in the song Marie Lloyd had made her own 'My Old Man said Follow the Van'.

The three of them all had favourites they wanted to include, and finally after some hard bartering it was agreed. Daisy would sing 'There was I waiting at the church', with Mari in suffragette outfit singing 'Fall in and follow me'. Chris's favourite was also included 'If you were the only girl in the world'. At the conclusion of their discussions and with the all important nods of approval from Rose and Monty, they heaved a sigh of relief and satisfaction. Performing was wonderful.   Performing something you especially liked, was even more so.

Estelle's absence from this meeting was explained to the girls by Rose. She was pregnant again. Steve had to be in town all week and she wanted to be with him, so they were staying in their flat. In this way, as Steve said, he could keep a closer watch on her activities, or as he would prefer, lack of them. He wanted her to take every precaution and not become overtired during these early weeks.

"That doesn't mean that as soon as he thinks it's safe for her to do so, she won't be back here and giving us all the run around. She'll certainly be more than happy to advise you on how to present the numbers you've selected and will contact the choreographer again on your behalf."

Following Lester's comments on the way he saw his career progressing, there was a cooling of the relationship between him and Mari. As Daisy said to her,

"You should have seen this coming. He's always loved church music and high opera."

"I never thought it would make much difference to us as a pair, but I can see now I was wrong. We'll always be going in opposite directions, besides…"

"Yes, besides…?"

"I did sometimes think he was getting a bit…well, stuffy."

"I think you're being very unfair. Just because he's serious minded and shows it from time to time, doesn't mean he's stuffy."

"I know, I know, but I am only twenty after all, well almost, and I want to have fun. Time enough to be serious later. No, I think he and I have come to the parting of the ways."

So once again a separation between Mari and the latest 'love of her life', Daisy began to wonder if Mari would ever find someone who fitted her exhaustive requirements.

Chris, meanwhile, had gone ahead with his plans to contact Justin Sudbery regarding the possibility of shares purchase. Justin had been both helpful and encouraging. He fully understood that Chris would have to pace himself with regard to any purchases, at the same time he pointed out that Orient Express shares were not available and would not be so for the foreseeable future. He did however advise investment in their own new hotel range, the Sudbery chain. Currently there were six hotels in the Cape Province, eight in the States and Lucy's brother was about to open the first London venue. This, with a view to expanding in the U.K. during the next ten years.

Excitedly, he explained to Daisy, what he had in mind.

"I know we're both still young and I'm not suggesting we get married right away, but will you wait for me Daisy darling?"

"Do I take it this is a proposal?"

"Too right it is. You must know by now, I love you to bits. If you say yes, I'll happily go out tomorrow and buy a ring, but if you'd rather wait, not be tied down, I will understand. You're already famous with everything going for you and…"

"Yes."

"Yes?"

"Yes, Chris darling. I love you too and I don't want to wait before letting everyone know we're promised to each other. And as for all that stuff about being famous forget it. I'll be proud to wear your ring and I don't mind what it is, or where it comes from. After all when all these shares you're going to buy rocket in value, you can always change it for the biggest diamond you can find."

"Darling." And, if there had been stage curtains, this would have been an ideal time for them to close.

Lucy's brother Nick, descended on them during a Music Hall rehearsal. As Mari said, 'descended' was the most appropriate word, because Nick did nothing quietly, always making his presence felt. Even the Director's scowl at the sight of someone he didn't know, watching from the stalls, was no deterrent for Nick Jameson.

Medium height, slightly built, with his sister's black hair and very blue eyes, he spoke rapidly, with a patter which as Daisy said, would have 'stopped a market stall holder in his tracks'. However, after the hospitality the girls had received in France, they were anxious to make Nick feel as welcome as possible. With the exception of various visits to oversee conversion of several buildings in the creation of the new hotel, Nick was unfamiliar with London. Now the first U.K. Sudbery was ready for opening and he was in permanent residence in the hotel apartment created for him.

It would have been churlish not to have invited him to their birthday party at the cottage, so it was there that he met Rose and Monty. Rose he knew by reputation and Monty, Nick had already met in the States. At his theatre visit he'd been briefly introduced to Chris.

He was amusing company, but after he had left, Mari commented,

"Too full of himself by half. Typical American, tries to hog the conversation. I mean, who does he think he is? It was our party and he practically took over."

Later, Rose tried to defuse the situation, "You have to accept Mari, that in new situations, people do often talk too much, it's a way of covering up their nervousness or apprehension."

"I can't believe he's got a nervous bone in his body. He's a hotel owner for heavens' sake, has to make people feel at ease."

"Exactly, and sometimes the way to do that, is to allow them to be silent while he does the talking. It's probably a habit he finds difficult to break. I think you're being rather harsh on him, I thought him a most pleasant young man. But, changing the subject, Daisy and Chris are looking very comfortable together. How do you feel about their engagement?"

"I think it's premature, they should have waited. There is so much Daisy and I want to do and I didn't really envisage Chris being a part of that. Now I suppose he'll always have to be considered."

"You're not jealous, feel you're being usurped?"

"I don't think so…I just wanted us to go on as we were for much, much longer."

"I can understand that, but I can't see Chris ever wanting to impede your careers in any way, he's far too generous by nature and he does understand the necessity for you to continue to experience new ventures. I think Chris himself will be doing just that.

"He was telling me this evening that when his contract with the Doylys comes to an end in the spring, he will not ask for it to be renewed. He too, has his eye on the new musicals in the pipeline and as an experienced tenor, there should be plenty of scope. Would you believe he's asked me to contact the dance teacher you have, to arrange lessons for him? He wants to learn as many basic steps as possible, so that he's prepared for whatever is on offer. Now that really is forward thinking."

Mari, remembering her own lukewarm reaction to Daisy's engagement felt somewhat chastened.

"Daisy, you're not yet twenty, don't you think you should have waited until you were older, shopped around a bit?" Mari's question was for once, tentative.

"No I don't. Chris is as steady as a rock. He was, after you, my best friend for some time before this. We've got so much in common with our professions and we love each other...end of story."

"I hope it is. If it's what you want, then I'm happy for you."

"You know, Mari, nothing and no-one is ever going to come between you and me. You're my other half, I won't say my better half, because there have been times..."

"Don't say any more, I was just getting all dewy-eyed and now you're beginning to spoil it, so stop right there." And she did.

Contrary to what they believed, the Music Hall rehearsal was not the first time Nick Jameson had seen the Golden Girls. A visit from the States several months earlier had left him one evening at a loose end. Wandering through the West End he had seen the posters of 'Double Trouble' and enquired at the box office if any seats were still available. Yes, he was told one or two singles were free and within minutes he was ensconced in the stalls. He was riveted by the two female leads. Both slender and beautiful and, absolutely identical. Several months later after his arrival in London, a letter from his sister had informed him that the same two girls, the Golden Girls and their partners were staying at her home in Nice. She also exclaimed about them.

"Nick, you must be losing your touch! Two gorgeous girls right on your doorstep and you haven't managed to seek them out. Amazing. Use me as an introduction if you wish, but do something, now! One is in a partnership which looks pretty stable, but the other... well it's worth finding out about that. They're already 'stars' in U.K. and I think

it won't be long before America discovers them. You've got a foot in both camps with hotel rooms as an extra incentive to anyone on the move. All this sounds very mercenary, but Daisy and Mari are in fact, as pleasant as they are lovely to look at. Go for it!"

And so, on that dull December afternoon he had gone into the Reece Theatre with every intention of making their acquaintance. The invitation to their birthday party the following week had been an unexpected bonus. He'd arrived with flowers, chocolates and balloons and from then on it had been plain sailing. With two major snags. Daisy it appeared, was already engaged to her singer boyfriend Chris and the other girl, Mari, didn't like him.

He had rarely met this reaction. Popular at school and college, successful at sports and with wealthy parents able to afford a home in Virginia, a New York apartment and a hunting lodge in the Rockies he was never short of friends. Driving back to the hotel after the party he began to wonder about that. Had they really been friends, or just hangers-on? Perhaps after all they, like Mari, didn't like him for what he was, but liked the rather wealthy baggage he carried with him. One half of him said it was better to walk away from the situation now, but the other told him to stay put, find out why she apparently found him objectionable and do something about it. There was something else. Seeing her against her home background he found her more attractive than ever. He'd followed up his sister's suggestion as something of a joke, now he found himself very attracted to a girl who obviously couldn't stand him. Whilst Daisy was fairly quiet, Mari was what the Americans would call 'sassy' and he liked that in a girl. She had an answer for everything and sometimes, judging by the anxious looks from her sister, spoke before her brain had really engaged with what she was saying. No, he wasn't going to give up without a fight.

Watching the twins at the Christmas Music Hall underlined what his sister had said. The audience loved them. He tried to analyse why this was. Obviously their talent was huge and they were undeniably beautiful. But he suspected the real admiration stemmed from the fact that everyone around him, as youngsters, had had aspirations to do well and now were witnessing two young women who had made their own dreams come true and the people around him were happy for them.

Meeting their co-performers after the show, Nick was impressed. This world was far removed from his own business empire, but it was filled with a wealth of creative talent. If some of them were a little well…flamboyant, with so much to offer in the way of literary and musical ability, that was excusable. Listening to Ivor and Noel talk, Nick was, to Mari's astonishment, silenced. She was unaware that his shrewd business brain was already going off at a tangent and considering the viability of after-dinner one man shows and cabaret.

So, Nick was actually capable of listening. In the presence of such masters as Coward and Novello, that was just as it should be, and Mari smiled at him warmly. It was this that prompted him to invite her to dine with him at the new Sudbery hotel. One week later, arriving in a haze of perfume, she was escorted from her car by a liveried doorman, greeted by Nick and shown to her seat. Service in the palatial dining room was deferential. Clearly as Managing Director, Nick was much respected.

At his suggestion they adjourned to his flat for coffee and she was able to see that the view of the city at night-time was, as he had said, spectacular. His two-bedroom flat was tastefully decorated, but thought Mari, so obviously a bachelor flat, lacking a woman's touch.

She asked him about his family. "Dad made his money from soup. Yes, soup. You won't know it over here, but Jameson soup is a household name in the States."

"All soups?"

"You name it, we sell it. A few years ago he branched out into ketchups and pickles, what you call chutneys. They're popular too, but it's soup that made the money initially."

"Has your father retired?"

"No way. I don't see that ever happening. He and Mum are always on the move. Our home is in Virginia and that's where most of our factories are, but Dad has offices in New York and they often stay in our apartment there, or they did. I think now we'll have to consider having a permanent flat in one of the New York hotels for them."

He hesitated, "Sorry, I'm talking too much, it's a habit I have…"

Now why did he say that I wonder? Mari thought, perhaps he knew it had annoyed me. Aloud she said, "No, no I did ask. I like to hear about the States. I'm hoping Daisy and I will go there in the not too distant future."

"When that happens and I'm sure it will be 'when' rather than 'if', don't forget I would want you to be my guests at one of our hotels in New York, the one that's most convenient for Broadway. Now, what about you, is that right you were born on an island?"

"A tiny island off the South Coast. It's very pretty and in the summer when it's surrounded by yachts of all shapes and sizes, it's really quite something."

"Then that I must see. We Yankees are really fond of sailing, everyone who can afford it has a boat, however small. I guess I was all of eight years old when I learned to sail the tiniest dinghy you've ever seen, but that love of the water stays with you forever. It certainly has with me."

And so the evening concluded. No animosity. A growing admiration on her part for what Nick had to cope with and clearly did well, the welcome knowledge on his part that she was at last talking to him, but most of all the delight that she was not only a beautiful girl, but sassy with it.

Chapter 15

Estelle's baby was born in the Spring. 'Our Easter chick' as Stephen said. His wish for a miniature Estelle was realised, a baby girl, dark-haired and blue-eyed. The bad news was given to him, before it was relayed to his wife. There were to be no more babies. Estelle's tiny frame had resulted in a high forceps difficult birth with a huge loss of blood and the inevitable weakness afterwards. She was heart-broken when told that her dream could not be realised. Constantly he reassured her.

"Estelle my darling, we have a beautiful baby, a daughter to love and cherish. There are many, many people who would give a great deal for that."

"I know, I know. I should be, and I am grateful, but I'd so hoped we'd have several babies and that I'd be able to give you a son."

"It's not to be and we must think positively. Just concentrate on the fact that this little one is healthy, has all her faculties and is already our joy and pride. So, first things first, she hasn't a name yet, what is it to be?"

"I think you've just said it. As she's our joy, that's what we must call her, Joy."

"Lovely, Joy, yes I like that. And now, Mrs. Vickers, I have my own suggestion with regard to names. I know how much Rose means to you and your regret that you were not recognised as her daughter years ago. I think our little princess, Rose's granddaughter should have Reece in her name. How does Joy Reece Vickers sound?" Estelle dried her tears, "Brilliant, my darling. How soon can we tell Rose?"

Rose had agonised over her daughter's difficult birth and now worried about the distress Estelle was suffering that there could be no further children. Realistically Rose knew Estelle was probably coming to the end of her child-bearing years and that further pregnancies would have taken their toll. At least her new grandchild was whole and healthy, so there was much to be thankful for. It was so often said, 'God moves in mysterious ways'. Perhaps what had happened was for the best.

Her own plans for the new restaurant adjacent to the Reece theatre had now come to fruition, Sebastian's paintings had been hung and on the launching day two of the four she had allocated, had been sold. Surprisingly, one had been purchased by Nick Jameson, who had insisted that living in a bachelor flat was not ideal and it would be nice to have at least one striking item to return to each evening. He was an unpredictable young man. Was he trying to demonstrate to Mari in particular, that he was not such a plebeian after all or was he genuinely trying to get to grips with as many aspects of the creative arts as possible? Clearly that would not prove difficult for someone as highly intelligent as he undoubtedly was. Whatever his aim, Mari was impressed. Not, Rose felt and hoped, because it was an expensive purchase, but because Nick had asked searching questions about the mode and techniques involved in the production of Sebastian's work.

Theatregoers were now flocking into the restaurant for snacks at lunchtime, afternoon tea and light suppers. A number of artists had been anxious to display their work for sale in the anterooms and Rose had acquired a good cross-section of water-colours, portraits and oils, trying to keep the prices reasonable. As she said to Monty,

"It's not my intention to go into competition with the major art galleries. People today want nice things in their homes, but the prices have to be realistic. This way the purchasers select exactly what they like and what suits their homes and the artists are rewarded for the work they've done. Sebastian's paintings are just a draw and will hopefully encourage them always to look for the best, whatever the genre."

Often now Rose wondered about her father. Theirs had been a dysfunctional family, brought about by his own philandering. Had there been more depth to the wager he had left in his will than she had first imagined? He had certainly known about Estelle, had known that in order to further her career Rose had sacrificed the opportunity of a mother/daughter relationship from birth. His barb about how long it had taken Rose to become a major actress was perhaps indicative of how seriously he had taken her decision, comparing it with his own lack of commitment to his family. Had he thought that in this respect she had been deprived? Perhaps the challenge had been not after all a challenge of her coaching ability. Had he believed that the introduction of another young person into her life would in some way compensate for the years of motherhood she had missed? There was no doubt about it that she had hugely enjoyed having Marigold and later, Daisy in her home, watching them develop from schoolgirls into young womanhood. But Estelle had always lived on her doorstep, close enough for Rose to watch her grow and learn, surely Sebastian had realised that. Whatever she had done at the time, she had done for what she thought was best and there was no going back.

Having learned from Daisy of Chris's intention to purchase shares in the Sudbery hotel chain, Rose enquired of Monty, "Is it a safe investment? I had thought of giving the girls some shares for their twenty-first birthday present. I know Chris is very conscious that Daisy is now earning more than he is and that the position is likely to accelerate. I'd like to see that pairing continue and it would help provide a firmer footing if Daisy could also contribute shares."

"Safe? I've known Lord and Lady Baring, Justin Sudbery's parents, for twenty years. He's as honest as they come and I don't see how the hotel industry can possibly fail in the big cities where they're establishing a hold. More and more people can now afford to travel and visit places of which they'd previously only dreamed. I know these hotels are the top of the price range, but there's certainly a market for them. I'm thinking of investing myself."

"In that case, they've got to be good! I'll go ahead."

At the London Sudbery Nick had put into practice the idea he'd been mulling over since meeting Noel Coward on the Music Hall night. Although Rose had said a number of offers had come in for the twins, things were thin on the ground until the end of April. A meeting with Noel and the girls confirmed that they would be happy to reprise their 'Don't put your daughter' number from the Music Hall at an after- dinner cabaret at the Sudbery. The early months of the year were usually quiet in the trade and Nick felt this could give it just the boost required. He was right. Suddenly the restaurant was fully booked for several weeks in advance and Noel was prepared to continue entertaining alone, after the girls started on their next assignment.

Before that, there was more excitement for Mari. Lord and Lady Baring, Justin's parents had been invited to host a table at a Charity Ball at the Savoy just after Easter. This was for one of Queen Mary's favourite charities and as her close friends they were anxious to support it. They now had to withdraw because Lord Baring was ill. Justin and Lucy were unable to come over from South Africa but had suggested that Nick might be prepared to substitute. Nick, inviting Mari to join him in hosting the table, told her that the King and Queen would make a token appearance at the pre-dinner reception, but that the Prince of Wales would attend and stay for the evening.

"What exactly does this entail, Nick?"

"It entails raising as much money as possible. Every guest will have paid a great deal for a ticket, they will have contributed gifts for a massive lottery and there'll probably be an auction of some sort when people are expected to dig deep in their pockets."

"Am I going to be able to afford this?" Mari was half joking and half serious.

Nick looked horrified. "You are my guest, any contributions I make are on behalf of the two of us

309

and remember many of these guests represent different organisations so much of the money is coming, not out of their personal pockets, but from business sources. Inevitably because these are people who own companies or, are in very senior positions, I should warn you that they will probably be at least middle-aged and possibly older."

In spite of his warning, for Mari it proved to be a very special evening. The King and Queen as promised, paid a token visit during the reception and were introduced to each one of those hosting tables. As Mari made her much practised curtsey, the Queen said to her,

"I understand, Miss Gold, that you are a protegée of Miss Reece, and won for her that intriguing wager. My congratulations."

"Thank you, Your Majesty."

"Is your sister with you this evening?"

"No Ma'am."

"Ah, a pity. I would have liked to see you together. Perhaps another time."

"I trust so, Ma'am."

Mari was shaking by the time the royal party moved on, through a wave of bows and curtseys. Nick smiled at her, "You did well, it's a bit nerve-wracking isn't it? Whoops, here's another one."

The 'other one' proved to be the Prince of Wales, who was as charming as Mari had heard. By the time they moved in for dinner, her appetite had quite vanished.

At their table were three other couples, the owner of a steel firm and his wife, the Managing Director of a building conglomerate and his wife, and a man who, as far as Mari could ascertain, owned half the London docks. He was accompanied by his daughter who was a great deal nearer Mari's age, which helped her cope with what was as Nick had warned, a mainly middle-aged gathering.

Nick was an attentive host, danced with each of his lady guests and escorted Mari to the lottery table, where from a block of tickets she found she had won a beautiful and expensive pair of ear-rings. "Probably donated by Asprey's," Nick whispered in her ear. Mari gazed in astonishment as one of their table guests returned with her prize, a set of teaspoons from Mappin and Webb. It was all a far cry from the raffles she had seen at the Swanmore Village Hall, but the proceeds were going to sick children so, Mari reasoned, the end must justify the means.

Nick was a good dancer and obviously enjoyed it. As he explained later, "During the last two years, there hasn't been much time for dancing, or for anything other than work, to be honest. Once Justin found he had his hands full with the South African hotels I was given the chance to take over in the States and then here in U.K. It was quite a thrill for me. Normally a chance like this doesn't come until you're well into your forties. So…it was a challenge and I decided everything else would have to go until I felt on top of my job. I think at last the time has come when I can relax and enjoy both work and play. And make no mistake about it I do enjoy my work. A hotel is like a huge machine, every piece has to be well oiled in order for it to run smoothly.

"It's my job to ensure our guests go home feeling they have had a truly wonderful experience and would like to come back for more."

Mari was impressed. Rose had been right, it was only now that she was seeing the real Nick, who was proving to be more sensitive than she had thought possible.

The birth of Joy, whilst gladdening Rose's heart, had had an even more profound effect on Monty. Having just come to terms with the fact that he was a father and still finding himself gazing disbelievingly at Estelle for long periods of time, he now found another being existed, also flesh of his flesh and tied inextricably by blood. To see Estelle holding baby Joy, was for him a moving experience. The parameters of his world previously limited by business and friends were now redefined. With that realisation, came considerations of the future. Whilst telling him about Estelle, Rose had tentatively suggested that he might want to amend his will to ensure his daughter benefited. Now there was another reason for doing so.

But there was something else troubling him. He and Rose had been lovers for a time and since then the dearest of friends for many years. She was no longer in good health. At their age neither of them would wish to alter the way in which they lived and certainly not want to co-habit. But, it may be that for both of them and certainly for Estelle, marriage would put the final seal on a love which had survived the years, at the same time setting the records straight for his daughter and granddaughter.

The thoughts put into words, the arrangements were promptly made. No fuss, no publicity. The venue for the marriage, a registrar's office with just Estelle and Stephen as witnesses. The few newspapers into which the information inevitably seeped, handled it discreetly; Rose, was after all, the darling of the journalists. If some made the assumption that this was just a pairing between two old friends they were not enlightened, those who hinted at other reasons were ignored. Within two days it was stale news and forgotten.

Rose now glowed with happiness. It had never been her wish to disrupt Monty's lifestyle but now, in this way, they could occasionally all enjoy being together as a family without any feelings of recrimination. Her life was still full as was Monty's . When Estelle was not at Greenacres there was much still to be done on the twins' behalf. The offers of work for them still on the table covered more Shakespeare at Stratford, Gilbert and Sullivan, Restoration Comedy , two thrillers and a comedy by a new author Anthony Woods. The latter she thought was a must. 'Three's a Crowd' concerned two sisters vying with each other to secure the same young man and was a witty well written account of sibling rivalry. Yes, she would definitely earmark that one, on the others she'd prefer to hold back for the time being. It was reassuring to know that they were so much in demand. I think if I could choose I'd like to see them do the comedy next and then perhaps a full musical where they would get plenty of on-stage experience of dance routines. To date, what they've done in that line has been chorus work or limited to one or two people dancing with them. What they really need is working as the principals with a chorus line. Keeping up with the standard of professional dancers is always the acid test. I remember… And suddenly she was back on stage in a diaphanous gown, in a haze of dry ice and rose petals, whilst a stringed orchestra played somewhere in the depths of the orchestra pit. Ah, those were the days...

Mari had always known that it was inevitable that she would at some time bump into Lester on the theatrical circuit. She had not however, expected him to come knocking on the door of the cottage so soon after the end of their courtship. He was there one morning and to her amazement, without preamble, said he had made a terrible mistake and realised now that he was in love with her and could they please start all over again. Uncharacteristically nonplussed, she played for time. "Let's go and sit down and I'll ask Sue to bring us some coffee." She'd never seen him nervous before. Now he sat on the edge of his seat and seemed to be constantly fingering his shirt cuffs. Yes he said, he'd had a successful tour in Germany and was now very fluent in the language. Yes, he had enjoyed singing lieder. The coffee arrived and they started again.

"Lester, I'm more than happy to see you, and glad everything has gone well. But in all truthfulness, I can't see our relationship going anywhere. I'm just twenty and there are so many things I want to do and experience. We're in the same profession but poles apart really. How often is our work likely to overlap, as it did on that one occasion at the Music Hall? We'll always be going in opposite directions and involved in very different productions, that's no basis for a sound courtship."

"I can't go along with that Mari. All over the world there must be couples who operate in very different spheres of work, but happily co-exist."

"Perhaps, but I feel it must put a strain on them. One of the joys of being together must surely be comparing notes about something you both understand and are part of.

"In any event, it's fair to tell you that I'm currently seeing someone else."

"And he's in your profession?"

"Well no, actually…"

"So, your point was?"

"Alright, touché. Nick's in business, but he does have some involvement with cabarets, that sort of thing…"

"You're stalling."

"Yes, I am. I don't know that I can put this any more plainly. Happy as I am to see you now and again as a good friend whose company I enjoy, I want you to be absolutely certain of the fact that I am making no promises whatsoever about the future."

Disconsolate, he left, but she felt Lester had at last realised that he was wasting his time. Daisy did not mince her words,

"What is it about you and your men friends? Nothing ever seems straightforward, there are always complications. You're not seeing the Prince of Wales I suppose?"

"Daisy, what a ridiculous thing to say. Of course I'm not seeing the Prince of Wales, why on earth would you think that?"

"Only joking, it's just that I'm hearing all sorts of rumours about his lady-friends and that there could be trouble there and as you seem to have a nose for that sort of thing, I wondered…"

"Then put it right out of your head. I might have friends in high places but, so sorry to disillusion you Sister dear, they're not that high."

"And while we're on the subject of men friends, what about Nick? After your complete volte face in that direction, has he suddenly won your heart?"

"Now you're being ridiculous. No, he hasn't won my heart. But I have changed my mind about him, quite considerably, now that I know him better. He's a lot more sensitive than I thought an American could possibly be and, well, I'm biding my time."

"Well I'm glad to see you've at last realised that making generalisations about people of different nationalities, colours and creeds is a waste of time."

"Yes Ma'am! Here endeth the first lesson."

Nick had been more persistent of late. She had finally agreed to accompany him on a trip to Bath, where he wanted to explore the possibility of it being a suitable venue for the next U.K. Sudbery hotel. It had been an enjoyable weekend. She now realised that it was only when Nick was meeting business colleagues that he seemed to acquire a slightly different persona, with the rather incessant patter which had irritated her at their first meeting. Daisy was right in one respect, her own first impressions had been ill-judged and were wrong. This change in Nick occurred only when he was in a new situation, so that contrary to her belief, he *was* nervous. When they were alone he was on occasions quiet, often witty, and always courteous. He now kissed her in greeting when they met in the hotel dining room for breakfast and again when he left her at her bedroom door. Never did he presume any further intimacy and for that she respected him.

The invitation to the Golden Girls to attend the June Garden Party at Buckingham Palace arrived at the beginning of May. Now it was Daisy who was beside herself with anticipation. What to wear? Which was the correct type of curtsey? Justin's parents Lord and Lady Baring were to be present and wrote suggesting that if the girls were able to attend, then they would be happy to collect them from Richmond. Their daughter-in-law's brother Nicholas would also be there, but had arranged to meet them at the Palace.

The girls finally settled on shell-pink silk dresses with matching jackets and accessories. Although the latest fashion in hair-styles was the bob, at Rose's advice they had kept their own hair long, pinning it into chignons when necessary. As Rose had pointed out, in so many plays long hair would be necessary because of the period and whilst wigs were available it was always preferable to have one's own hair. "Wigs can get very hot under the lights, especially in a heat-wave. At some point you will obviously succumb to the fashion, but I would suggest holding back as long as possible." On the morning of the Party, a local hairdresser came to the cottage and dressed their hair, so that it fitted neatly under their hats, but at the sides gave the appearance of stylish bobs.

At the Palace, an equerry was grouping together those the King and Queen had wanted to meet and Daisy and Mari, with Nick as their escort were delighted to find themselves marshalled into one of these groups. Queen Mary's austere appearance relaxed into a smile when she caught sight of Mari and then seeing her identical twin, made a slight exclamation of amazement. "Miss Gold," Mari curtsied, "I'm delighted to see you again and this of course is your sister. They told me you were identical twins, but the resemblance is really quite amazing. Miss Gold," this to Daisy, "I am most happy to welcome you here. I trust you will have a pleasant afternoon. It will be my pleasure on a future occasion to see you both on stage."

Two pink-clad figures bobbed as one and two voices exclaimed in unison "Thank you Ma'am."

After that the tea and cakes, the music of the brass bands and the cloud of perfume surrounding the elegantly clad guests all merged into one. But as Daisy said "What a memory for us to treasure. Isn't the Queen wonderful, she's so regal?"

"Yes," said Mari, "but my feet don't feel regal, they're killing me!"

318

Chapter 16

Back to reality and Stratford, where they met up with Tessa Rainer once again and were pleased to learn they would all be in the same guest house. Tessa and Daisy were in 'As you Like It' whilst Mari had the coveted role of Cleopatra and was playing opposite a man who had had extremely good press, Graham Line. He was as delighted to have secured the part of Antony, as she was to be playing Cleopatra.

As he said, "It's quite awe-inspiring when you think of the famous people who have almost made the role their own."

"We have to put that right out of our minds," Mari knew she sounded rather prissy, "and be the characters as we ourselves see them. After all when we start on a new part, we're all in the same boat and can only try to pick up clues from the text. Who knows what was really in the author's mind? I always like that quote from Robert Browning, whether it's true or not is anyone's guess, when asked what something in one of his poems meant he said..."

"When I wrote that only God and Robert Browning knew what it meant, now only God knows."

Mari laughed, "It's so true though isn't it? We can analyse until we're blue in the face, but we don't really know. All we have to rely on is what the character says and of course the reaction of others to him."

"Right, so if I say I think Antony is vain and a lecherer, you would say?"

"That I'm inclined to agree with you and that he has met his match in an equally vain, supercilious creature who thinks she's God's gift to men."

And having neatly allocated two of history's most famous figures to very ignoble categories, they laughed together as they went in to rehearse.

Daisy too, was very impressed with Graham Line. He was tall and broad with dark hair and the brownest eyes she had ever seen, but it was the sum of these parts which made him on stage quite electrifying. In his Roman uniform he was devastatingly handsome with a directness which was so acute that once he appeared on stage he seemed central to everything that was said and done.

Rose had once warned the twins, "There are some performers who have such charisma that acting with them is a remarkable experience." (Daisy felt Rose had not mentioned that she herself had by all accounts been one such performer.) Rose continued, "You might think there is then the danger that no-one else on stage would be noticed, but in fact the reverse happens, such a performer will always bring out the best in everyone else and that is when a production will move from being a mere re-enaction of a plot to something quite outstanding."

Well, Daisy decided, if they were talking charisma, then Graham certainly had it in abundance. She herself was riveted watching him in rehearsal and for the first time ever, felt jealous that it was Mari and not herself, who had the role opposite him. When the twins were both in his company he was equally charming to them. Having quickly noted and remarked upon the unusual eyebrow which signified Daisy's identity, she was more than surprised when he asked her to have Sunday lunch with him.

Hesitantly she said, "I'm Daisy you know, you're not thinking…?"

"No, my dear, I'm not confused. I know exactly who you are. Isn't it time we got to know each other better?"

It was impossible to keep this from Mari, but embarrassing to have to tell her. She shrugged it off, saying he perhaps liked 'playing the field'. But Daisy decided following Graham's persistent advances on their afternoon country walk, that if this was a case of 'handsome is as handsome does', he had this afternoon turned from a prince into a frog. Perhaps he got some vicarious thrill from trying to make love on stage to one sister and off stage to the other. He might have succeeded in theory on the set, but had definitely lost out off-stage.

I am writing this down on Tessa's advice. She told me that psychiatrists always advise people who have had a traumatic experience to try and write down what happened, in that way they release a lot of pent-up anguish. So here goes…

A week after my unpleasant walk in the park with Graham, Mari and I decided to make the most of a free day. 'As you like it' had finished its run and the following night was the final one of 'Antony and Cleopatra'. We drove to Warwick, picnicked by the river and then stretched out in the sun. Bliss.

On our return to the guest house still exhausted after a busy week, we each decided to have an early night. Our twin-bedded room was at the back of the house and we had become accustomed to the background noise of Stratford's traffic. We each read for a while then switched off our bedside lights I was just drifting off to sleep when there was a tap on the door. Mari, the nearest, put her light on. "Who is it?" she called.

"Urgent message for Miss Gold" came a man's voice in reply. I suppose we both immediately thought of Rose. Mari leaped out of bed and I sat up as she rushed to unlock the door. There was a flurry of movement, a gasping sound and Mari was flung backwards on her bed. At the same time I was aware of a peculiar smell which I later learned was chloroform. Mari was still, very still, and as the figure silhouetted against Mari's light moved towards me, I now recognised the shape and build…it was Graham Line.

I grabbed my bedside light and hurled it in his direction, screaming 'Get out', then jumped out of the bed on the far side shouting 'Help, help!' The lamp was heavy and struck him in the stomach. He faltered and then, as sounds of activity came from further down the corridor, he turned and ran from the room. Banging the door behind him I turned to Mari, who was just stirring. Later we worked out he must have given her only a whiff of the anaesthetic to keep her quiet whilst he entered the room.

People were banging on the door and I called to them to come in. Tessa was first and I sobbed in her arms, incoherently trying to tell her what had happened. Mari was helped to the open window and the extra oxygen inhaled soon roused her. She was stunned, but totally unaware of the sequence of events.

The owner of the guest house had been at her desk. She said a man had come rushing in saying he had an urgent and serious message for the Golden Girls, which she had assumed to be genuine. With hindsight she realised that he had kept well back from her desk and nightlight so that she had not actually seen his face. Eventually at one o'clock in the morning, we tried to sleep, Tessa insisting on bringing eiderdowns and blankets and sleeping on the floor of our room.

We had no proof. Only Mari and I had seen Graham. Mari only momentarily, before the chloroform pad was thrust into her face and I, in what others might classify as half light.

We were plagued by thoughts of what he had intended. Did he hope that after the first shock, we would welcome him into our beds? Had he planned to sedate me also and then perform some vile three-party sex act on us whilst we were still semi- conscious? The whole event beggars belief. Mari and I had early been made aware that there are men around who are to be watched carefully, particularly if the stage outfit you are wearing is in any way revealing. They are referred to as 'the gropers'. But this, this was in a different league altogether.

The next morning Tessa got in touch with the Director, Gordon, and asked him to call. Shocked, he yet had to consider practicalities. A full house was booked for that night's final performance. Did Mari think she would be able to play opposite him?. An unequivocal 'No'. In that case he must go and alert the understudy that she would be performing. He asked if we intended pressing charges and we said that lack of concrete proof and identification would make this too difficult, in any event we just did not want that sort of adverse publicity. Gordon's next request was that we discuss it with no-one until the final performance was over. He would say merely that Mari was very unwell and had sent her apologies. With regard to Graham, he decided that no mention of the incident would be made to him until after the show. Gordon would then interview him and tell Graham that although we were not pressing charges, Gordon had accepted our story. And, a surprise to Mari, Tessa and me, there had been another complaint about Graham's unwelcome advances from one of the girls in the 'Cleo' cast. In view of this, and the seriousness of the offence against us, Gordon planned to tell him that he would not be appearing at Stratford again and that word of his sexual proclivities would soon spread and mar, if not curtail completely, his future career.

We were badly shaken. Yes, we had often talked about love and sex as young people do, but in romantic terms. What had almost happened last night would have been a violation of our personal liberty, the right to make our own decisions about such matters. Suddenly we realised that we often placed ourselves at risk. Making ourselves attractive for the stage, we could inevitably be a target for perverts and people like Graham, who seemed to imagine themselves above the law and were determined to satisfy bodily urges at all cost.

This was a lesson learned in the hardest of ways. From now on we are going to be much more careful of our personal safety. With so many kind people around, it saddens me that we should have to curtail our own freedom because of those with ugly minds and ugly tendencies.

Back to the cottage and there was concern from everyone at Greenacres about what had happened. Although the twins were now almost twenty-one, Rose had since their first arrival at her home, regarded herself as in *loco parentis* and now felt she had been neglectful of her duties. Perhaps, as before, she should have organised some sort of chaperone, another older woman to whom the twins would have been able to turn when a problem arose.

Seeing her distress, Mari said quickly,

"But one thing we have learned from this is how careful we must be in the future, so you're not to worry about us."

And Daisy added, "We realise now how stupid we were to open our door late at night, without being absolutely sure who it was."

Then Mari chipped in again with, "And we've also realised what a good friend we have in Tessa, she was brilliant, looking after us and staying with us when we still felt rather shaky."

Chris had learned of the incident, probably on the theatrical grape-vine, and was on the phone at once to see if the girls were unharmed or if there was anything he could do. Nick was next, arriving in person, furious at Graham Line's behaviour and quite set on having him charged. Patiently the girls explained the lack of proof about the intruder's identity. The chloroform pad in their bedroom could have come from anywhere and put there by anyone. No, there was nothing for the police to go on, but equally patiently they explained they didn't want the publicity.

"Surely you theatrical people always say 'Any publicity's good publicity'."

"In this case we don't agree," Mari said.

Daisy added, "Think about it, the last thing we want is for people to say when they hear we're in a play, or whatever, 'Oh yes, the Golden Girls, they're the girls who were in that peculiar bedroom case'. Ten to one there would be someone who would suggest that we must have been asking for trouble. Our audiences can be quite fickle you know, they will go along with you up to a point, but after that…"

And Mari added rather wistfully, "As it is, the fact that I was supposedly ill on the last night of 'Cleo' meant that reports were rather more concerned with what was wrong with me, than about the show as a whole…"

Nick's parting shot was, "You two had better just hope I never come across that fellow, because I make no promises that if it happens, I won't break his neck."

They endeavoured to put the whole incident to the back of their minds. But sometimes they would discuss the nasty problems they had had with Celia and then that awful night in Stratford. From that point on, as they had promised Rose, they were very wary of their mutual safety and security.

Two weeks' break and they were due to start rehearsing "Three's a crowd," Estelle ruefully remarked to the girls. "Your next play couldn't have had a more unfortunate title if you had set out to find one."

The girls agreed, but as Mari said, "We have to live with it and perhaps it will help us lay the ghost of that night."

There were three pleasant surprises in store for them. The first was that Tessa read for and secured one of the lesser roles, the second that the play was to be staged at *their* theatre, the Reece, and last of all that Nick was insistent that there would be a double room at their disposal in the Sudbery for the length of the run. He brushed aside their protestations.

"I do not like the thought of you having to get back to Richmond each evening after a performance, when you're tired. In this way you will have a base in the city and, from a purely selfish point of view, I'll know that you are safely installed in my hotel. Your laundry will be dealt with and there will be no shortage of food available. There will be some occasions of course, when you want to go home, at the weekends for instance and to see Rose and Estelle. As long as I am made aware that you are doing so, I will not worry. Please say yes, if only to prevent my hair turning grey very, very quickly."

In the face of such kindness they agreed it would be churlish to refuse. There was a postscript from Nick "All I ask is that you keep me a seat on both the opening and closing performances, so that I can encourage you at the start and congratulate you at the finale."

As Mari said afterwards, "I really got it wrong about him, didn't I? I can't believe how thoughtful he's been about all this."

"Now there's an admission, Big Sister. Could it be that the first hint of love is in the air?" Daisy was laughing.

"You'll be the first to know. Now can we get on with these scripts?"

The comedy, as Rose had decided on her first perusal, was well structured, with Anthony Woods capturing brilliantly the quick-fire repartee between two young girls, each anxious to win the same beau, but at the same time hoping that to do so would not mean the losing the love of their sibling. The scenes where each pretended to be the other, were hilarious and soon, as Rose and Monty had anticipated, the comedy was playing to packed houses at the Reece.

The hotel arrangement worked very well. In fact, as Mari said, they were being thoroughly spoiled there. "Room service on demand," she told an astonished Rose and Estelle. "Nick says if we're hungry, we've to ring for food, rather than go into the dining room, especially if it's late. As you both know it takes a while at the end of an evening on stage for the adrenalin to stop pumping, so we need a hot drink before retiring and sometimes a snack too... we never feel like eating much prior to the show. It's such a delight when the scrambled eggs and bacon arrive at ll.0 p.m. and a gorgeous pot of hot chocolate. By that time we've bathed and got into our night things and dressing gowns and can put our feet up and be utterly and totally relaxed."

For Rose, the relief was tremendous. Nick had struck her from the start as an efficient administrator. The success of his hotels to date was evidence of that. He was also a thorough gentleman and although unfamiliar with the theatrical scene had gone to great pains to ensure that any plans were always built around the rather erratic life-styles the girls inevitably lived. He had discussed this with her on one occasion.

"But Miss Reece, Rose, this is in fact very similar to the sort of life I lead. Mine is determined by the volume of guests in the hotels, the efficiency of my staff, but often a problem is brought to my door and I must deal with it at whatever time of day or night. I think it would be very difficult for any woman to marry a man such as me. What sort of a life would she be able to lead?"

This sounded to Rose very much like a young man needing help as to if, and how, he should progress in a courtship.

"I think, Nick, you would find that if you are ideally matched, then the two of you together would be able and willing to make all the necessary adjustments to your life-styles. We've moved on since the war. Once it became clear that women could hold down jobs whilst men were away fighting, massive social changes occurred. Women no longer are expected to stay at home all day and just raise families. Now many of them are attempting both to go out to work and enjoy having children. If they have talents they can share with others that would seem reasonable, especially if there is sufficient money to ensure children are not at risk. But," seeing he was about to continue the discussion, "these are momentous decisions and only the people involved can make them."

On the surface, life at Greenacres maintained its usual tranquillity, but there was an ominous undercurrent. Stephen was aware that Rose was becoming increasingly unwell. His medical knowledge had alerted him to symptoms which might have passed unnoticed to others. On several occasions watching Rose replacing her cup onto the saucer, he saw that she no longer did so with her usual precision. Sometimes she would have two or three attempts before the cup sat properly in the well of the saucer, to avoid spillage. Clearly her reflexes were no longer one hundred per cent normal. Meeting her on the landing he had noticed an increased breathlessness. Reluctantly, he decided it was time to alert Estelle to these facts,

"I don't want to alarm you, my darling, but there are things you need to be aware of. For instance Rose so loves holding Joy. Do try to ensure that she does that only when seated. You must deter Rose on whatever pretext, from moving around carrying the baby. If heaven forbid, Rose did collapse, then Joy would go down with her, perhaps under her. Say that Joy was just going to have a sleep, any excuse so that Rose herself doesn't become aware and frightened."

Estelle *was* frightened. Having just 'found' that her dearest friend was also her mother, even the suggestion that Rose's life might be in jeopardy was hard to contemplate. But she took to heart Stephen's warning that Rose herself must not be worried and nervous and tried to maintain a cheerful disposition when in her company. The baby's presence helped. Gurgling and smiling at anyone and everyone she had imperceptibly added to the quality of their lives.

In view of Stephen's warning, Estelle was even more alarmed when Rose started to make noises about the twins' twenty-first birthday. As she said to him later, "I can't say this will be all too much for you, let's keep it very low-key, she would immediately be suspicious of my motives."

"No, I agree, but what we can do is ensure that the majority of the planning is taken out of her hands. There are after all party organisers who would handle everything. Has she given any indication of where she wants this to be?"

"No, I did wonder..."

"Yes, you wondered...?"

"Whether a quiet word with Monty would be the way forward. He is probably the only person to whom she'd raise no objection. And then of course there's Nick, he has been so kind to the girls and I understand there are all sorts of different sized function rooms at his hotel."

"Brilliant my darling, on both counts. I always did say you were not just a pretty face. Why don't I telephone Monty, you contact Nick and we'll ask them if they would get together and make some preliminary plans? That way as soon as possible we can present Rose with a fait accompli and it will appear to be their idea."

The men met and decided that a room at the Sudbery would be ideal. The girls were to be told merely that they were all going out to dinner, but as a surprise, as many of their friends as could be gathered together, would be invited. Nick would phone Rose and agree on a menu and table flowers, so that she would feel involved and Estelle would start to compile a list of people with whom the twins had been closely associated over the past few years. Noel and Ivor were to be invited and asked if they, together with Estelle and Chris, would provide a short cabaret after the meal.

It was a happy chance that their birthday fell on a Sunday. Once Sarah had arrived with morning tea into each room, Daisy picked up her tray and moved in with Mari.

"Many happies dear Sister. Can you believe that we're now twenty-one and presumably fully-fledged?"

"Many happy returns to you too little one. I'm not sure about the fully-fledged bit, if that entails everything I think it should, then I don't think we're quite there yet."

"As far as I'm concerned, life already seems complicated enough, without any further distractions."

"Couldn't agree more. You have your lovely Chris, who seems happy enough to wait until his bank account is loaded and I have…"

"Yes?"

"Well I have Nick, who's a wonderful escort and I'm very fond of him."

"I sense a 'but' there…and that's all?"

"Yes, for the time being. Now about this dinner tonight, what are you wearing?"

"Tea first, then let's sort something out for tonight. Bath time next and up to see Rose and the family, for coffee at about eleven."

"Daisy Gold, you're becoming more like a major domo every day. Today is for relaxing, remember?"

"Feeling our years are we, Sister dear?"

Gifts awaited them at Greenacres. Double ropes of pearls with a diamante clasp from Rose, gold chains with a small medallion, each inscribed with their initials from Estelle and Stephen and marcasite brooches from Monty. Nick's present had already been delivered and there were more exclamations of delight when they unpacked two matching short fur evening capes. Both girls were in tears at their astonishing array of gifts and were joined by Rose, who said "Tears of happiness are the sweetest tears of all."

Their delight at finding the Magnolia Room at the Sudbery awash with friends was very obvious. Fellow artistes, directors, producers, stage managers and stage hands, to all of whom they had been particularly close were included and the girls were showered with gifts and good wishes. Looking around Rose felt a glow of satisfaction. The twins were not just good on stage, but they were kind and thoughtful and this was very apparent from the cross-section of people who had been thrilled to join them on this occasion. All the hard work has been worthwhile, they have done me proud. I now have a wonderful family of my own with a beautiful granddaughter and as a bonus a talented surrogate family. Receiving my medal from the King was such a wonderful honour but this is the legacy of which I'm proudest, it's worth more than all the medals in the world.

Only Noel Coward was allowed to make a speech. His tribute to the Golden Girls and to their tutor was witty and concise; then a signal from him to the Maitre d' Hotel, and the cake was brought in. It was a huge iced key, decorated with tiny golden marigolds, golden-hearted daisies and twenty one golden candles. A toast in champagne was proposed by Noel and the company drank to 'The Golden Girls, Mari and Daisy'.

Happy and tired, when it was all over, they went their separate ways. Stephen was particularly solicitous of Rose and ensured that her car left first and that Estelle accompanied her to help her to bed as quickly as possible.

Mari and Daisy waited with Nick and Chris until they were at last alone. There were thanks of course to Nick for all that he had done and for his wonderful gifts, then Chris and Daisy excused themselves and said they were retiring to one of the smaller lounges.

Mari laughing said, "They've gone to have a cuddle."

"Would we could do the same," was Nick's response.

Unusually, Mari was at a loss for words.

"I have never presumed on our friendship Mari, but I have for some time wanted, no *longed* to take it further. You must know by now that I care for you a great deal and want us to be like Daisy and Chris, a couple. I know my occupation has not the glamour of the theatrical world and I must seem a very humdrum sort of chap..."

"Humdrum never. You really are the limit Nick. Give me a hug for heaven's sake my love and let's get all this preliminary stuff out of the way."

Without further ado he embraced her and stayed holding her in his arms for several moments. Her silky hair, her perfume enveloped him, stunned him for a moment then,

"Am I really?" He gazed deep into those azure eyes.

"Are you really what?"

"Your love."

"Do you know I didn't really know until tonight, but I think you have been for quite a while," Mari smiled back at him. "You see I'd always told Daisy I would marry a rich man and I was worried that that might be what drew me to you. You always seem to cushion our lives to make things more comfortable. Now I see any spoils you might have are, like ours, the results of a great deal of gruelling commitment."

"So... are you my golden girl?"

"I'm not sure about the golden bit, but indisputably and without a doubt, darling Nick, I really am your girl."

"And I can tell the world?"

"We'll tell the world together."

It was a relatively quiet Christmas, the highlight of which was watching Joy's expression struggling with paper wrappings, to discover the exciting things underneath. Then at a small twelfth night party at Greenacres, Mari and Nick to everyone's smiling approval, announced their engagement.

Casting understudies for their roles in 'Three's a Crowd' was virtually impossible, as the parts had to be played by identical twins, so Monty ensured the girls had a break over the Christmas period by staging Music Hall for three weeks at the Reece. Now the time was up and they must go back to a full working week, with the show expected to run for at least another two months. Once again they were installed in their comfortable quarters at the Sudbery and as Mari said, it was "Back to scrambled eggs and bacon and cocoa at eleven."

The call from Estelle came late one Friday afternoon. Her voice breaking, she told Mari that Rose had had a severe heart-attack and was in a coma. Stephen then took over the call and said Rose's condition was being monitored all the time, she was comfortable, not in any pain and there was nothing any of them could do, but watch over her. The girls were devastated and said they felt they ought to be there. Estelle came back on the line and said, "I know how you feel and we appreciate it. Monty is here with us of course and what we all would say to you both, is what Rose would say, 'The show must go on'. Many people will have paid to see you this evening and you must honour that."

Monty came on the line next. "Girls, I know how difficult it is for you, but your acting skills will enable you to do this and as Estelle has said, it is not only what Rose would have wanted, it is what she would have expected from her two outstanding pupils."

And so they went through the motions, raised the laughs in all the right places and took their curtain calls, smiling. That night they returned to Greenacres and saw Rose. Her own doctor had arrived and he and Stephen agreed that the end would be within a few hours. Nervous and tentative, they entered Rose's room, her own private sanctuary. She was like a small, perfect porcelain doll, her alabaster-like skin smooth and unlined and Estelle had ensured that her hair was tidy and the nightdress she wore was in her favourite rose colour. There were roses in her room and music softly playing. In fact as Mari said afterwards, "It was totally fitting for such a great actress, like looking at a stage setting and yet you knew it was for real."

Rose died at 3.0 a.m. without recovering consciousness. A distraught Estelle was given a sleeping draught by Stephen and sent to bed. Monty, shrunken with grief, drank a double whisky and also went upstairs to try and unwind. The girls, comforting each other, left for their cottage and Stephen lit candles and went to sit with the lady who had proved the catalyst in all their lives.

The news of Rose's death had come too late for the daily papers and there was a family consultation about how they should proceed. The twins were included in this.

It was decided that Saturday night's performance must go ahead, again requiring the twins to draw on all their resources, acting out their roles normally. No announcement would be made prior to the show, but at the final curtain Monty would tell the audience and ask for a minute's silence before they left the theatre. The next day being a Sunday, would enable them all to have some respite and allow the girls to grieve in their own way. The funeral for family and close friends would take place on the following Wednesday in Richmond and the theatre would close that day. At a later date to be agreed, there would be a full memorial service at the Actors' Church, St. Martin's in the Fields.

Somehow the girls once again got through the play, but their relief at the final curtain was tremendous. Then Monty went onto the stage and at his announcement there was a wail of grief from the audience, then the silence and through it the sobs were clearly audible, whilst behind the curtains the twins and the cast were at last allowed the luxury of their own tears. The orchestra played 'Auld Lang Syne' as people left the theatre and Nick and Chris hastened to the girls' dressing room to comfort them.

As planned, the funeral was quiet and contemplative. Rose's favourite hymns were sung and if the singers' voices faltered from time to time that was only to be expected.

Back at Greenacres there was the customary wake, but Rose's chair remained empty and there were frequent rapid disappearances from the room as first one and then another succumbed to their grief. The twins returned at last to their cottage, leaving Monty with Estelle and Stephen and the baby, who alone was helping to lighten the atmosphere. Mari said, "I feel all cried out and so tired...What was it someone said about the labour of mourning?"

"I don't know", Daisy replied, "but whatever it was, it's true. It is exhausting and I think I need to be on my own for a time."

"Me too," and they each disappeared to their own rooms.

Rose's will was read the following day and the twins were asked to attend Greenacres. A vast sum of money was left to Estelle, plus all Rose's jewellery, with the rider that Estelle was asked to put several items of her own choosing on one side for Joy. For her granddaughter there was a bequest of £5,000 to be held in trust until she was eighteen, plus all the Sebastian Reece paintings currently in Rose's possession. All other paintings to be held in trust by the British Arts Council and displayed as wished. The Reece Theatre, Rose had left to Monty, *'He already manages the theatre and has its success at heart. I know he will ensure that it eventually stays in our family'*.

Each of the twins was to receive £2,000, the cottage to be made over into their names and in addition, a further 100 each of the Sudbery shares with the proviso that these shares were non-transferable and could only be disposed of if their owners, Mari and Daisy, so desired. *'In this way I hope to ensure that you are truly independent and that should there be any long periods of 'resting', you will not be seriously inconvenienced.'* Further bequests to the staff and to Biddy and a substantial donation to a home for retired actors and it was finished.

The girls were stunned by what they had heard. Rose had kept Mari, fed and clothed her since she was fourteen and had similarly looked after Daisy for a number of years and now all this. No longer need they worry about having to vacate the cottage, it was theirs. And, as Daisy pointed out, "She has even made sure that if we married, our husbands couldn't just claim our possessions, everything has been well and truly tied up legally."

Mari added, "The very first day when I met Estelle at Waterloo station, one of the first things she said to me was that Rose was the most generous person she knew. How right she was."

A sea of condolences flooded in from all parts of the world and Estelle had to employ a temporary secretary to ensure they were dealt with efficiently. "I will eventually reply to everyone, but for now they are being separated into countries and counties and kept in that order." Hundreds of roses were sent to Greenacres from dignitaries abroad, organisations large and small in the United Kingdom and transported thence to hospitals and nursing homes in and around the area.

Six weeks later and St. Martin's was filled with the 'great and the good', the queue for entry stretching for a mile and a half. A broadcast system was in place so that those who couldn't get into the church would hear the service. With the permission of the clergy, roses filled St. Martin's. Monty had felt unable to present the eulogy without breaking down and had asked Noel to deputise for him. This Noel said he was happy to do so for such a dear friend. Rose's favourite hymns were sung, her favourite pieces read and there was humour too when her comedy roles were remembered and quoted. Thanks were expressed for a life so rich in talent and a generosity of spirit which had embraced everyone with whom she came in contact. It was, as those present said, a very suitable tribute to a life-enhancer, an exceptional lady.

Inevitably, her passing left a void in all their lives, but as she would have wished they picked up the threads and started again. For Mari and Daisy it was the end of an era and the beginning of what Rose had always anticipated would be their golden time.

Chapter 17

For the next ten years, the world was their oyster. In 1926 Daisy, a vision in white charmeuse married her Chris, their happiness in each other a joy to see. And as Chris had always intended, a part of their honeymoon was spent on the Orient Express. The year was marred only by the fire which completely destroyed the Shakespeare Memorial Theatre. Mari's escape from this being due entirely to the quick thinking and bravery of the Stage Manager.

The invitation to take 'Three's a Crowd' to Broadway followed and with it the magic of travelling there by P. & O., in style, and seeing the New York skyline for the first time. Staying at the Waldorf Astoria and meeting the extraordinary Nancy, Lady Astor and her husband, entertaining the U.S. President at the White House with some of their Music Hall numbers, all truly wonderful experiences. Mari, meeting Nick's parents for the first time, found out again how wrong she had been about Americans.

Back in England they drank Pimms at the Henley Regatta, cheered the Oxford crew to victory in the Boat Race and then in the autumn of 1928 the joy of Mari and Nick's wedding with Daisy, Tessa, and a tiny, bewitching

Joy, as bridesmaids. Honeymooning in Europe, dancing until dawn in Paris and being serenaded by gondoliers in Venice, Mari and Nick watched the sun rise and set over the Alps and loved and delighted in each other. Another Broadway visit and visiting Nick's parents again, this time travelling to their hunting lodge in the Rockies. Always and everywhere the Golden Girls were feted and acclaimed. Designer houses anxious to dress the twins in their own brand of haute couture, tempted them with offers of free garments, jewellers showered them with gifts, ever hopeful that the Golden Girls would wear their products and so advertise their wares.

And in 1929 the twins celebrated the birth of two girls, one in May to Daisy and the second in June to Mari. In the certainty that any offspring of theirs would gravitate towards the stage, their names were determined before birth. And so Mae Manning and June Jameson, sharing a birth year, arrived to form the next step in the Rose Reece dynasty. Increasingly Estelle had taken over the role of Rose and as soon as they were walking and talking the three girls, Joy, Mae and June were all taught the rudiments of performing. They learned ballet and tap dancing, recited poetry, learned elementary French and by the time they reached school age were precocious in talent and articulate in speech.

Invitations for Mari and Daisy and their husbands to attend weekend house parties came in thick and fast. Impossible to accept them all, but there were notable exceptions; Hever Castle, the home of Lord and Lady Astor, the mansions of Lord and Lady Baring and the Cranbournes. Suddenly, learning to ride became a necessity for Mari and Daisy, and shooting almost obligatory for their partners. On these weekends, meets were followed by magnificent pageants, staged by professionals, with the hostess always playing the most prominent role, but the beautiful Golden Girls invariably being asked to participate. As Mari said, tongue in cheek, "We may not have anything to say, but we do dress the stage."

Both the marriages were stable. Whilst not affluent, Chris was now in a position to hold his own amongst the rich. His astute ongoing purchasing of Sudbery shares, together with those held by Daisy, meant they were now holders of a substantial number of shares which were appreciating annually. The house they had purchased at Strawberry Hill was testimony to this. The Sudbery chain having now extended from Bath to Manchester, York and Norwich, of necessity Nick had to be near London, the centre of his business empire and it was to no-one's surprise when he and Mari found a Georgian house just a quarter of a mile from that of Daisy and Chris.

This was the era when Coward and Novello at last reached their own pinnacles of achievement. Noel followed 'Bittersweet' with what was to become a classic, 'Private Lives'. Then came 'Cavalcade' at Drury Lane, also playing to packed houses. For a time London theatre seemed to be in the doldrums until Ivor's 'Glamorous Night' took the London scene by storm.

Whilst 'Keep the Home fires burning' written by Ivor for the first World War, had been a success with the troops and with the public, there had been much criticism of it in musical circles, where the experts dismissed it as trivial. There was nothing trivial about the response of theatregoers to his 'Glamorous Night', a happy marriage between old fashioned melodrama and modern operetta.

'Careless Rapture' in which Mari played the lead and 'Crest of a Wave' with Daisy, rapidly followed, 'Glamorous Night' was made into a film and Ivor's place in history was assured. A revival of 'The Quaker Girl' saw Daisy centre stage and Mari in the opening production of the new Shakespeare Memorial Theatre at Stratford. But the Golden years for the twins, the theatre and the British public were about to wane.

The desire for European supremacy, already rooted in the youth of Germany, could not be easily ignored or quashed and a generation which had already endured the horrors of four years of conflict, watched in dismay as the clouds of war gathered momentum. The death of George V and the Abdication of his son, the Hunger marches in the North and the clashes in London, involving Mosleyite Fascists and their opponents, added to the increasing feeling of unease.

In 1939, following the Anschluss, Ivor's submission of the script of 'The Dancing Years' with overt references to the Reich Chancellor Adolf Hitler,was only accepted by Drury Lane directors after a great deal of 'watering down'. It proved a triumph. Following the declaration of War on the lst September 1939, every theatre was told to close and there was an emotional scene at Drury Lane when Ivor asked the small audience to gather close to the stage for a final performance, as cast and theatre staff wondered when they would ever be together again.

But members of the theatrical profession are nothing if not resilient. Accustomed to being out of work, often for long periods, they adapt to any given situation, and so it was now. Within a few short months the Lane became the home of the Entertainment National Service Association,

E.N.S.A. and Ivor was making plans to take 'The Dancing Years' on tour in Great Britain.

Meanwhile Chris Mason and the twins started to make their own plans. Chris and Nick had already been conscripted and the former had been given permission to form, under the ENSA umbrella, his own entertainment group. Their children's safety had to be catered for, but Stephen was outside the age group for enlistment, so Estelle and Stephen would be on hand in case of emergency. Chris and the twins decided to go ahead and gather together one or two friends in the profession and take entertainment to the troops. Lester, Mari's erstwhile boyfriend, was their first recruit. Singing in Europe was now out of the question for him and with a heart murmur he had not been eligible for conscription. He declared himself delighted to assist, as did Tessa, the girl who had been a tower of strength during what the twins called 'that nasty bedroom scene'. She assured them that although first and foremost an actress she could 'hold a tune with the best of them'.

Daisy's comment was "It never ceases to amaze me just how many in our profession are both singers and actors," whilst Mari grinning said, "It's the breathing exercises m'dear, all that attention to the diaphragm and the intercostals."

But it was Ivor who pointed out that there was a danger here, in not assuring that every part was played to the highest standard and it was he who later introduced actors into his musicals, giving them non-singing roles and thus strengthening his productions.

Estelle enthusiastically gave their plans her blessing. "I'll be more than happy to watch over our three darlings.

There's school during the week of course except for the holiday periods but I'll organise something for those. We've now got the tennis court and I'll invite some of their friends to make up foursomes. But…?"

"Yes, but?"

"Well, wouldn't it make sense for them to move in here with me? I would feel much happier having them all under the same roof and we can hire just one nanny for supervision. The girls go to school together any way and Stephen is often working late so they would not only have each other for company but they'll be company for me too. Let me have keys and we'll ensure that a check is kept on your properties and also that rooms are ready when you are due home."

"Estelle, you're an angel. We feel guilty enough about leaving, but we must do something to help. Knowing they're in your capable hands we won't be worrying about them all the time. It's so kind of you…" Mari was beginning to get emotional and Estelle responded quite brusquely, "Don't forget, if I can help in any way at all, just let me know."

And they didn't forget. Soon Estelle too, was involved in the choreography for musical numbers, making valuable suggestions as to what should work and more importantly, what would appeal. With two more male actors, two female singers, and a pianist added to their list, they felt they were a sufficiently strong group to perform sketches, musical routines and cabaret style entertainment. Props and costumes for the numbers were kept to a minimum, a theatre basket containing wigs, cloaks, feather boas and hats of all types being their major support system. For the sake of safety, scripts and musical scores travelled with their personal belongings. They targeted Army and Air Force camps first of all and visited dockyards where Naval personnel were based, then, as the wounded arrived back from the front lines they went into hospitals, performing wherever there was an open space.

A visit to the Naval dockyard at Portsmouth found Daisy and Mari reunited with two members of their family. At an introductory meeting with the Commanding Officer of the base they were informed that there were twins there from the Isle of Wight who said they were related to the Golden Girls. There was a slight embarrassment as the girls explained why they had been unaware of their brothers' whereabouts but found real delight in meeting Joe and Timmy, now strapping six footers. From the twins they learned their father was frail and that Sue had terminal cancer and was unlikely to survive the year.

Guilty that they had made only the briefest of contacts during the past years, the girls resolved to visit the Island at the earliest opportunity. They were assured that there was a huge deployment of army there, it being the first landing stage for a possible invasion and that any entertainment they could take would be welcomed with open arms.

It proved a bitter sweet visit. Sue was being nursed round the clock by nurses and kind-hearted neighbours. No longer sharp-tongued, her sickness had left her frail and vulnerable. The girls did what they could, arranged and paid for extra help and attempted to stir their father from his depressive state. The farm was almost devoid of cattle, the Griffins dependent upon what remained of these and the food from their own gardens. Deciding that the boys must have a home on their return the twins provided finance for the purchase of new stock and organised an experienced retired farmer to take over and assist where necessary. He and his wife had been evicted from a tied cottage and would live in the Griffin farmhouse indefinitely on the agreement that when Sue died and should there be any other change in the circumstances there, they would move into the unoccupied farm labourer's cottage on the Griffin farm. Daisy and Mari left with heavy hearts, feeling they could do no more.

Their travels around the country were proving exhausting but rewarding. Their reception everywhere overwhelmingly enthusiastic. In the hospitals they had to suppress their emotions on seeing so many young men disabled and sick and fulfil their original intentions to make their audiences forget, if only for a short while, the inhumanity of war. Always they were aware that Estelle provided for them the bedrock of stability which enabled them to continue. They knew their girls were being not only well cared for, but loved, and whilst feeling keenly that they were missing some aspects of Mae and June's growing years, then this was a sacrifice they had to make, just as others throughout the country were making much greater sacrifices.

June 1944 saw Nick, now a Major, leading his regiment from the toe of Italy northwards, their orders being to secure Rome. This task achieved, Nick, still unkempt and dirty from the rigours endured en route, was astonished when his batman approached him with a message that he was to report immediately to a local college. There, joined by other commanding officers from his regiment, he was ushered into a room where he was told they were to meet the Pope. The general verdict was that this was impossible, but without warning the curtains at the far end of the room were drawn back and there, in all his splendour, was the Pope! Without more ado he thanked them all for securing Italy's capital and then moved amongst them presenting each one with a Papal medal. Nick's batman was a Roman Catholic and when on Nick's insistence that the medal was his to keep, was overcome with emotion and wept on Nick's shoulder.

Mari was delighted to receive news of Nick's safety and to learn that he was due for some leave. Now they would be able to enjoy a few blissful days together and for a short time forget the problems of war. It was not to be. Within two days of his joyful reunion with Mari and his daughter June, he was informed that one of the dreaded buzz bombs now striking London had demolished a wing of the London Sudbery Hotel and he was needed on site to make some serious decisions with regard to reconstruction. All too soon it was time for him to return to barracks and await his next deployment.

Novello's 'Perchance to Dream' opened in April 1945 and until the end of 1947 there was never an empty seat. 'We'll gather lilacs' became to World War 11 what 'Keep the Home Fires burning' had been to the first World War and the line 'until our hearts have learned to sing again' epitomised the feelings of a nation weary of the war years. Soon the twins were in the thick of theatrical life again, with Mari securing the lead role in 'The Winslow Boy', which ran for several months and   Daisy playing the central figure in 'The Lady's not for Burning', by a new playwright, Christopher Fry. The Savoyards re-formed and a delighted Chris was soon heavily involved in casting, performing and learning his new role as a Director.

The end of the War saw a desperate attempt to return to normality. Evacuees returned home as did husbands, fathers and sons, unfamiliar now to many of their kin.

The Reece Theatre re-opened for the Christmas of 1945, with the ever popular Music Hall. In it the twins had two show stoppers, 'A Pretty Girl is like a Melody' and their favourite comedy piece, previously performed to soldiers and airmen all over the country, 'We're two of the ruins that Cromwell knocked abaht a bit".

In due course, Mari and Daisy were informed of Sue Griffin's death and that Joe had elected to remain in the Royal Navy. With the input of some financial assistance from the twins to restock the farm, Tim took control and the temporary manager and his wife moved out into the cottage, with Mrs. Bailey still cooking and generally keeping house for the menfolk. However, further information from Mrs. Bailey was that this was not likely to be needed for much longer, as Tim was already seeing a young lady from the village and the relationship looked a serious one.

1948 and London hosted the first post-war Olympic Games and to the twins' pleasure, Lester was invited to sing at the opening ceremony. His choice of Ivor's 'Rose of England' was approved, as was 'Maybe it's because I'm a Londoner', sung with gusto by a nation determined to enjoy themselves, after years of rationing and emotional trauma. The whole family were present to enjoy Lester's success and the thrill of being part of such an exciting occasion.

Mae and June, the twins' daughters, were now nineteen, and Estelle's Joy was in her twenty-third year. Whilst they had all been steeped in theatrical lore, Joy had no desire to tread the boards and had recently completed a course in business management. This at the suggestion of her grandfather Monty, now almost eighty. He was determined that she should, if and when necessary, be able to take over the running of the Reece Theatre.

Mae and June were different in looks and temperament. Mae had inherited her father's rather tentative approach to new situations, together with her mother's ash-blonde hair, whilst June had Nick's dark colouring but like her mother, was extrovert and unfazed by anybody or anything. Stephen in his late fifties was still the typical surgeon, practical, authoritative when called for and, whatever the situation, never at a loss. Nick had undergone a significant change during the war years. In 1945 he had taken his troops into Belsen and the horrors of that experience lived with him still. Chris, now a senior member of the Doylys, assured of the devotion of his wife and family, was confident as never before, in his own ability to succeed. Surveying their family group Estelle felt a pang of grief, that Rose was not able to witness their respective developments. How proud she would have been of all of them.

At this point Stephen looked at her anxiously. He and she were both aware that her own time now was limited. Tests he had insisted upon had revealed the leukaemia he had suspected and now they could hope for, at best, two years. Just how he would be able to carry on without her bright, effervescent persona beside him, he didn't know.

A loving smile of reassurance, a squeeze of her hand and she knew he was with her, willing her on. How fortunate she was.

Estelle clung to her two years, then the twins and their families had to say goodbye to their dear friend. Quietly and without fuss she was laid to rest, but for each one of those who loved her it was a hard and bitter separation.

Another year, another parting. Ivor Novello died a few hours after performing in 'King's Rhapsody'. Now the nation mourned the loss of a matinee idol and undisputed king of the musical stage. Thousands flocked to his funeral, the line stretching several miles, people of all classes, patiently waiting, having come to say goodbye to a friend. Sound was relayed from inside the chapel and flooding out into the spring air came the music of the man who had won their hearts. Inside all was white lilac, a great cross of it on the coffin. Flamboyant yes, but echoing his character and lifestyle and fittingly, his final exit was to 'We'll gather lilacs'.

For the twins these years proved a watershed in their own careers. Now the emphasis was back to the classics, 'Macbeth', 'King Lear' and the Restoration Comedies. Occasionally a cameo role in a contemporary drama presented itself, Mari was a magnificent Lady Bracknell and, blessing Ivor for his foresight in employing actors in musicals, Daisy relished her role as Mrs. Higgins in 'My Fair Lady'. Always though at Christmas they enjoyed the sheer fun of the Music Hall.

As anticipated, on his death, Monty had left the Reece Theatre to Joy and she became a very hands-on Managing Director. Now the mother of two sons, she was already planning that they could, if they so wished, eventually join her in the business of running both theatre and adjoining restaurant and art gallery. Mae and June had started to carve out their own careers from the age of sixteen, and were now established performers, June having already starred in '42nd Street' and Mae in 'Me and My Girl'.

The 1950's saw the birth of the hovercraft, by an Isle of Wight designer and Mari's pithy comment to her husband, *'You see! Daisy and I are forever being taunted that we come from the back of the beyond, where nothing ever happens and no-one knows anything about anything. Eat your words, we are now at the forefront of technology!'*

In this decade Britain saw the death of its monarch and a second Queen Elizabeth on the throne. Agatha Christie's 'Mousetrap' began a run which was to run for many years, Everest was conquered and Roger Bannister ran the first four minute mile; Mae married a choreographer and June tied the knot with one of Joy's sons, David, who managed the Reece Art Gallery and Restaurant.

Chapter 18

Sunday 1964

Mari awoke to a bright frosty day and the rattle of tea-cups. "Happy birthday Darling," a smiling Nick set down a tea tray and deposited a pile of cards on the bed before embracing and kissing her warmly. "Many, many happy returns. How does it feel to be an old lady of sixty?"

"I refuse to be sixty, as I told you yesterday, I am sticking at thirty-nine, well perhaps, forty-nine."

"Whatever, you still look a radiant twenty year old as far as I'm concerned," Nick grinned back at her.

"If only... oh this is so nice," Mari surveyed him pouring tea thinking, 'There may be quite a lot of silver in that dark hair now, but he's still a handsome fella.'

"Make the most of it, we're usually rushing off somewhere and all too often in opposite directions. Whatever happened to retiring?"

"I was just thinking..."

"Yes?"

"Fifty years ago at this same time of the morning, Daisy and I were on our way to school for the last time. Fifty years, it sounds absolutely ages, but it hasn't seemed like it."

"And think what you've achieved my darling. *I'm* so proud of you and I don't have to tell you that June and her little family think you're the bees' knees."

"Well whatever successes I've had it's been through a lot of love and assistance on the part of a great many people, dear Rose, Estelle, you my love and of course Daisy, I couldn't have done any of this without her."

Not far away, a similar scene was being enacted, as Daisy and Chris also enjoyed the peace of a leisurely start to their day. The evening they knew would be far from tranquil as the whole family was due to celebrate with a dinner party in one of the private function rooms at the London Sudbery.

Nick surveyed the scene both as a competent, observant manager and as the devoted husband of one of the principal guests. They were, he thought, an elegant group representing a wide spectrum of ages, from Stephen, now an old man, to Joy's sons in their middle twenties. Theatrical people he thought were fortunate. Whilst dancers had a limited stage life, the acting and singing professions provided work for all age groups and, importantly, that work was invariably both emotionally stimulating and a continuous learning process. Often he had found that Mari was surprisingly well-informed about an unexpected subject, merely because it had been referred to in a play and she had had to do her own research before playing the role. Her vocabulary and her general knowledge were both extensive.

Stephen now made a suggestion, "I know that over the years Mari and Daisy must have had some amazing and probably funny experiences, perhaps they would like to share a few of them with us." Nick noticed the quick glance which passed between the sisters and knew instinctively that it was a 'This is not the occasion for remembering any of those nasty happenings in the Celia years' look. Daisy was the first to speak,

"I did witness something almost unbelievable when I was performing with Ivor in his production of 'Perchance to Dream'. He was on the stage alone, playing just a few bars of music on the piano, when the butler went on and announced that a young lady would like to see him...me, waiting in the wings. What was supposed to happen was that Ivor said "Show her in", but to the butler's amazement he said instead,

"Ask her to wait a few moments would you?" Dazed, the butler walked off the stage. The Director and the Stage Manager were immediately at my side and we looked at each other in total disbelief. What on earth was Ivor up to? He, meanwhile continued playing odd bars of music and then making notes on a musical score. I suppose the audience thought it was all part of the show. Suddenly he called "She can come in now," in I went, and we resumed the show. What I found out later, much later, was that in those few moments, he had written the song which regularly brought the audiences for his next show, 'King's Rhapsody' to their feet, 'Some Day my heart will awake.'"

"Astonishing!", "What a talent", "Imagine". The family were quite rightly taken aback.

Next it was Mari's turn. "My anecdotes both involve costumes. When Daisy and I were in one of the Music Halls we shared a dressing room with the soloist dancer. One night she had a very quick change from an evening dress into a leotard which zipped up and fitted very tightly. She was quite adept at doing this, but that night there was a sudden wail from her, "The zip's stuck!" With the body part still only half zipped up she made her way into the wings and whilst someone held a light she started to work at the zip, brushing away all offers of help. The opening bars of her music cue were actually playing, when she suddenly freed the zip and burst onto the stage. It was a really close call.

"The second incident was in 'Romeo and Juliet'. I was on the balcony doing my sorrowful wailing bit, 'Wherefore art thou?', etc., etc., when someone sidled as close to me as they could get, behind the rear flats, and whispered loud and clear "His trousers have split, keep stalling for as long as possible, whilst we get him into another pair". I must have paced up and down that blasted balcony weeping and wailing about ten times, I can't imagine what the audience thought, but at last my hero, Romeo, arrived, complete with trousers."

She and Daisy were amazing, Nick decided. Still beautiful in spite of their sixty years, with Mari always insisting that grease paint was good for the skin, because it was pure and acted as a moisturiser. Whatever they had used, she and Daisy had gorgeous skins. Some wrinkles now of course, or 'laughter lines' as Mari insisted on calling them. Perhaps now they were just starting to look, ever so slightly, matronly, although Mari would kill him if he'd even hinted at the possibility! They had now excused themselves and were leaving the room, Daisy's arm round her sister's waist and giggling together like a couple of schoolgirls. What now, Nick wondered? I never know just what they're going to do next.

Their departure was in fact for the totally innocent reason that they wanted just a few precious moments together. In the quiet corner of an empty lounge they sat and for a short while neither spoke.

"Sixty, can you believe it?" Mari spoke first.

"Don't have any choice do we? The thing is, apart from a few creaks in the joints now and again, I don't feel it. What about you?"

"I'm the same, but putting aside the gloom and despondency at our great age, what a whale of a time we've had in getting here." Mari smiled.

"I thank God every night for what we've done, what we've seen, it's all been wonderful." Daisy smiled back and took Mari's hand. "We were so fortunate having each other, I certainly couldn't have done any of it alone."

"You probably could, but the point is we've been together, Daisy. It's been such an exciting and occasionally hazardous journey and I wouldn't have missed any of it for the world."

"Nor me, but please don't make me emotional, it will ruin my make-up," Daisy grinned.

"You know you said about thanking God for what's happened to us, what's that phrase in the Bible, where the angel tells Mary she's going to have a baby?"

"For heavens' sake, I know we welcome publicity, you're not pregnant are you?" Daisy teased.

"Don't be daft… It's that phrase the angel used, I'm trying to remember."

"Oh you mean 'Blessed are you amongst women'."

"That's the one, that's what I feel. We've been blessed in each other, our husbands, our children in so many, many ways."

"You're doing it again, getting me all emotional, I think it's time we joined the others, come along."

"I'm on my way and I've got something to dry your tears. You know we were always taught to be on cue? Well, we're right on it now, little Sister, they must be expecting us, you see they're playing our song."

"And which particular song might that be, Sister dear?"

"The one which was obviously written with us in mind, 'We're two of the ruins that Cromwell knocked abaht a bit'."

And arms round each other, laughing helplessly, they moved towards the music.

Printed in the United Kingdom
by Lightning Source UK Ltd.
122686UK00001BA/1-39/A